CITIES

SUNY SERIES IN URBAN PUBLIC POLICY
JAMES BOHLAND AND PATRICIA EDWARDS, EDITORS

SELLING CITIES

Attracting Homebuyers through Schools and Housing Programs

DAVID P. VARADY
JEFFREY A. RAFFEL

STATE UNIVERSITY OF NEW YORK PRESS

8-28-96

Published by
State University of New York Press, Albany

© 1995 State University of New York

Printed in the United States of America

For information, address State University of New York
Press, State University Plaza, Albany, N.Y., 12246

Production by E. Moore
Marketing by Bernadette LaManna

Library of Congress Cataloging-in-Publication Data

Varady, David P.
    Selling cities : attracting homebuyers through schools and housing
programs / David P. Varady, Jeffrey A. Raffel.
        p.   cm. — (SUNY series in urban public policy)
    Includes index.
    ISBN 0-7914-2557-6 (acid-free paper). — ISBN 0-7914-2558-4 (pbk.
: acid-free paper)
    1. Urban renewal—United States. 2. Community development, Urban—
United States. 3. Metropolitan areas—United States. 4. Housing
policy—United States. 5. House buying—United States. 6. Magnet
schools—United States. 7. School integration—United States.
8. Public relations—Municipal government—United States.
I. Raffel, Jeffrey A. II. Title. III. Series: SUNY series on urban
public policy.
HT175.V38   1995

307.3'416'0973—dc20   94-23443
                                                       CIP

CONTENTS

FIGURES

TABLES

ACKNOWLEDGMENTS

While both authors are planners by nature, neither planned for the complexity and difficulties of this joint venture. The collection of data, linking of the survey data to administrative records, joining of the two data bases, garnering of financial support for the data collection and analysis, and communicating across a thousand miles necessitated the support of a great many people and institutions. It is our pleasure to thank them here.

The University of Cincinnati, University Programs Advisory Committee (UPAC), the Cincinnati Department of Neighborhood Housing and Conservation, and the Cincinnati Housing Resources Board provided the funding for the Cincinnati portion of the research. UPAC funding came from the Ohio Board of Regents. The Cincinnati Department of City Planning made available the real estate transactions set, which was used to create the sample for the Cincinnati survey research.

Thanks are due to the organizations that funded the New Castle County data collection: the Christina School District, Red Clay School District, Delaware Homebuilders Association, and the College of Urban Affairs and Public Policy, University of Delaware. The New Castle County Planning and Housing and Community Development departments helped to support the analysis. Individuals who helped provide this support were Marvin Gilman, Ed O'Donnell, and Tim Barnekov. The New Castle County Assessment Division and its director, Fran Lally, provided some of the data that made this study possible.

Jay Chatterjee, dean, College of Design, Art, Architecture, and Planning, University of Cincinnati, provided David Varady with a special duty leave of absence, fall 1991, to work on this book project.

Tom Bier, Urban Studies Center, Cleveland State University, provided Varady with the initial idea for this research project through the series of surveys of homebuyers he has been conducting in Cleveland. The survey questions we used in Cincinnati and Wilmington build directly on his work in Cleveland. We also appreciate Tom's willingness to serve as a "sounding board" for our ideas throughout the history of the project.

Jan Bending, doctoral student, Department of Sociology, University of Cincinnati, competently carried out data collection for the first wave of mailed surveys in Cincinnati. The Institute for Policy Research (IPR), University of Cincinnati (Al Tuchfarber, director) expertly carried out these tasks for the second and third waves.

Ed Ratledge, director of the University of Delaware Center for Applied Demography and Survey Research (CADSR), played an indispensable role in accomplishing the complex computer work necessary to develop the New Castle County database and was a source of critical insight throughout this effort. Gi Yong Yang, doctoral student, College of Urban Affairs and Public Policy, University of Delaware, served as the research assistant for the Delaware component of this project and mastered the intricate computer instructions necessary to do everything from linking data bases to running multivariate analysis. He tirelessly and competently conducted the computer runs for this project as well as provided advice and good questions along the way. Yang and Mary Cannon, also a doctoral student in the College of Urban Affairs and Public Policy, ensured that the quality of data was high. Phyllis Raab, assistant director, CADSR, did her usually friendly and superb job of supervising the data collection through this center.

We have been fortunate in having excellent consultants available throughout the course of this project. Roger Steuebing (IPR) provided critically important statistical advice for the chapter on housing market segmentation. Sadly, Roger died before this book project was completed. Robert Oldendick (IPR) merged the three waves of Cincinnati surveys into one. Ben Hawkins assisted David Varady throughout the project in utilizing the University of Cincinnati mainframe computer; we are especially grateful for his help in "exporting" the merged data set to the University of Delaware computing center, where the Cincinnati and Wilmington data sets were combined and then for shipping the merged data set back to Cincinnati where it was computer analyzed.

We are grateful to Joe Hamburg, computer coordinator, School of Planning, University of Cincinnati, for preparing the path diagrams, even though we decided not to include them in the book. Two of Varady's research assistants, Mustafa Bootwala and Solomon Tadese, prepared the computer- generated map of Cincinnati for chapter 6 (Housing Market Segmentation). Ed Ratledge, director, Center for Applied Demography and Survey Research, prepared the corresponding map for Wilmington. We are grateful to Dick Moran, Planning and Management Support System, City of Cincinnati, for preparing the Cincinnati map included in chapter 9.

Dave Varady feels fortunate to have had an excellent secretary—Dorothea Cloke (School of Planning)—for most of the research project. Ms. Cloke typed most of the tables and, in addition, transformed the rough documents that came off the word processor into polished professional papers.

Dean Dan Rich and MPA program director Betty McCummings of the University of Delaware's College of Urban Affairs and Public Policy supported Jeff Raffel's devotion to this book for several years, and he is most appreciative of their strong support and counsel. Carole Hermes played an important role in facilitating communications between the two authors. Judy Byerly helped check and correct the references.

Charlotte (Tommie) Birdsall was coauthor to earlier drafts of chapter 7 and helped the research in ways too numerous to mention. Chapter 7 is based in part on Varady's participation in the Housing Blueprint Technical Working Group. Dave Varady would like to thank Wayne Chapman, director of the Cincinnati Department of Neighborhood Housing and Conservation, for involving him in the project, as both a participant and consultant.

In preparing chapter 8, David Varady drew heavily on interviews he conducted with practitioners and planners in seven cities in the United States and Canada. We are grateful for their assistance:

Baltimore: Richard Bird and Sarah Buikema, Baltimore Department of Housing and Community Development; Dan Evans, Baltimore Community Development Financing Corporation; Richard Hurley, Baltimore Economic Development Corporation; Tom Jaudon, Home Ownership Institute; and Reggie Stanfield, Baltimore Vacant House Program;

Cleveland: Norman Krumholz and Thomas Bier, Cleveland

State University; Ron Thomas, Cleveland Action to Support Housing; and Anda Cook, Living in Cleveland Center Inc.;
Montreal: Claire Piche-Cyr, planning officer, City of Montreal; and Martin Wexler, City of Montreal, Housing and Urban Development Services;
New York: David Listokin, Rutgers University; Peter Salins, Hunter College, City University of New York; and Katherine Wylde, New York City Housing Partnership;
St. Louis: Charles Kindleberger, St. Louis Community Development Agency; Peter Sortino, director of intergovernmental affairs, office of the mayor;
St. Paul: Frank Jossi, Macalester College; and Katy Sears Lindblad, St. Paul Department of Planning and Economic Development;
Wilmington: Alan Matas, Wilmington Homeownership Corporation, and Robert Weir, Wilmington Partnership.

Chapter 9 also draws heavily upon personal interviews conducted by Varady with participants in the Eastern Riverfront planning process. Dave Varady would like to thank the following individuals for their time and insights: Jackie McCray and Doug Ruwe (Cincinnati Department of City Planning); Ken Bordwell and Gerard Hyland (Cincinnati Department of Neighborhood Housing and Conservation); Arnold Bellow (Office of the City Manager, City of Cincinnati); John Schrider (Legal Aid Society of Cincinnati); and Lynne Coward (Riverfront Advisory Commission).

Larry Adams of the Data Service Center and Larry Gabbert of Delaware's Department of Public Instruction provided valuable data for chapter 10. For chapter 11, Jeff Raffel conducted interviews with Duane Holm (Metropolitan Area Religious Coalition of Cincinnati, MARCC), Ed Burdell (Applied Information Resources, AIR Inc.), and several current and former Cincinnati school district administrators including Lynn Goodwin, Jack Lewis, Joe Timmons, and Bob Townsend, about Cincinnati's magnet schools and would like to take this opportunity to thank them.

We want to take this opportunity to thank five of our colleagues for reviewing an earlier version of this monograph: Thomas Bier (Cleveland State University), Dennis Gale (Florida Atlantic University), Daniel Monti (Boston University), Tim Barnekov (University of Delaware), and Barry Cullingworth (University of Delaware and

Cambridge University). Their suggestions strengthened the book immeasurably. Ted Koebel of Virginia Tech and two anonymous reviewers for SUNY Press also provided excellent suggestions for improvement of this work. Bob Warren, University of Delaware, helped identify relevant literature for our discussions in chapters 2 and 12.

Margaret Pyle Hassert, director of the University of Delaware's Writing Center, expertly helped us turn a rough manuscript into a book. We thank her for her skillful, professional editorial advice. We also thank the College of Urban Affairs and Public Policy for making the use of her fine services possible. Diana Simmons did an excellent job of typing the final drafts of the manuscript. We thank her, too, as well as the College of Urban Affairs and Public Policy for supporting her work.

Family support makes difficult jobs more doable and pleasant. Both authors had great support throughout this effort. Dave Varady dedicates this book to his wife (Adrienne) and children (Julie and Aaron). Without their patience and encouragement, this book would not have been possible.

Jeff Raffel thanks his parents, George and Renee, for impressing on him the value of diligence, and his wife, Joanne, for impressing on him the value of brevity and clarity. They, along with children Ken, Lori, and Allison, provided support, as well as diversion, during the production of this volume.

For permission to reprint material from previously published works, or to publish revised versions of previously published works, we are grateful to the following publishers and/or authors:

From James Cibulka, "Choice and Restructuring of American Education," in William Lowe Boyd and Herbert J. Walberg, *Choice in Education: Potential and Problems.* Copyright 1990 by McCutchan Publishing Corporation, Berkeley, CA 94702. Permission granted by the publisher.

From Mary H. Metz, "Potentialities and Problems of Choice in Desegregation Plans," pp. 131–32, in *Choice and Control in American Education* vol. 2, edited by William H. Clune and John F. Witte (Bristol, PA: Falmer Press, 1990). Used with permission of Falmer Press. (Copyright 1990 W. Clune and J. Witte)

From Mitchell Sviridoff, "The seed of urban revival," *The Public Interest* (Winter 1994), 94, 101. Reprinted by permission of *The Public Interest.*

From Peter Mieszkowski and Edwin S. Mills, "The causes of

metropolitan suburbanization," *Journal of Economic Perspectives* 7 (3) (Summer 1993), 135–47. Reprinted by permission of the American Economic Association.

From David P. Varady and Jeffrey A. Raffel, "Changing demographics and lifestyles. What are recent homebuyers really like?" *Journal of Urban Affairs* 14 (2), (1992), 161–72. Reprinted by permission of the *Journal of Urban Affairs.*

From David P. Varady, "Influences on the city-suburban choice," *Journal of the American Planning Association* 56 (1) (Winter 1990), 22–40. Reprinted by permission of the *Journal of the American Planning Association.*

From David P. Varady, "The impact of city/suburban location on moving plans: A Cincinnati study," *Growth and Change* 20 (2) (Spring 1989). Reprinted by permission of *Growth and Change.*

From David P. Varady. "Segmentation of the home-buyer market: A Cincinnati study," *Urban Affairs Quarterly* 26 (4) (1991), 549–66. Reprinted by permission of the *Urban Affairs Quarterly.*

From David P. Varady, "Middle-income housing programs in American cities," *Urban Studies* 31 (8) (October 1994), 1345–46. Reprinted by permission of *Urban Studies.*

From David P. Varady and Charlotte T. Birdsall, "Local housing plans," *Journal of Planning Literature* 6 (2) (November 1991), 115–35. Reprinted by permission of the *Journal of Planning Literature.*

From David P. Varady and Jeffrey A. Raffel, "Two approaches to school desegregation and their impacts on city-suburban choice: Cincinnati, Ohio and Wilmington, Delaware," *Journal of Urban Affairs* 15 (3) (June 1993), 259–74. Reprinted by permission of the *Journal of Urban Affairs.*

From William Julius Wilson, editor, The Ghetto Underclass: Social Science Perspectives, Special issue of the *Annals of the American Academy of Political and Social Science* (1989). Reprinted by permission of Sage Publications.

DAVID P. VARADY
JEFFREY A. RAFFEL

PART I

THE PROBLEM OF CITIES

1

The Importance of Attracting Middle-Class Homeowners to Cities

The riots in Los Angeles that followed the verdict in the trial of four white policemen accused of beating black motorist Rodney King have led to a renewal of concern about America's cities. *Time Magazine*, a good bellwether of American attention, sounded like the Kerner Commission (U.S. National Advisory Commission on Civil Disorders 1969) of twenty-five years earlier when it concluded that the result of "suburbanization, the most irresistible demographic trend of the past 40 years . . . is an America that is rapidly dividing into two worlds separated by class, race, and drive time" (Lacayo 1992: 31).

This book analyzes how cities can help to overcome this irresistible force—relentless suburbanization and the resultant neglect of urban social problems. We believe that the vitality of American cities depends in part on their ability to retain and attract the middle class. While the focus of recent years has appropriately been on equity and minorities, cities have been losing their middle-class

3

base. We believe that policies and programs can be developed to begin to reverse this trend, thereby making it possible to address urgent social problems. We believe that cities can take actions to become more attractive to both middle- and lower-income individuals.

Our focus in this book is on homebuyers. We review the literature on mobility as well as on housing and school policies to determine what we know and what we need to find out about why households stay in and are attracted to cities, and what role housing and school policies play in this process. We examine two metropolitan areas—Cincinnati, Ohio, and Wilmington, Delaware—in depth to further understand this process. Homebuyer surveys and case analyses serve as the basis for our exploration of city-suburban housing choice and related policies and programs. Finally, we propose a number of actions that cities and other jurisdictions could take to begin to reverse the so-called irresistible force of suburbanization.

City advocates looking for a "magic bullet" to reverse historical trends will be disappointed with this book. While we have identified segments of the homebuyer market that are and could be attracted to cities, we also confirm many strong decentralizing tendencies. For example, we show that Wilmington's metropolitan desegregation plan may have changed attitudes about city schools without changing decisions about city living. We confirm that many urban amenities are now as likely as not to be found in the suburbs, attracting those with urban values to urbanized suburbia. Therefore, the types of programs that will attract middle-class households (especially those with children) will require resources and awareness of trade-offs and, ultimately, strong political leadership.

Suburban apologists will also be unhappy with our findings. We have identified households that would like to live in cities and have willingly moved to city neighborhoods. We have found successful efforts to blend the needs of lower-income city residents with middle-class desires for various services and amenities. Thus, prophecies of "doom and gloom" for central cities are, for the most part, premature.

We conclude that programs and policies can be shaped to encourage middle-class homeownership in cities, and we try to specify what will be necessary to do so. Our perspective is empirical, local, pragmatic, and programmatic. We are interested in what cities can do within the current political and economic structure to attract and retain middle-class homebuyers. We indicate that appropriate financial incentives, marketing of city homes and neighborhoods, and educational initiatives can improve the ability of cities to revitalize, even within the current structures of the economy and government. While recognizing an equity issue—the need to address the issue of the underclass—we feel that there is a need for a balanced approach, which addresses the housing and schooling needs of middle-class households. Unless cities are sensitive to middle-class householders' search for educational quality for their children and housing quality for their families, cities will continue to lose such families to the suburbs. In this case, cities will lack the tax base to fund programs for the underclass.

Our conclusions indicate that, while in the short run cities will not be able to reverse long-term patterns of suburbanization, empirically based programs could help slow down this trend, especially in cities that have amenities (for example, panoramic views of rivers, hills, and parks; lively downtowns) attractive to the middle class. The success of such programs will require improved leadership at the local level as well as access to greater financial resources from state and federal governments. At the present time, only meager resources are available. Furthermore, there is a lack of awareness of the need to fund these efforts. But to judge our recommendations, the reader should begin with our more detailed argument concerning suburbanization and the need for cities to attract middle-class homebuyers.

THE SIGNIFICANCE OF CENTRAL CITY REVITALIZATION

Since the mid-1970s, journalists and social scientists have observed the increased incidence of neighborhood revitalization in American cities (Black 1975). Neighborhood revitalization is a product of a number of forces—one being demographic and lifestyle changes at the societal level. For the last twenty years, researchers have pointed to a new generation of young people who place less emphasis on childrearing and a traditional family lifestyle and to women who work outside the home as increasing the demand for central city living (Gale 1984, 1987; Palen and London 1987). Some scholars, such as Alonso (1982), believe that these changes will lead to the rebirth of cities.

Countering these optimistic writings is the reality that in American metropolitan areas, the long-term trend is suburbanization. During the 1970s and 1980s, many medium and large cities in the northeast and upper midwest experienced population decline (Holthaus 1991). Twice as many people were moving from the cities to the suburbs as in the opposite direction (Goodman 1978). Finally, most of those moving to revitalizing neighborhoods were coming from other city neighborhoods rather than from the suburbs. Therefore, the notion of a "return to the city" was a widely believed myth.

The 1990 United States census indicates that metropolitan areas grew in the last decade, but most of the population growth continued to be in the suburbs (U.S. Bureau of the Census 1991b). Central cities did fare better in the 1980s than in the previous decade, when most cities lost population at a rapid rate. The census bureau reports that only thirteen of the forty largest cities lost population in the 1980s. The midwest had the largest number of population losers—Chicago, Detroit, Milwaukee, Cleveland—but the south and east had some declining cities—Memphis, New Orleans, Baltimore, Philadelphia. The most rapidly growing major metropolitan areas are in the south or the west. So while the south and west continue to grow, in each region there are cities that are demographic winners and losers.

A disproportionate number of families moving to the suburbs are middle-class, and thus the city-suburban income gap is widening (Long and Dahmann 1980). Furthermore, the dispersion of multifamily housing and entertainment spots to the suburbs has increased the attraction of "nontraditional households" such as singles, couples without children, and gays to suburban areas (Gross 1991; Nemy 1991). These demographic shifts have increased the seriousness of problems facing central city policymakers, problems that include a declining tax base as well as declining political power, difficulty in achieving racial and class integration in the public schools, and difficulty in attaining cooperation with suburban governments because the service priorities on both sides of the city-suburban boundary are so different.

The preceding urban problems are exacerbated by the mismatch between the limited skills of the remaining urban residents and the requirements of the postindustrial white-collar jobs that have been created. Most of these jobs have gone to suburban commuters. The inability of central city residents (many from minority groups) to take advantage of these jobs has contributed to high levels of unemployment, poverty, welfare dependency, and related social ills.

As suggested by the census data cited above, the seriousness of the problems of suburbanization and increasing inequalities varies by metropolitan area. Some cities are adapting to the postindustrial era more successfully than others. In these locations, as service jobs replace manufacturing ones, middle-class householders are replacing blue-collar workers in gentrifying neighborhoods, and this partially compensates for the urban-to-suburban flow. In contrast, in many other metropolitan areas, central city living is not perceived as desirable; as a result, the suburbanization rate is greater.

How can we account for continued patterns of migration from central cities? Human ecologists, geographers, and other social scientists have debated the importance of different "pull" and "push" forces in explaining suburbanization. The "pulls" include the wider availability of jobs and housing along the edges of the metropolitan area; the "pushes" encompass inadequate schools, crime, and similar problems.

Demographers (Frey 1979, 1985; Frey and Kobrin 1982) have tested for the importance of these push and pull forces, using aggregated data and examining, among other things, the correlation between citywide crime rates and both the overall mobility rate and the incidence of city-to-suburban moves. This type of research, which uses aggregated data, is deceptive because it produces assertions about individuals based on the examination of groups. (This is called the ecological fallacy.) It is conceivable, for example, that those people least concerned about crime in high crime areas are the ones most likely to choose suburban locations.

For this reason, survey analysis that focuses on individual households is the appropriate analytic approach to improve understanding of mobility decisions. Unfortunately, there has been a large gap between theoretical models of household choice that have been developed (see chapter 4) and over descriptive empirical research. In recent years, social scientists concerned with intraurban migration have chosen the individual household as the unit of analysis and have conceptualized mobility as consisting of two steps: the decision to stay or to move, and the search for and selection of an alternative (Herbert 1973; Knox 1982; Moore 1972.)

Unfortunately, there has been limited research on the second issue. Most recent mobility research has focused on the decision of *whether* to move, and has ignored the decision of *where* to locate (Moore 1972; Simmons 1968).[1]

Research on factors affecting the likelihood of moving generally shows policy variables having little ability to hold middle-

income families in central city locations. Whether these policy variables can help to attract such families to the central city is an un-
answered question, however (Varady 1983). According to Rossi and
Shlay (1982), the critical issue for mobility research is why families
choose a particular location and whether public programs might
influence this decision:

> The problem is not why families move but why families choose
> to move where they do. . . . The prospects of addressing social
> policy issues through the study of residential mobility can be
> considerably enhanced if the focus of such research shifts to
> residential location processes. (25)

This book represents an effort to reduce the gap in existing
research on relocation decisions by considering the relative importance of different background demographic characteristics, such as
marital status and the presence of children, and residential attitudes,
such as the quest for urban or suburban attributes and concerns
about public schools and housing prices, in distinguishing city and
suburban homebuyers and in distinguishing between those planning
to remain and those planning to move in the near future.

RETAINING AND ATTRACTING THE MIDDLE CLASS

One approach to solving the existing ghetto problem is to
disperse the poor of central cities by building low-income housing in
the suburbs. The obvious advantage of this strategy is to better link
low-income householders with suburban jobs. However, this strategy faces formidable obstacles, including entrenched patterns of racial discrimination and the unwillingness of central city minority
politicians to give up their political power (which would occur if a
massive dispersal policy were implemented). Thus, for the foresee-
able future, the most realistic policy to deal with America's urban
problems will be a core strategy aimed at improving housing and
social conditions in the central city.

In order to implement a core improvement strategy, cities need
to expand their tax base. This will require better linking housing and
economic development. More specifically, cities have to replace
those activities that they are losing (typically manufacturing) with
ones where they are competitive (specialized service jobs like finance and advertising). The problem for large cities like New York is

that the companies that they are trying to attract find that their middle management staff tend to live in the outer suburbs. Given the costs and uncertainties of commuting, such firms find it increasingly tempting to locate in the suburbs. The challenge for cities is to stimulate the production of market-rate housing for such white-collar workers.

Thus, to be successful in the long run, cities need to meet two distinct types of housing needs; or to put the matter somewhat differently, cities need to develop balanced housing policies encompassing both equity and economic growth considerations. Emphasizing equity alone is impractical and counterproductive:

> One group of low- and moderate-income people, the "shelter society," requires the basics of adequate physical housing. Members of a second, more affluent group, the "post shelter society," want housing to serve also as a symbol of prestige and a vehicle for capital accumulation. The primary consideration in choosing a dwelling for these people is not whether one can afford the investment, but whether it is retrievable at a profit. For the young members of this group, location close to core areas of jobs and consumption is an equally key concern. (Sternlieb and Listokin 1985: 385)

Up to now, we have stressed the need for a middle-income housing policy to expand the tax base so as to fund programs for the underclass and, more generally, to adapt to the transformation from an industrial to a post-industrial society. Such a policy has other advantages. Because of its purchasing power, a larger middle-class population would improve the prospects for viable downtown and neighborhood shopping districts. In addition, because of their greater political acumen, middle-income families would probably pressure local bureaucracies for better services. Finally, a larger middle-class population (including families with children) would facilitate neighborhood class and racial integration as well as integration in the schools. If the latter occurred, this could help to raise test scores among low-income minority students.

Programs like tax abatements have been shown to be effective in stimulating middle-income housing construction. Furthermore, empirical studies have shown that these programs pay for themselves within a relatively short time (Sternlieb and Listokin 1985). However, the programs have sometimes been viewed as controversial. Opponents contend: (1) that the benefits of such programs rarely, if ever, filter down to the poor; (2) that city efforts to work with private developers often hurt the poor (through either direct or indirect displacement, the latter referring to relocations resulting from general price rises in the area); (3) that these funds are more appropriately spent helping the poor; and (4) that the middle-income families locating in the city under these programs would have done so anyway.

The debate over these middle-income subsidies is partly empirical in nature, including the issue of whether these programs do in fact have spillover benefits for the poor. The research on this subject is, in fact, meager. More basically, the argument revolves around ideology. Those who are against such subsidies on principle are not likely to change their minds even if they are provided with evidence demonstrating the existence of spillover benefits.

Our aim in writing this book is not to convince the reader of any ideal balance between equity and economic growth considerations. Rather, we attempt to answer several more straightforward empirical questions. For example, are middle-income economic incentives such as tax abatements as controversial as might be expected, based on academic journal articles? Can coalitions be developed at the citywide and community levels willing to address both types of housing needs, or are the two positions so strongly held that compromise is impossible?

This book would hardly make sense unless we were convinced of the importance of addressing middle-income housing/schooling needs. We have found Daniel Monti's 1990 study, *Race, Redevelopment and the New Company Town*, persuasive. Paraphrasing him, cities can be rebuilt in a way that accommodates both the rich and the poor. A review of the literature and a case study of private sector redevelopment in the central corridor of St. Louis make him (and us) relatively optimistic about the prospects for such a balanced approach. It is worth reviewing the major points of his argument.

Monti begins by noting that, historically, there is much basis for skepticism about the desirability of these efforts based on governmental programs in three types of communities (downtowns, gentrifying communities, and neighborhoods experiencing incumbent upgrading). In all three, minority and low-income families have tended not to benefit from redevelopment. Urban renewal is probably the best known example of a well-intentioned program aimed at promoting the return of the middle class that hurt the poor.

Turning from history to theory, Monti notes that both Marxists and ecologists are pessimistic about the ability of private corporations to address the needs of poorer citizens as part of redevelopment efforts:

> Ecologists would not argue that private corporations have an obligation to remedy these problems or to rebuild the city in a way that its citizens deem responsible. Marxists would argue that private corporations should do this, but rarely do. In neither case does it seem that theorists offer an especially hopeful view of cities or the ability of persons living in cities to shape the world in which they live. (9)

The "city as polity" perspective, held by only a minority of academic experts on the subject, is much more optimistic about the role that private corporations might play in efforts to redevelop particular areas:

> Some thirty years ago . . . political scientist Norton Long had hoped that business leaders would find a responsible way to reassert themselves in the daily affairs of cities. He viewed the modern corporation as competing with the city itself for the loyalty of its personnel; and he worried about the loss of civic-minded stewards who could help guide the city. He thought that if unions and corporations found an agreeable way to invigorate the political process, it might be possible to build a more united community and a set of ethical standards everyone could adopt. . . . Long resurrected the nineteenth-century American idea that the city's business leaders could be instrumental in drawing everyone else together. (xvii)

In reality, Monti's case studies of redevelopment in five communities in the central corridor of St. Louis supported the third perspective, "city as polity." That is, on the whole, the redevelopment process in these communities worked out rather well, certainly better than would have been expected based on Marxist or human ecological writings:

> Today, these areas not only look better but they also have a racially and economically mixed resident population. The political debates inspired by redevelopment work did not ignore

the problems inherent in building a more pluralistic neighbor-hood. Indeed, the behavior of public and private leaders fueled such arguments. The lessons learned in these areas have yet to be widely shared with other parts of St. Louis. Nevertheless, they are readily available for others to adopt as they see fit. (xviii)

Thus, the St. Louis study seems to show that, in order to make redevelopment happen, it is necessary to create a coalition of busi-ness leaders, elected officials, civil servants, and some grassroots leaders. Whether the coalition will be effective is dependent on local circumstances (for example, the personalities of leaders) rather than on external forces (for example, broad economic trends, national housing policy).

Monti's work makes us optimistic about the possibility for developing and implementing "balanced" housing and schooling policies—that is, policies addressing both economic growth and eq-uity concerns. This premise provided the basis for our doing this research and writing this book. We believe that cities need middle-class homeowners for their financial, political, and social viability. They can address their needs while simultaneously helping lower-income families.

Our premise—that cities need middle-class homeowners and should shape policies to retain and attract them—may be controver-sial. The thrust of much of the literature about cities and the recent politics of cities focuses on the search for more equity in cities and for the empowerment of minorities. The pronouncements from aca-demics and politicians after the Rodney King verdict show how tempting it is to stress equity (and to sound politically correct) rather than to face the more difficult and controversial task of developing housing/schooling policies that promote equity in the context of expanding the city's economic base.

We believe, as most Americans probably do, that the time for white-led divisive racial policies, inequitable service delivery, and government school segregation has long passed. But we have also witnessed an overcorrection as reflected by those who want to stress equity to the exclusion of all other factors. Cities cannot afford to ignore or discourage homeowners, of whatever race, who can help finance equitable policies, share leadership in city and community organizations, and support policies of higher jurisdictions that im-pact on cities. Yet they have. Writers such as Davidoff and Krumholz have opposed virtually all efforts to fund middle-class housing/ schooling programs (see, for example, Krumholz and Shatten 1992).

As Tom Bier, who read an early draft of this manuscript, argued, "I believe that you could go as far as to say that the history of the past forty years demonstrates that there is no hope for most cities until government policies that influence the location choice of middle-class people are changed." Bier's comment reflects an understanding that so many governmental programs have had the net effect of stimulating suburbanization. These programs include overgenerous funding for highway construction and the lack of effective regional planning. Such programs have enabled the proliferation of development and suburban malls, thus undercutting the viability of central cities. We agree with Bier and in this book address how this could be changed.

Cities need to attract more middle-class householders whether they rent or own. However, we have decided to focus on homebuyers because the goal of homeownership is so strongly held by members of the middle class, because homeownership has been promoted by federal tax/housing policy, and because owners usually have stronger residential ties to their areas than renters. Thus, attracting middle-income owners is a way to strengthen the fabric of cities. We therefore use "middle-income" as shorthand for middle-income homeowners.

If policymakers are to develop effective policies to stem population loss, they will require improved information on the composition of the homebuying population, the structure of metropolitan housing markets, the factors affecting locational choices, and the extent to which different homebuying subpopulations are attached to their current locations. Revitalization is also related to the nature and the quality of the public schools serving city residents, for perceptions of schools can be a significant factor in homebuying decisions of families. The chapters that follow address gaps in research in all of these areas.

Organizational Framework

This book seeks to answer three sets of questions. First, what are the gaps in existing research regarding the underlying causes of suburbanization and central city inmigration? What insights does our analysis of recent Cincinnati/Wilmington homebuyer mobility offer into the underlying causes of these trends? Second, what does the research literature suggest concerning the conflict over middle-class housing and schooling programs developed and implemented towards these ends? What additional insights do our Cincinnati/ Wilmington case studies offer into the ability of cities to simultaneously address middle- and lower-income needs? Finally, based on our empirical analysis and case studies, what additional research is needed and what types of programs ought to be tried?

More specifically, this book examines the problem, process, politics, and potential of central city revitalization and metropolitan development through a comparative analysis of homebuyers in Hamilton County, Ohio (which includes Cincinnati and many of its suburbs), and New Castle County, Delaware (which includes Wilmington and its suburbs). The analysis helps us to understand what factors play a role in homebuying decisions, especially with respect to city-suburban choices. We focus on the role of schools and housing characteristics in this decision. The inclusion of the major Cincinnati metropolitan county allows us to examine the impact of the city's historic magnet school plan on homebuyers. Similarly, the inclusion of the Wilmington metropolitan area permits us to analyze the effects of a metropolitan school desegregation plan on home-buyer attitudes and decisions. Although both metropolitan areas have school plans that should make the central city more attractive to middle-class homebuyers, New Castle County's metropolitan school districts probably offer more potential for stemming white middle-class outmigration. In addition, both cities have begun to struggle with the issue of providing housing for the middle class in the context of economic difficulties. This provides us with a context to examine the bureaucratic and political issues involved in implementing housing programs aimed at middle-class families.

ORGANIZATION OF BOOK

In this introductory chapter we have stated our premises and our research questions. Chapter 2 places our work in the context of the larger literature on central city revitalization. In this chapter we review selected works in urban political economy, urban sociology, and metropolitan planning. We specify research questions from these three literatures. Chapter 3 discusses the setting for our research and our methodology (the types of questions that we included in the mailed questionnaires, the numbers of survey forms that were sent out and that were returned, and so forth). In order to provide a base for the chapters that follow, we present and discuss statistical profiles of recent homebuyers in the two metropolitan areas. In doing so, we seek answers to two questions. To what extent has the homebuying population been affected by the demographic and life-style changes discussed earlier in this chapter? To what extent is it possible to identify (using a technique called cluster analysis) a "cosmopolitan" group of buyers, and how large is this group, if it does exist?

Chapter 4 begins the second part of the book, The Mobility Process. The merged Cincinnati/Wilmington homebuyer survey data set is utilized to examine the types of families most likely to make city choices.

Even if certain types of young householders are attracted to cities, there is no certainty that they will remain there through later stages of the life cycle. Chapter 5 seeks to determine what types of recent homebuyers are most likely to move quickly and what the relative importance of particular background attitudinal and demographic characteristics is in influencing moving plans. An especially important issue that we examine is whether urban-oriented buyers who have purchased in the city plan to stay put (because of the match-up between their values and their current residential situation) or whether they intend relocating as they anticipate moving through later stages of the life cycle.

Whereas chapters 4 and 5 focus on the determinants of mobility decisions (where and when to move), chapter 6 looks at the consequences of these decisions—that is, how recent homebuyers are distributed in space. We use cluster analysis to test for the existence of identifiable groupings of neighborhoods defined by demographic and attitudinal characteristics. The results show that Cincinnati (and to a lesser extent, Wilmington) contains cosmopolitan neighborhoods where the level of affluence and housing prices approach that of the most expensive suburbs.

Part 3, Developing Programs to Attract Middle-Income Families, examines the political and bureaucratic issues that cities face as they try to stimulate the production of market-rate housing. In chapter 7, we assess whether it is possible for cities to prepare citywide housing strategies that address both market-rate and below market-rate housing issues. As we point out, American local housing efforts during the last twenty years have tended to focus exclusively on low-income housing problems. Most of the initiatives and funding have been federal, and the delivery local (Nenno and Brophy 1982). The chapter uses an "insider's perspective" to evaluate why it was possible for a Cincinnati task force (the Housing Blueprint Technical Working Group) to produce a plan dealing with market-rate as well as below market-rate housing. (The Ohio author of this book was a member of, as well as a consultant to, the Technical Working Group, thereby facilitating an insider's viewpoint.)

Chapter 8 examines the practicality of local government efforts to use tax abatements and other economic incentives to attract middle-income families. It may come as a surprise to some readers of this book to learn that a number of cities, including Cleveland, Montreal, and St. Paul, have used these incentives and have been able to do so with relatively little controversy based on the equity issue. Those raising this issue ask: How can middle-income programs be funded when there exists so much low-income housing need? The chapter explains the lack of controversy. Later in the chapter, we use the results of the Cincinnati/Wilmington home-buyer surveys data set to examine a related set of questions. What is the level and nature of demand for tax abatements and below market-rate mortgages among homebuyers? What factors are most important in predicting interest when we take into account the interrelationships among the different determinants?

Programs like tax abatements have a spatial dimension; they are often implemented in conjunction with projects aimed at constructing new market-rate units (or rehabilitating existing ones) in declining central city neighborhoods. Frequently, these projects are resisted by residents from the surrounding area because these residents fear being displaced as a result of conversions or because of rent/property value increases. Chapter 9 first looks at the social science literature to see what suggestions it offers to cities facing this manifestation of the "not in my backyard" (NIMBY) syndrome. From the literature review we turn to a case study of Cincinnati's East End, where the city was able to overcome community resistance to a land use plan that included additional market-rate housing. To achieve community approval, the city involved the community in preparing a plan much broader than the one originally envisaged, one including regulations to protect the character of the area and to address the area's low-income housing needs.

In the following two chapters we shift from housing to school programs. In chapter 10 we analyze the court-ordered metropolitan school desegregation plan implemented in the Wilmington area. We examine the legal basis of this plan, as well as a number of implementation issues, focusing on whether this metropolitan plan has successfully served the needs of low- and middle-income families. Our analysis indicates the limitation of this approach—for example, the busing burden on city children, the refocusing of attention from educational quality to racial equity and discipline—for retaining and attracting middle-class families to cities. In chapter 11 we analyze the Cincinnati public schools, examining closely the city's alternative schools program and whether magnet schools can help retain and attract middle-class families to cities. We see some hope in the reform of this city's schools, and an attractive magnet and a selective college oriented junior and senior high school. We also point out the limits of this approach—concerns about student selection to magnets and discipline/safety in the schools.

Chapter 12, Future City Revitalization Efforts, outlines the major lessons to be derived from our analysis and offers an agenda for future research.

CENTRAL CITY REVITALIZATION: THREE DIFFERENT PERSPECTIVES

Selling Cities is by no means the first book to examine efforts to revitalize central cities. The motivation and context for our book derive from three different literatures concerned about revitalizing cities, but looking at different aspects of the current and future situation. Urban political economists have examined the declining economic status of cities in the postindustrial era and debated the role that government can play in city revitalization. Urban sociologists have focused on the urban poor and have discussed the role of culture and economic opportunity in changing their plight. Planning practitioners have broadened their visions to analyze the maze of governments in metropolitan areas and considered how decision-making structures could be changed to revitalize cities. As we summarize these three literatures below, we show how our book relates to, and builds upon, these works by empirically examining the pushes and pulls of city/suburban moves, by examining programs to hold and attract the middle class in central cities, and by proposing policies to revitalize cities through middle-class enhancement while serving those in need.[1]

URBAN POLITICAL ECONOMISTS: AN ECONOMIC DEVELOPMENT FOCUS

Since the 1970s, economic decline in cities in Europe and North America has provoked a debate as to whether cities can be saved. One side says that it is unwise or impossible to reverse the market forces creating decline. The other side says that the abandonment of urban policy is a form of Social Darwinism with devastating social impact on local communities.

The debate on urban policy includes academics as well as politicians and has centered to a large degree on Paul Peterson's influential 1981 book *City Limits*. Peterson argues that, because cities are in competition for scarce but mobile economic activity and people with resources, cities must avoid redistributional policies. That is, social welfare policies, which take from those with resources to provide for services to the disadvantaged, provide an incentive for individual and business taxpayers to escape from the city to the suburbs. In such havens the taxes households and businesses pay will provide them with services not diluted by helping others. Peterson also argues that redistributive policies are conflictive, for they pit class against class.

On the other hand, developmental (or growth-oriented) policies are supported by the elites and masses of cities. Such policies, which enhance the economic position of the city, include attracting new industry, expanding the tax base, increasing tourism. Developmental policies are necessary for city survival and "create an overriding unitary city interest in meeting the demands of above-average taxpayers" (Henig 1992: 373). A third type of policy, allocational policies, are those basically neutral in their economic effects; these are the so-called housekeeping policies.

The *City Limits* thesis has many critics, and a number of their arguments help to set the context for our book. While accepting that cities are in competition for economic activity and individuals with resources, critics have argued that cities can (and should) still serve the disadvantaged and lower-income groups (Waste 1993). Critics have argued that developmental policies that have focused on upgrading economic activity downtown have led to uneven development, a booming downtown serving middle- and upper-class workers surrounded by decaying neighborhoods housing the poor. Examples of more balanced growth have been identified, where extractions have been made from downtown developers to help city neighborhoods. Fainstein (1990a) argues that the absence of "a unified counterforce to finance- and development-led capital" (142) leaves it for the left to devise a program with a universalistic premise, "promising growth and benefits for the middle class," not simply benefiting labor unions and ethnic minorities. Rosdil (1992) has identified Boston, San Francisco, and Seattle as cities in the United States with progressive policies, policies that Peterson's model would find hard to explain. Such cities mobilize middle- and lower-income neighborhood groups to restrict the role of business leaders in development and "extract resources from downtown investment in order to satisfy neighborhood needs and assist disadvantaged groups" (1).

Peterson's book has also been criticized for its economic determinism. Critics have argued that, despite the pressures for all cities to attract and retain economic activity, different cities have responded in quite different ways to the challenge (Logan and Swanstrom 1990) and that these responses have been tied to political leadership (Molotch 1990). Redistributive policies and programs have been reframed as developmental or allocative policies by mayors and policy entrepreneurs (Waste 1993). "A skilled politician can make a vital difference" in whether a jobs program targeted at low-income residents is viewed as a redistributive or developmental program (Waste 1993: 449). For example, policies fostering uneven growth could be modified by progressive policies "requiring a quid pro quo in exchange for subsidies" and linkage programs, which "permit developers to build high-profit projects only on the condition that they build accompanying low-profit projects . . . or contribute to funding them" (Clavel and Kleniewski 1990: 208–9). Localities are far less constrained to enact such policies than Peterson has argued. Most policies, including educational policies, do not fit easily into one of Peterson's three categories (Henig 1992).

In fact, these policies and their implementation are also differentially impacted by leadership within various institutional sectors such as public schools and housing departments (Wong 1990). We need to explain "how differences in places are coming about and how political initiatives, historic idiosyncrasies, physical constraints, or just plain luck affect outcomes" (Molotch 1990: 177). Furthermore, the notion of a clearly defined economic self-interest of city residents is impossible to sustain (Henig 1992). City residents are motivated by more than economic self-interest, and their definition of interest is influenced by multiple roles and contexts. Henig therefore asks, "Why is it that potentially mobile businesses and middle- and upper-income residents remain in central cities in spite of high tax rates, service cutbacks, infrastructure deterioration, and an apparent decline in social order?" (Henig 1992: 382).

One recent book illustrates the critics' point that leadership and differential responses to economic change can make a difference in city fortunes. *Urban Leadership and Regeneration* (Judd and Parkinson 1990) indicates that the question is no longer whether cities will be able to survive, but rather what strategies they will use. This is a study of how twelve cities on both sides of the Atlantic have responded to economic crisis (Baltimore, Buffalo, Houston, Pittsburgh, Montreal, Vancouver, Glasgow, Liverpool, Sheffield, Rennes, Hamburg, and Marseilles). All are "second tier" cities, which lack major corporate headquarters; all were historically important as port, commercial, or industrial centers. As Susan Fainstein notes in her chapter, these cities have had to respond to the same economic forces and have had the same limited options (that is, promoting an expanded service sector). However, because of differences in history and culture, the cities have responded differently. Those with the highest quality public and private leadership have been able to develop the more complex regeneration strategies.

Judd and Parkinson classify the twelve cities into four categories based on their response to economic restructuring: (1) cities that have developed a capacity to define and implement coherent strategies for regeneration (Pittsburgh); (2) cities that have produced leadership capable of guiding regeneration but where the coalitions are fragile (Glasgow); (3) cities where regeneration operates out of public view in semiautonomous public agencies (Baltimore) or out of the private sector (Houston); and (4) cities that have serious leadership problems (Buffalo).

Pittsburgh demonstrates how important leadership is. Deindustrialization could have led to the type of decline in jobs and population that occurred in Buffalo, but the expected scenario did not occur. Pittsburgh has been able to restructure its economy to one based on corporate headquarters and advanced biotechnology in association with its two major research universities.[2] "It appears that Pittsburgh was able to substantially direct—if not control—its own destiny (298)."

Judd and Parkinson emphasize that the type of economic regeneration that has taken place in Pittsburgh has not benefited all segments of the population equally:

> The existence of a strong leadership in support of regeneration
> . . . does not guarantee that the benefits of regeneration will be
> equitably distributed. In Pittsburgh, the people thrown out of
> work by deindustrialization are not the same people who qual-
> ify for the well-paying jobs in the hospitals, medical laborato-
> ries, research parks or universities. (306)

They conclude by noting that this type of limited success remains
better than failure.

   Urban Leadership and Regeneration therefore raises an important question. What can cities do to address equity issues—that is,
poverty and inner-city decline? Should cities try to upgrade existing
ghettos and create a new middle class? Should they try to eliminate
the ghetto by relocating inner-city residents to the suburbs? Should
they try to attract more middle-class people to the city and create an
"integrated core"? Which one of these approaches (or which combination) is best?

   Our work is certainly based on the premise that cities need to
retain and attract individuals with resources. The central question of
our research is: What will help cities to retain and attract middle-
class homebuyers? Although not the primary focus of our research,
we do show that cities have varied in their responses to the challenge
of retention and attraction of middle-class homebuyers—based on
political leadership and competency in the policy arena.

   Most importantly, in this book we have tried to identify how
cities can retain and attract citizens with resources while still meeting the needs of the disadvantaged. Unlike much of the recent work
on downtown redevelopment, we focus on housing and schooling as
means of middle-class retention and attraction. Instead of assuming
that middle-class homebuyers view their self-interest in the suburbs
rather than the city, we utilize survey research to assess their own
vision of the pulls and pushes of the city as compared to suburbia. We
examine views about the cost of housing as well as the cost of
services, the benefits of neighborhood living as well as the fear of
crime. We discuss how a number of cities, but most specifically
Wilmington and Cincinnati, have tried within the political context
to attract and retain middle-class homebuyers. That is, what kinds of
constraints do politicians and administrators face in formulating
middle-class housing and schooling programs?

   As we see it, two key lessons from the writings on economic
regeneration provide a basis for our book *Selling Cities*. First, cities

are able to intervene in response to economic shifts and direct their own destinies. Second, quality of leadership makes a difference. Both of these lessons are echoed now as we turn to antipoverty strategies and neighborhood stabilization.

URBAN SOCIOLOGISTS: FOCUS ON URBAN POVERTY

The urban sociology literature seeks to improve the lot of the urban poor through essays on inner-city conditions and the "underclass" as well as through empirical studies related to neighborhood development. The relation of this objective (helping the poor) to revitalizing cities and retaining and attracting the middle class is highlighted below. We examine two relatively representative books from this literature, as well as two very recent articles.

Inner-City Conditions and the Underclass

The New Urban Reality, edited by Paul E. Peterson (1985), reports the state of the literature as of the late 1970s. It includes papers by some of the most well-known scholars involved in the debate on how to address urban decline: Anthony Downs, William Julius Wilson, Gary Orfield, and John Kasarda. Typical of this genre, it offers a gloomy assessment for prospects for revitalization. The contributors differ on the causes of urban ills, and consequently the book does not offer a coherent strategy for improvement.

The pessimistic tone is most evident in the first chapter by Peterson (1985) and in the last one by Downs (1985). Peterson itemizes the familiar litany of problems facing central cities: the migration of jobs and people, ethnic tensions in racially changing neighborhoods, the deterioration of the black family, and the inability of cities to address the problem of violent street crime. He not only questions the feasibility of efforts to stem decline; he suggests that they may no longer be desirable: "Industrial cities must simply accept a less exalted place in American political and social life than they once enjoyed. Policies must adapt to this new urban reality" (1). This pessimistic prognosis leads Peterson to the conclusion that the federal government should not help cities as places, but should help the poor as individuals or families. His "nonurban" policy involves the federal government taking responsibility for both the costs and administration of welfare programs; currently, the federal government shares these responsibilities with state and local governments.[3]

Anthony Downs (1985) is also pessimistic about the fate of America's cities but for different reasons. Downs is familiar with the three types of strategies discussed elsewhere in *The New Urban Reality,* having reviewed them as a member of the Kerner Commission in 1968: (1) ghetto enrichment; (2) integrated dispersal; and (3) a combination of dispersal along with a program to strengthen the central business district. Since the commission's recommendation of an integrated dispersal strategy was not acted upon in the succeeding seventeen years, he is pessimistic that any change would occur through the publication of this volume.

Downs's own "realistic strategies" prove not to be very practical at all. His first recommendation—that the black community assume more control by electing more black mayors—has been superseded by events of the 1980s and 1990s. In the four largest American cities, black mayors have been replaced by white ones, as voters have expressed increased concern for "nuts and bolts" issues like street crime and balanced budgets. His second proposal—for more internal discipline within the black community—is one made rather frequently today by black politicians and black scholars, but we see little evidence of action following rhetoric.[4]

One aspect of Downs's call for improved discipline should be emphasized because of its relevance to this review. He recommends that blacks form alliances in order to improve their situation. Such alliances would include downtown property owners; "they might support more ghetto enrichment as a quid pro quo for further integrated core development benefiting them" (292). Thus, Downs acknowledges that a middle-income development strategy could provide spillover benefits for the inner-city poor. *Selling Cities* examines the feasibility of such a strategy, based on the locational preferences of middle-income families and the political practicality of addressing both middle- and low-income housing/schooling needs.

There are a surprising number of optimistic nuggets throughout this generally pessimistic book. For example, John Kasarda (best known for his recommendation that the federal government do away with place-oriented programs like public housing) recommends that cities take better advantage of their competitive advantage in attracting particular businesses (those involved with information processing) and in attracting particular groups (childless couples with dual incomes, "empty nesters," households pursuing nontraditional lifestyles).[5]

Brian Berry (1985) warns against the type of media hype concerning gentrification that was so common during the late 1970s.[6] Policymakers should not, however, understate the substantial impact of this trend in cities that are on the whole experiencing decline:

> Decreased vacancy rates, increases in property values, stability in once declining neighborhoods, encouragement of other forms of development in or near the neighborhoods, and increased interest in the central city to live . . . (81)

The challenge for city leaders is how to nurture this trend of gentrification, while at the same time addressing the displacement concerns of residents of established areas. *Selling Cities* discusses this balancing act through a case study of the East End of Cincinnati.

Gary Orfield's chapter (1985), "Ghettoization and its Alternatives," suggests that both suburban dispersal and an integrated core strategy may be more feasible than Anthony Downs thinks. A large-scale experiment in Chicago arising from the Gautreaux decision shows that it is possible to relocate inner-city blacks to the suburbs. As of 1984, the program had resulted in the relocation of two thousand blacks, and an evaluation indicated that participants had benefited through better schools and better job opportunities.[7] Orfield also offers some surprisingly good news about the prospects for integration in central cities. Analysis of Chicago census data for the 1970s indicates an astonishingly high degree of stable racial integration in the city: "Redevelopment and gentrification have created a cluster of stably integrated communities close to the Loop on all sides, in Hyde Park, and in the Near North Side" (185). Thus, integrated neighborhoods may be one of the unrecognized benefits of gentrification.

Selling Cities seeks to answer empirically two questions raised by Orfield. First, does the trend toward central city integration reflect the search for mixed neighborhoods by highly educated home-buyers, or does it reflect childless couples insensitive to racial tension moving into gentrifying areas?[8] Second, does the existence of magnet schools or metropolitan school districts make white families with school-age children more willing to move into central city neighborhoods?

The part of Kenneth Small's chapter (1985), "Transportation and Urban Change," most relevant to this review is his discussion of a statistical simulation (in which he participated) that tested for the impact of five revitalization policy "packages" on one city, Cleveland. The five included: a job stimulus package, a housing rehabilitation package, a fiscal equalization package that merged all municipal and country governments within Cuyahoga County, a transit improvement package, and a suburban growth package containing constraints that reduced suburban growth by twenty-five percent from what it otherwise would have been.[9] When all five packages were combined, they reduced the city's job loss by fifty percent, completely offset its loss of households, and cut its population loss by about two-thirds. These are no mean achievements and indicate that it is possible to slow, if not reverse, central city decline, at least in simulations.[10]

Terry Nichols Clark offers some good news about the ability of cities to react to population and job losses. In the first place, population loss is not entirely bad: "local officials in Pittsburgh . . . point out that population decline helped eliminate slums and crowding, permitted construction of more spacious parks, and allowed for more desirable land use" (262).

Furthermore, as we noted above in our discussion of Peterson's *City Limits*, economic forces do not "mechanistically" determine how cities adapt. Individual solutions are forged as a result of the interaction of citizen preferences, organized groups, and political leaders, in addition to the economic base.[11] In other words, leadership matters in dealing with inner-city decline just as it does with economic regeneration. What city leaders can do is to devise better ways to "satisfy the demands of local citizens for both low taxes and good services [in order] to improve productivity in city government" (280).[12] Achieving these goals could go a long way towards attracting and holding middle-income families and in promoting social mobility among the poor.

Thus, a close reading of *The New Urban Reality* suggests much basis for hope. Efforts to attract more middle-income families to the central city could help to slow decline and could have a particularly marked impact on areas near to downtown.

Selling Cities builds upon the kernels of hope found in *The New Urban Reality*. We provide badly needed empirical research on the types of families moving into central cities to supplement gentrification research carried out almost fifteen years ago. Furthermore, we examine the role of leadership in developing housing/schooling programs that are sensitive to the needs of both middle- and low-income families. Much of the urban poverty literature has focused on the growing "underclass," rooted, persistently destitute ghetto dwellers, typified by single-parent households, out-of-wedlock births, little formal education, joblessness, and crime. Local leaders recognize that unless they tackle this issue, the prospects for maintaining the economic and social viability of their city are poor.

"The Ghetto Underclass: Social Science Perspectives" (Wilson 1989a), a special issue of the *Annals of the American Academy of Political and Social Science,* shows the experts sharply divided on the causes of the growing underclass, but in some agreement on possible remedies. We will focus on this book because it contains articles by some of the most prominent researchers in the field.

Wacquant and Wilson (1989) are representative of those scholars who stress economic and social factors in creating the underclass. According to them, the worsening conditions of the inner city result from the relocation to the suburbs of blue-collar jobs and the migration of middle-class blacks who had served as role models. The organized ghetto of the 1940s is, as a result, being replaced by the disorganized ghetto of the 1980s and 1990s.[13]

Several of the chapters support Wacquant and Wilson's argument. John Kasarda (1989) documents the growing disparity between skill requirements of central city jobs and skill levels of black residents. Elijah Anderson sees the growing number of unwed parents as a response to worsening job prospects: "partially in response [to job conditions], the young men's peer group emphasizes sexual prowess as a mark of manhood, at times, including babies as evidence" (59). Testa et al. find that employed fathers are much more likely than unemployed fathers to marry the mother of their first child.

Lawrence Mead, on the other hand (1989), is typical of social scientists who argue that cultural factors play a role in creating and maintaining an underclass. According to him, members of the underclass want to work, but they do not feel very strongly about it; "it is an aspiration not an obligation" (162). Several of the articles support Mead's thesis. For example, cultural factors help to account for the ability of some recent immigrant groups (Koreans, Dominicans) to succeed despite facing the same structural impediments as inner-city blacks: "[Their ethnic] businesses are characterized by thriftiness and long hours of intense, hard work, with continuing reinvestment of profits" (Kasarda 1989: 43).

Along similar lines, Nathan notes that it will be hard to solve the problem of the underclass because of the attitudes of many ghetto residents: "The people who need help are often resentful, alienated, and prone to hostile acts. This makes the politics of response much more difficult than in an earlier period" (172).

The gap between "structuralists" like Wilson and "individualists" like Mead is not as great as it appears throughout much of the book. In the final chapter, Wilson concedes that there is a ghetto culture, a subset of dysfunctional attitudes that are more prevalent in the inner city, such as an overt emphasis on sexuality. These attitudes are reinforced by the social and spatial isolation of residents. Where Wilson and Mead disagree is on the long-term impacts of these attitudes. Wilson asserts that these attitudes would disappear (or not be transmitted to the next generation) if the structure of opportunities changes. Mead, on the other hand, speculates that the ghetto culture will not pass so quickly; he sees it as influencing residents' ability to take advantage of opportunities. This collection of essays, "The Ghetto Underclass," provides little concrete evidence at the individual level with which to resolve this debate.

The discussion of solutions provides some basis for optimism. The contributors offer an eclectic mix of recommendations focusing both on individuals and on economic structures. Kasarda, not surprisingly, recommends programs offering spatial mobility—for example, public-private efforts to van-pool unemployed inner-city residents to suburban businesses facing job shortages. However, he also calls for strengthening the black family and for upgrading public schools so as to take advantage of central city job opportunities. Similarly, Sullivan recognizes the need for both long-term solutions (addressing the structural economic factors that concentrate poverty in the inner city) and short-term ones as well (for example, including males in programs for preventing unwanted pregnancies).

A number of the contributors see the development of workfare requirements as part of welfare reform at the state level as a positive sign. Mead notes that workfare helps the poor with the job search and also helps them to be more assertive. The fact that workfare has been developed at the state level is a strength; this quiet incremental approach avoids the expansive rhetoric associated with new federal programs.

Whether workfare will lead to a more comprehensive approach to the underclass is uncertain. There has been some convergence between liberals and conservatives leading to a consensus in favor of a workfare requirement. Nevertheless, many liberal legislators still play down the work requirement (in favor of additional social services) in order to avoid upsetting some advocates for the poor. Wilson's rather shrill criticism of workfare in this volume certainly hurts the prospects for using "new style workfare" as the basis for an incremental approach to dealing with the underclass.[14]

Unfortunately, Wilson (in the concluding essay) does not offer a cohesive strategy to address the underclass issue. He does repeat a suggestion made by Robert Reischauer, one of the contributors, that a public sector job strategy be implemented as a last resort. Because of its exorbitant cost, such an approach would not be politically feasible.

"The Ghetto Underclass" and *Selling Cities* are linked in two ways. First, the former provides a moderate degree of confidence about the ability of government to tackle the underclass issue. Being able to do so is a prerequisite to improving the quality of life of the central city and attracting the middle class, which is the focus of our book. Second, Wilson's writings in that volume raise a question that we examine. Would it be possible to slow the migration of the black middle class and in this way provide the types of role models that are sorely missing in inner-city areas today? Such a strategy would only be appropriate if it were implemented in conjunction with efforts to reduce suburban housing discrimination. In other words, efforts to retain and hold middle-class blacks would be part of a larger effort to provide the emerging black middle class with as many options as possible—that is, to remain in the city, or to move to the suburbs.[15]

Two recent articles—by Nicholas Lemann (1994) and Mitchell Sviridoff (1994)—highlight the continuing debate among scholars concerning the feasibility of efforts to achieve inner-city revitalization. Both are skeptical about the prospects for President Clinton's Empowerment Zone legislation under which six large swaths of big cities will be selected to receive tax breaks and other benefits.

Lemann points out that Empowerment Zones are a continuation of a failed series of policies over the last thirty years, policies that assume the only long-term solution for poverty is revitalization through neighborhood economic development. In fact, according to Lemann, "it is . . . extremely difficult to find statistical evidence that any inner-city neighborhood in the country has been economically revitalized" (30). Among the factors making economic development nearly impossible are high crime rates, low skill levels among residents, continuing population migration (in areas supposedly experiencing revitalization), and the absence of homegrown business activity.

Both Lemann and Sviridoff see community development corporations (CDCs) as a ray of hope in the midst of inner-city decline, but interpret CDC successes differently. (A CDC is a nonprofit community-based organization governed by a board consisting of neighborhood residents and business leadership dedicated to the revitalization of a defined area. CDCs focus on economic development, jobs, housing, and other aspects of area livability.[16]) Three of the most successful CDCs have pursued a housing strategy of increasing the degree of income and tenure mixing.

(1) In Newark, New Jersey, the Central Ward's New Community Corporation has built, owns, and manages upwards of twenty-five hundred apartments. One measure of its success is the development of more than one thousand middle-income condominiums immediately adjacent to the NCC development area.

(2) The Charlotte Street Area of the Bronx has experienced a dramatic physical transformation as a result of the Mid-Bronx Desperadoes. The area now has ninety privately owned, white-picket-fenced ranch houses, which have attracted moderate income families. "On a given block, privately-owned houses sit side-by-side with small-scale projects for the elderly, single-parent families, or the once-homeless" (Allen 1992: C3).

(3) Large-scale funding from foundations and corporations has allowed the Bedford Stuyvesant Restoration Corporation to pursue a balanced housing strategy:

> Restoration's community organizing strategy centered around the rehabilitation and stabilization of the area's handsome brownstone blocks, in addition to highly productive efforts to increase the supply of new and rebuilt housing for poorer residents. (Sviridoff 1994: 94)

CDCs have, therefore, shown that they can improve the livability of inner-city areas by improving the delivery of social services, including housing. The lesson, according to Lemann, is that politicians should seek increased funding for CDCs, based on what they do (housing production) rather than what they do not do.

Sviridoff draws a wider set of implications from the CDC experience. According to him, "by the late 1970s, a dozen or so major CDCs akin to [Bedford Stuyvesant] Restoration Corporation had proved themselves effective agents of neighborhood revitalization" (94). Successful revitalization, according to Sviridoff, has to do with a greater degree of social organization in areas where this feature was not present previously[17]:

> At its core, field experience suggests social organization is about the ways in which people behave in relation to their neighbors and community. It is about how neighbors organize themselves to deal with problems that go beyond food, shelter and clothing . . . [to] the quality of the schools, or its PTA, or adult literacy. (101)

Sviridoff's article must be considered a preliminary foray into this subject. He provides no evidence that the above areas are more viable socially. Equally important he does not address directly Lemann's assertion that to be successful, a neighborhood revitalization effort must yield more local jobs. Had he done so, he would have seen a fairly gloomy picture: "in the neighborhood where New Community [Corporation] operates there is almost no private sector economic activity" (Lemann 1994: 54).

For the purposes of this review, we would stress the areas of agreement between Lemann and Sviridoff—that is, that CDCs can improve the livability of inner-city areas and that they can do this through a "balanced" housing strategy involving assistance to moderate/middle-income families as well as to lower-income ones.[18] Thus, despite the generally gloomy tone of the urban sociology literature, it does provide some basis for hope for central city revitalization. Furthermore, there is a clear-cut link between these writings and our focus on attracting middle-class families. The latter would be part of a broader effort aimed at strengthening downtown and near-downtown areas; an effort which would provide badly needed low-skill jobs. Furthermore, middle-income housing programs could strengthen the already promising work of CDCs by increasing the level of income and tenure mixing. Minority middle-class families living in these communities could provide badly needed role models for poor youths. The blending of families from different backgrounds could begin to unravel the cycle of poverty.

Empirical Studies of Neighborhood Development

The preceding highlights the importance of promoting a mix of housing (by income, tenure) as part of CDC revitalization efforts. If local governments and foundations are to nurture such mixing, better information will be needed on the types of families who are attracted to such communities as homebuyers as well as their willingness to invest in home improvements. That is, what types of families seek to or are willing to live in such mixed areas? To what degree could economic incentives (cheaper housing prices, below market-rate mortgages) increase willingness to locate in such neighborhoods? Would the existence of rehabilitation grants and subsidized loans contribute to an increased likelihood of making home repairs and improvements than would otherwise be the case?

Unfortunately, the urban sociological writings that we have reviewed up to this point do not provide decisive answers to these questions, since the works are based on casual observation or impressionistic evidence. Conclusions regarding mobility from this body of research may not be valid. We now turn to empirical research dealing with *when* to move and *where* to locate. The key question here is: What do we know about the impact government programs can have in holding existing families in cities and in attracting other families?

Varady's 1983 residential mobility research is typical of this recent scholarly work; it suggests that government possesses limited ability to hold families in cities.[19] His study using 1974 to 1977 national data from the longitudinal version of the Annual Housing Survey (now called the American Housing Survey) showed that concerns about public services did not play a meaningful role in the analysis, implying that efforts to hold middle-income residents in declining neighborhoods through improved services would not succeed. His 1984 study using a data set from the longitudinal survey of residents of the U.S. Department of Housing and Urban Development's Urban Homesteading Demonstration neighborhoods found that the demonstration itself had no impact on moving over and beyond background characteristics. This finding highlights the difficulty of holding middle-income families in this particular type of inner-city area.

Similarly, Galster's 1987 research shows government housing programs having a limited stabilizing effect. Based on a sophisticated multivariate analysis of homebuyer survey results for Minneapolis and Wooster, Ohio, Galster finds that the receipt of a loan for home rehabilitation is directly related to short-term moving plans. It therefore appears that an unintended side effect of such programs is to permit short-term capital gains recouping. The rehabilitation loans clearly were not helping to hold participants at their locations.[20]

Up to now we have discussed research on the determinants of mobility (the decision to move or stay). Scholars generally agree that the factors affecting mobility are different from the determinants of locational choices (for example, city versus suburbs). Thus, it is conceivable that government could play a meaningful role in influencing migration flows into cities even if it cannot affect residential attachments.

Unfortunately, there has been far less research on these locational choices than there has been on mobility plans/behavior. Furthermore, what is known about locational decisions in regard to central cities is largely based on case studies of gentrifying communities carried out in the 1970s (see, for example, Laska and Spain 1980). It is a mistake to generalize from gentrifying neighborhoods (which comprise only a small proportion of the land area of cities and are atypical in terms of the presence of amenities) to central cities as a whole. Furthermore, conclusions derived from these studies in the 1970s may no longer be applicable because of changes in cities and suburbs—for example, the development of apartment complexes and entertainment strips in the suburbs appealing to precisely those demographic subgroups such as college-educated couples without children, who have been presumed to have a high propensity for central city living.

In addition, there has been a paucity of research up to now on the importance of residential preferences in influencing residential choices. Research carried out during the 1970s focused on demographic characteristics such as education, and made inferences regarding attitudes such as a taste for cosmopolitan living. Such inferences may not be valid. Finally, gentrification research was relatively unsophisticated statistically, relying almost exclusively on bivariate statistical techniques. Consequently, relatively little is known about the importance of particular variables controlling for others (for example, the impact of education controlling for marital status).

Selling Cities addresses all of these weaknesses in the locational choice literature. The book builds upon Varady's research on mobility plans and Galster's research on housing improvements in three specific ways. First, following the approach used by Galster, we use a combination of path analysis and logit analysis to analyze the impact of background demographic characteristics through neighborhood assessments and preferences to city-suburban choices. Second, we examine in much more detail the role of public schools in affecting residential choices than has been the case in previous research. We ask: What proportion of homebuyers consider public school quality important in locational choices, and to what extent do concerns about public schools influence choices when other demographic and attitudinal characteristics are controlled? What impact can metropolitan school districts and magnet schools have in making central city public schools more attractive to families with children? Third, we, like Galster, are interested in the degree to which housing programs can stabilize middle-income populations in central cities. However, whereas Galster focused on how governments could use repair loans and grants to hold such families, we focus on the extent to which other housing programs (tax abatements and below market-rate loans) could influence the willingness of such families to locate in central city neighborhoods.

Planning Practitioners: Focus on Metropolitan Cooperation and Planning

Three recent books dealing with metropolitan planning provide a rosier picture regarding the prospects for addressing urban poverty: *Cities Without Suburbs* (by David Rusk 1993, former mayor of Albuquerque, New Mexico), *CitiStates* (by Neal Peirce 1993, noted journalist), and *Old Problems in New Times* (by Oliver Byrum 1992, planning director, Minneapolis, Minnesota). Aimed at practitioners and informed citizens, readability is stressed, and statistics are kept to a minimum.

In the 1960s, metropolitan planning was seen as a way to make local governments more efficient; today metropolitan planning is seen as a means to address urban poverty and to stem central city decline.[21] City-suburban cooperation could help to remove disparities in tax rates, which drive families and businesses to the suburbs.[22] Further, better metropolitan planning could help to link inner-city poor with suburban housing and employment opportunities. Finally, American metropolitan areas functioning as integral units could compete better with conurbations from around the world for office headquarters, factory sites, and convention business; some of the resulting economic activity would filter to the inner-city poor.[23]

There have also been some encouraging signs of increased interest in metropolitan cooperation and metropolitan planning. The Twin Cities implemented fair-share housing legislation in the 1960s, and in the 1970s instituted a unique metropolitan tax-base-sharing effort. Portland, Oregon, has a metropolitan planning mechanism that not only limits growth at the edges but also requires all local governments to develop a full range of price and density housing within their borders, regardless of federal funding for that housing. Two federal initiatives (the Federal Clean Air Act and the Intermodal Surface Transportation Efficiency Act [ISTEA]) also contribute to some optimism about the future.

Although legislation to permit metropolitan planning must come from the state level, the impetus for change will have to be local in the form of citizen-led metropolitan lobbying groups.[24] Furthermore, central city politicians will have to address weaknesses of city government if they are to help create a sense of regional citizenship and to obtain the needed cooperation of their counterparts on the other side of the municipal boundary.[25]

All three authors see the attraction of middle-class families as a key component of a central city revitalization policy. Rusk highlights the primacy of these programs as part of inner-city regeneration efforts, noting "a revived middle-class in the cities . . . must be the leavening of inner city revival" (122). Byrum emphasizes the need to "make the distinction between shelter programs for those in severe need and efforts to economically and physically revitalize a neighborhood, the two being quite different" (117). According to him, attracting middle-income families to the city is a key to central city revitalization. A ghetto enrichment policy alone will not succeed.

Peirce and Byrum identify a number of specific approaches toward attracting and holding middle-income families, including: (1) quality public schools, (2) neighborhood organizing to create a sense of community, (3) marketing and public relations,[26] (4) financial incentives such as below market-rate loans to rehabilitate inner-city housing, (5) sustaining existing stable middle-income areas by addressing crime, reducing ethnic tensions, and keeping taxes as low as possible.

Byrum and Peirce's recommendations are valuable, but it is important to recognize that they are assertions without empirical backing. Byrum concedes this point: "The reader should read this report as the academic synonym for assertion—that is, an hypothesis needing examination, testing and discussion" (v).

Selling Cities responds to the above noted gap. We examine the empirical basis for the above suggestions (for example, whether families without school-age children are unaffected by public school issues) as well as homeowner interest in particular options such as governmental subsidized below market-rate mortgage loans.

The three authors differ in how far they would go towards eliminating existing local governmental fragmentation. Rusk advocates creating more metropolitan governments by consolidating particular central cities with their surrounding urban counties.[27] Peirce and Byrum, on the other hand, recommend more incremental improvements—that is, better metropolitan cooperation and stronger metropolitan planning.

Rusk argues that elastic cities, those that have been able to annex their suburbs, are healthier than inelastic ones, based on such measures as job and population growth, city-suburban income gap, residential and school integration, and bond ratings. According to him, cities that do not adopt the metropolitan government model are destined to decline as they run out of developable suburban-type land.

The main criticism of metropolitan government is that it is not feasible (Salins 1993). Rusk concedes this point late in the book when he notes that this is not a practical suggestion for larger, older cities, not only on political grounds[28] but also because, as a result of economic trends, these cities are "beyond the point of no return."[29] In these cities, Rusk sees improved cooperation and more effective metropolitan planning as a more appropriate strategy for dealing with urban ills. Thus, *Cities Without Suburbs* is not quite as radical as the title implies.

Rusk, Peirce, and Byrum stress different approaches to inner-city revitalization. Rusk basically ignores the subject, assuming that it will be possible to solve the poverty problem by dispersing the inner-city poor to the suburbs. Peirce emphasizes ghetto enrichment, an expansion of social welfare, housing and economic development programs that are targeted on the inner city. Critical to the success of these health, schooling, and policing programs, argues Peirce, is that they involve residents at all stages of development and implementation. The Atlanta Project (initiated by ex-President Jimmy Carter, see Knack 1993) is cited as an example of what can be done.[30] Finally, Byrum offers a "middle of the road" approach. He suggests funding programs that maintain the overall livability of the area (for example, better public education) but not funding place-oriented programs like housing, because they would anchor people in these areas.[31]

Improvements in metropolitan planning cannot alone solve the problems associated with inner-city poverty and central-city decline. Only the federal government has the resources to tackle the underlying causes of poverty, which include, but are not limited to, the lack of jobs for individuals with limited skills. Obstacles to developing a coherent antipoverty program include: (1) the limited funds available for domestic programs, (2) the ideological bickering between conservatives and liberals as to the ability of government to solve social problems,[32] and (3) the differences of opinions among academic experts regarding solutions.[33]

The preceding points can make one pessimistic about the future prospects for inner-city ghettos and, by implication, central cities. Byrum counters this sense of gloom by noting that we know enough now to do a better job than we are doing at present:

> It is clear from what is going on in Minnesota and around the country that we know a lot about solutions. A great deal more is being learned in research and demonstrations. The problem is not so much not knowing what works as knowing how to deploy what works at the scale needed. (65)

Demonstration programs in cities like Minneapolis and St. Paul, where the problems are still manageable, could result in insights for program development elsewhere. Byrum makes the same point as Nathan (1989)—that Americans need to be patient about antipoverty efforts; incremental improvement is the best that can be expected.

Selling Cities is based on the premise—drawn from the above literature—that it is feasible to deal with inner-city decline but only as part of metropolitanwide strategies that include attracting middle-income families to cities. Our book focuses on the question: What types of housing and schooling policies will be most effective in stimulating such migration to inner cities?

CONCLUSIONS

The three sets of writings reviewed in this section (central-city economic regeneration, urban poverty, metropolitan planning) provide some basis for optimism about efforts to slow, if not reverse, patterns of urban decline. Some cities, like Pittsburgh, have been able to stimulate service sector jobs. Some CDCs, like Newark's

New Community Corporation, have been able to begin to physically transform their area and to expand affordable housing opportunities. Finally, in a handful of metropolitan areas (most notably, Portland and Minneapolis/St. Paul), city and suburban officials are working together to deal with suburban sprawl and inner-city poverty. The key element in all of these successes is the quality of local leadership.

Although there are numerous serious obstacles to central-city revitalization, there is considerable basis for confidence about the prospects for addressing decline. Much more can be done in slowing decline with the information that is available.

However, critical gaps in knowledge exist about one key component of city revitalization, efforts to attract and hold middle-class families. The existing literature offers numerous hypotheses concerning programs that could potentially help cities to attract and hold middle-income families. Up to now, there has been little empirical research aimed at testing these hypotheses. *Selling Cities* aims to close this gap.

3

Two Cities and Their Recent Homebuyers

The first part of this chapter seeks to acquaint the reader with our two study areas (Cincinnati, Ohio, and Wilmington, Delaware) and with the surveys of recent homebuyers that we conducted in these two metropolitan areas. The second part of the chapter takes a look at the survey results as we seek answers to the question: What are recent homebuyers really like?

The neighborhood revitalization literature reviewed in chapter 1 implies that the homebuyer markets in Cincinnati and Wilmington contain an identifiable grouping of "cosmopolitan" buyers, singles and young couples predisposed toward urban living. The limited empirical research on the subject (Michelson 1977; Hanz 1971) provides no support for the existence of such a city-oriented segment. However, both of these studies were conducted prior to the mid-1970s, when an upsurge in city living occurred. Therefore, this chapter should provide some needed, up-to-date information on this subject, in addition to introducing the reader to our research methodology.

THE SETTING

Cincinnati, Ohio, is a central city of 364,000 population in a metropolitan area of about 1.4 million people. The metropolitan area is spread across eight counties in three states and encompasses 2,620 square miles (Urban Land Institute 1990, figure 3.1). Hamilton County, in which Cincinnati is located, has a population of 866,000, about the same as in 1960 (figure 3.2). Like other midwestern and northeastern cities, Cincinnati has experienced a drop in population, losing 140,000 residents from 1960 to 1990. During the past decade the population has stabilized (Sturmon 1989) because of the region's healthy economy and because of the drawing power of some of the city's older cosmopolitan neighborhoods. The area's diverse economic base (Cincinnati is the home base for Proctor and Gamble, Kroger Company, and Federated Department Stores, among others), means that unemployment rates have been relatively low and that the area has been shielded from the sharp economic fluctuations experienced by cities on the east and west coasts. Housing prices are moderate in comparison to other major American cities.

Cincinnati is well known for its viable, compact downtown, which contains a number of award-winning restaurants. During the past decade, college-educated white-collar workers have migrated to a broad band of communities extending from north of the central business district east to the Ohio River. Some of the communities, such as Mt. Adams, are well known as gentrifying areas. Others (Clifton, Hyde Park) are historically prestigious areas with attractive neighborhood business districts, which never underwent decline. Another more recent positive sign for the city has been the construction of expensive condominium apartments on the tops of hillsides, near downtown, with views of the Ohio River (Bolton 1990; Kent 1990). One of the challenges for city leaders (discussed in detail in chapter 9) is how to promote the construction of additional market-rate housing in these areas that would take advantage of these amenities without displacing the existing working-class and lower-class residents.

In the Cincinnati area, families seeking suburban attributes tend to look in suburban areas because of the city's older housing stock and because of perceived problems with the city's public schools. In 1984 the Cincinnati Board of Education adopted the Alternative Schools Program, a magnet school arrangement, as part of a racial desegregation settlement (the Bronson suit). While students

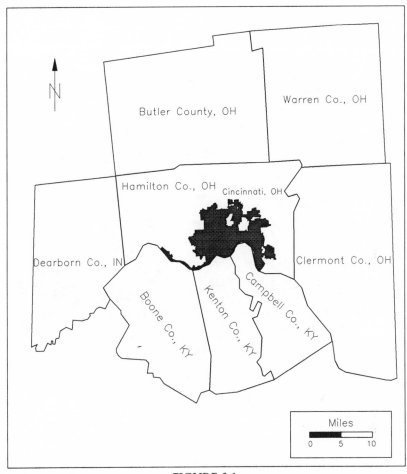

FIGURE 3.1
Hamilton County Primary Metropolitan Statistical Area. *Source:* Ed
Ratledge, Center for Applied Demography and Survey Research,
University of Delaware

can volunteer for these schools, student selection is a function of the
degree of integration at each school.

New Castle County, in which the city of Wilmington is located,
has continued to increase in population in the 1980s. In 1980 the
population was just under 400,000; today it stands at over 440,000
(figure 3.3). Wilmington, however, has had a constant population of

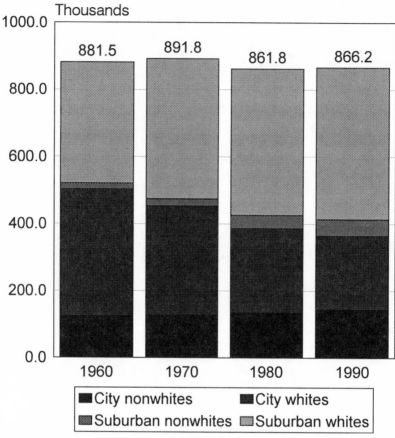

FIGURE 3.2

Hamilton County Population, 1960–1990. *Source:* U. S. Census

approximately 70,000 since 1980. This followed, however, its post-war drop from well over 110,000.

Technically, the Wilmington Metropolitan Statistical Area contains three counties in three states. In practice, most officials define the metropolitan market as just New Castle County. This area is 437 square miles (figure 3.4) and includes the university town of Newark, the historic city of New Castle, as well as the working class area of Elsmere. The county is bordered by the Delaware River and New Jersey to the east, Pennsylvania to the north, and Maryland to the

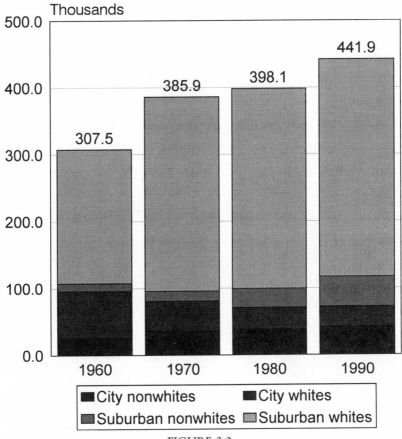

FIGURE 3.3
New Castle County Population, 1960–1990. *Source:* U.S. Census

west. The two remaining Delaware counties, Kent and Sussex, lie to the south.

New Castle County has experienced an economic and housing boom accompanied by inflation in the latter part of the 1980s. The boom has been the result in large part of the Financial Centers Development Act of 1982 and the Consumer Credit Bank Act of 1983, which brought major banking and credit card operations to Wilmington and New Castle County to join DuPont, Hercules, and ICI headquarters as well as General Motors (due to close in 1998) and

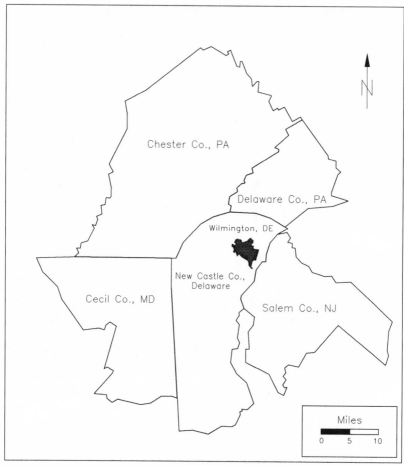

FIGURE 3.4
New Castle County Primary Metropolitan Statistical Area. *Source:* Ed
Ratledge, Center for Applied Demography and Survey Research,
University of Delaware

Chrysler assembly plants in the county. The average home price
increased faster than wages (O'Neill 1990; Applied Economic Research 1989). It has been estimated that only about 13 percent of
New Castle County's renters can afford to purchase the median
priced house or unit. As a result, many homebuyers are looking
outside the county, and even the state, for housing (O'Neill 1990).
    The population loss and shift in economic activity in the

Wilmington metropolitan area suggest that even those who prefer the more traditionally urban attributes may well find their preferences better met outside city lines. New Castle County's largest shopping center, the Christiana Mall, is in the suburbs. There is not a movie theater left in Wilmington. Although many restaurants remain in the city, there are certainly far more in the suburbs, including a majority of the best restaurants in a variety of categories, as determined by a newspaper poll and critic's views ("Readers Choice" 1992). That the nature of each of these two areas is different is illustrated by the fact that Cincinnati has a major baseball and football team in the city, while Wilmington recently lured a minor league team (Wilmington Blue Rocks of the Carolina League) with a new stadium.

In 1978 the federal court ordered the Wilmington public schools to merge with the ten surrounding suburban school districts after finding that the state had not desegregated the public schools in the city as per previous court decisions (Raffel 1980). In 1981 the state reorganized the New Castle County school district into four districts, each with a portion of the city and a larger portion of suburban New Castle County. The pupil assignment plan in each of the four districts was built on the principle of city pupils being bused into the suburbs for nine years and suburban children being bused into the city for three years. Kindergarten students were assigned to neighborhood schools. The grades offered in the city vary by school district, but by court order they must span grades 1–12. Two-thirds of the pupils in the public schools in the county are white, over one-quarter are black (28%), and the remainder are primarily Asian and Hispanic. Almost 25 percent of the county's school children attend private or parochial schools.

Although the major difference between the two areas is their approach to school desegregation, they do differ in other respects as well. Wilmington represents about 15 percent of the population of New Castle County, while Cincinnati represents about two-fifths (42%) of Hamilton County. The median household income in New Castle County was $38,617 in 1989 and $29,498 in Hamilton County (U.S. Bureau of the Census 1993b). While the density of Wilmington is somewhat higher than Cincinnati's (6,637 versus 4,740 persons per square mile in 1986), the density of Hamilton County is twice that of New Castle County (U.S. Bureau of the Census 1988). Over half of Wilmington and one-third of Cincinnati's populations are black, but the percentage of blacks in both counties is approximately 20 percent. The percentage of high school graduates and college graduates is slightly higher in New Castle County.

In general, Cincinnati and Wilmington are like many older American cities, especially those in the east and upper midwest. Cincinnati comprises 18.6 percent of the metropolitan area, compared with a mean of 16.1 percent for all "old" cities (Pollakowski and Edwards 1987). Similarly, 43.1 percent of Cincinnati's housing units were built before 1940, compared with 51.5 percent for all old cities. Wilmington is home to 13.4 percent of the metropolitan area's population, and half (47.8%) of its housing stock was built before 1940 (U.S. Bureau of the Census 1990). Pollakowski and Edwards define an old city as one containing 30 percent or less of the total urbanized area and having a housing stock of which 40 percent or more was built before 1940.

Both cities have features that help to set them apart from others. Cincinnati has two drawing cards that most medium-sized midwestern cities do not have: a relatively vibrant and well-defined downtown area and a large stock of well-maintained older homes, many from the Victorian era (Schwab 1987). Wilmington's main attraction is its role as a corporate headquarters city and home of the DuPont Company. We have chosen to study these cities because we know them well, and we could locate and collect the data needed for our analysis. We believe, and the data show, that the similarities between Cincinnati, Wilmington, and other midwestern and northeastern cities are great enough for us to offer insights to the reader about stemming central city decline.

Focusing on these two metropolitan counties thus allows us to examine the impact two different approaches to school integration have had on migration decisions. New Castle County has one of the few combined city/suburban school districts in the north. In the latter system, families cannot flee from the city to escape school integration without leaving the state. Hamilton County has a more typical setup, with a distinct city system and a number of suburban ones. Under the 1984 court mandate, the Cincinnati public school system has set up a series of alternative schools ("magnets") to promote integration. This book compares the effectiveness of Cincinnati's choice system with Wilmington's combined city/suburban districts with respect to their ability to attract and hold middle-class families. In addition, the book looks at other programs that the two cities have implemented (or have considered implementing) to attract and hold middle-income families.

Housing Supply

Previous writings on housing supply, primarily but not entirely from economists, make two key points. First, older landlocked cities like Cincinnati and Wilmington have a difficult time holding middle-income families. As middle-income families move up the socio-economic ladder, they seek larger and newer homes. As a result of the lack of developable land, cities cannot offer such housing options. Most new, upscale housing is, as a consequence, built on the suburban fringe. The new home construction on the suburban fringe pulls middle-income families from the city, thus undercutting the city's financial stability.

A second housing supply process also harms cities. Typically, the number of new housing units added through construction on the edge initiates a chain of moves eventually resulting in the abandonment of housing units near the center of the city. Below, we examine how these processes play out in Cincinnati and Wilmington.

Housing Supply and Suburbanization

An analysis of 1990 census results shows that families seeking new upscale housing had few choices in the cities of Wilmington and Cincinnati in the 1980s. The 1990 census indicates that 3,206 housing units were constructed in the city of Wilmington in this decade (U.S. Bureau of the Census 1992a). In comparison, over 30,000 were constructed in the suburbs of Wilmington during this period. Thus, the percentage of new housing units built in the city was just over 10 percent of the total built in the entire county. Furthermore, of the 3,206 units built in the city, only one-third (1,053) were owner-occupied. In the suburbs 19,995 owner-occupied units were built. Thus, the percentage of newly constructed owner-occupied units built in the city of Wilmington in the last decade was even less than the percentage of all new housing units, only 5 percent.

Relatively fewer new homes were built in the Cincinnati metropolitan area than in the Wilmington metropolitan area in the 1980s. As in the Wilmington area, the vast majority of those new homes built were constructed in the suburbs. There were 35,856 new units built in Hamilton County in the 1980s, but only 7,815, or 21.8 percent, were built in the city. The percentage of owner-occupied units built in the city of Cincinnati was only 7.8 percent during the 1980s.[1] This is a higher proportion than in New Castle County but a smaller percentage than the existing ratio of city/county housing units. Thus, while those in the Cincinnati area had more absolute and relative choices of new housing in the city than their Wilmington area counterparts, in both metropolitan areas new building was concentrated in the suburban areas.

Those looking for above-average priced residences also had to look to the suburbs. In 1990 the median value of an owner-occupied housing unit in New Castle County was $110,900, according to the 1990 U.S. Bureau of the Census (1993a). In Wilmington the median was $77,500, two-thirds of the suburban median of $118,233. In the city only 16.9 percent of these housing units had values equal or greater than $125,000 (and 26.2 percent over $100,000) in 1990 (U.S. Bureau of the Census 1993a). In the suburbs the percentage of owner-occupied housing units valued at over $125,000 was 36 percent. The proportion of units valued at more than $100,000 was over half (55.1%). Thus, those seeking above-average housing had few choices in the city of Wilmington and a great variety of choices in the suburbs.

While the prices were lower in the Ohio than the Delaware study area, the geographical pattern of housing prices was similar. Housing units in Cincinnati were valued at three-quarters of the price of those in the suburbs. The city median value was $61,700 in 1990, while the suburban Hamilton County median value was $80,867. Those seeking a home worth over $100,000 would have found 17.7 percent of the Cincinnati and 30.4 percent of the suburban Hamilton County housing stock at this level. Again, the Cincinnati area offered more middle-class and upper-class housing in the city than in the Wilmington area, but in both metropolitan areas the suburbs offered far more choices for the homebuyer with resources and the desire for superior housing.

The greater availability of upscale housing outside the city limits is driving suburbanization. This conclusion emerges from an analysis of a 1991 homesellers data set for seven Ohio metropolitan areas, which helps us to go beyond the federal census to determine the extent to which the availability of higher priced homes stimulates suburbanization.[2] Moves of homesellers were determined by matching names of sellers with names of buyers. Records used for matching were from recorded deed transfers. In order to determine the spatial patterning of the moves, family addresses were coded into census tracts. Each census tract was located in one of a series of one-mile rings emanating from the center of the city. The number of rings used varied by metropolitan area.[3] In all seven metropolitan areas, roughly four out of five homesellers moved up in price. The median price move up for Cincinnati (57%) is typical for the seven metropolitan areas.

The seven cities vary in terms of the opportunities offered for those moving up the housing stock. Cincinnati contains roughly one-fourth (24%) of the homes priced equal to or above the median for the metropolitan core ($75,000). This is a more favorable situation than in Cleveland (4%) but less favorable than that for Columbus (47%) or Toledo (50%).

Within Cincinnati, the concentration of higher priced housing varies by area. The downtown area (ring one) has the highest median sales price ($121,000). Ring one in Cincinnati has a higher median sales price than comparable ones in the other six cities. Cleveland is next with a median of $91,000. These higher priced units are mostly condominium apartments located in the central business district or overlooking the Ohio River. It is important to point out that the high median is based on only 24 sales, which comprises less than 2 percent of the higher priced sales in the city. Thus, while these downtown condominiums constitute a positive sign for the city, they have limited significance in terms of the overall housing market.

The availability of higher priced housing in the central city helps to account for variations in migration from the seven cities. As might be expected, Cleveland, lacking a supply of upscale homes, had the highest migration rate; 86 percent of the sellers moved out of the city. Also as anticipated, Columbus, with a relatively larger supply of upscale homes, had a relatively low migration rate; "only" 57 percent moved outside the city limits. The Cincinnati results are somewhat puzzling. The city ranked in the middle of the seven in terms of the proportion of higher priced housing within the city boundaries.[4] However, the migration rate was relatively high (74%).

The preceding indicates that supply factors are an important but not a sufficient factor in understanding suburbanization. If homesellers are moving primarily as a result of their desire to advance toward their housing ideal, there is little that a city can do to hold them if the city contains little upscale housing. However, the availability of higher priced homes cannot fully explain the rate of migration; some families look at combinations of housing and neighborhood factors, including the quality of the public schools and the level of public safety. Thus, it is necessary to look at demand side factors in addition to housing supply information. This is precisely what we do in later sections of this book.

New Construction and Abandonment

The 1990 census revealed that across the nation 13.8 million housing units were built from 1980 to 1990. While the number of housing units in the nation increased by nearly 16 percent, the number of households increased by only 10 percent during this time. Household size has continued to decline and across the nation there was an increase in vacant housing units. The census reported that "slightly more than 10 million housing units, 10 percent, were vacant in 1990, up by 2.3 million over 1980" (U.S. Bureau of the Census 1991a: 1). As Brian Berry (1985) has indicated, the increased building, primarily in suburbs, has not been matched by household numbers increasing at the same pace and this has led to housing abandonment concentrated in cities.

Census data for Cincinnati and Wilmington show that new construction in both metropolitan areas exceeded household growth. This surplus undoubtedly contributed to the large number of abandoned units near the center of both cities. Although census results do not specify the location of these abandoned units, casual observation of both cities indicates their concentration in the center city.

Specifically, in New Castle County the number of new housing units built, 33,249 (U.S. Bureau of the Census 1983; 1992a), exceeded the increase in households (25,217). Thus, the metropolitan area could not absorb all the new homes without some change in the vacancy or abandonment rate. Since the number of vacant units stayed approximately the same over the decade, the number of units withdrawn had to account for the difference. In the Wilmington metropolitan area 30 percent of the withdrawal took place in the city. Following a similar logic, two-thirds of the 17,785 units withdrawn in Hamilton County during the 1980s were located in the city of Cincinnati.

Mobility and Migration Patterns

The United States is a nation of movers. The 1990 U.S. Census of Population and Housing (1993a) indicated that almost as many people living in a metropolitan area in 1990 changed their residence between 1985 and 1990 as had remained in their home. While 93 million of those five years or older stayed in place for this five-year period, 86 million changed residences. Millions of individuals moved from suburbs as well as from cities; one-quarter moved from one metropolitan area to another. Although not analyzed by the census, a substantial proportion of these moves were city to suburban and suburban to city.[5]

Analysis of movers in New Castle County and Hamilton County challenges some myths about city-suburban mobility; 57.1 percent among New Castle County residents, and 55 percent among Hamilton County residents, were living in the same home in 1985 as in 1990 (U.S. Bureau of the Census 1993a). Thus, movers represent over 40 percent of the residents of each area.

About one-third of the movers crossed city-suburban boundaries in their moves. The Wilmington percentage of replanted suburbanites approaches one-third—20 percent from Wilmington's suburbs and 8.9 percent from the suburbs of other metropolitan areas. The fraction of those living in Cincinnati who came from the suburbs was smaller but still substantial. Among the 1990 residents of this city, 14.5 percent reported living in the Cincinnati suburbs in 1985, and 8.5 percent reported living in the suburbs of another metropolitan area five years earlier. Thus, while some individuals may be fleeing cities, others are being attracted to cities, at least to Cincinnati and Wilmington.

Among those who moved to a home in the suburbs of Wilmington from 1985 to 1990, only 18 percent had lived in Wilmington or another city in the earlier year. The city of Cincinnati lost far more residents, absolutely and on a percentage basis to its suburbs, during this five-year period. Fully 29.1 percent of the 1990 suburban residents over five came from Cincinnati to the suburbs from 1985 to 1990. Another 8.4 percent came from other cities.

Analysis of residential moves in New Castle and Hamilton counties leads to questions about prevailing stereotypes. Only a small proportion of the suburban increase reflects people moving from the core city. On the other hand, despite the attention given to headlines about "return to the city," this type of population flow is relatively small in the two metropolitan areas.

While the above information on the magnitude of population flows is helpful, policymakers require answers to a number of other questions in order to do a better job in attracting and holding middle-income families. They need to know: Who is moving into the city? How strong are the residential attachments of subgroups moving into the city? Why are some types of families making particular residential choices? What types of programs that could be implemented by cities might cause additional families to choose the city? These are precisely the questions that we examine in later chapters in the book.

Survey Methodology

In both metropolitan areas, surveys were mailed to recent homebuyers in order to study the location decision-making process and to gather information on demographic characteristics. Both surveys included similar sets of questions to measure the location decision-making process, moving plans, evaluations of city and suburban public schools, and background demographic characteristics. To better understand the criteria that homebuyers stressed in their housing search, we asked about the importance of twenty-one different factors, ranging from "close to work," "near to schools," to "quality of governmental services." For each factor, we asked whether it had been "very important," "important," or "not important" in the housing search. Table 3.1 presents the marginal results for the different locational choice items. In New Castle County the respondents were asked about their views of all five school districts in the county and three nearby school districts in Maryland and Pennsylvania. In Hamilton County the focus was on respondents' evaluations of the city schools in relation to those in the suburbs.

The Cincinnati sample, totaling approximately 6,600 households over three waves of surveys, consists of those who purchased homes during 1985, 1986, and 1987 (table 3.2). Almost 2,800 Wilmington householders who purchased homes in 1988 were also surveyed by mail. Budget limitations prevented us from sending another copy of the survey to nonrespondents. Such a follow-up would have raised the response rate but would not have eliminated variations in response rates by community. Consequently, the benefits of a follow-up mailing would have been marginal. Telephone interviewing, with its higher response rates than mailed surveys, was not a feasible methodology, since we did not have telephone numbers for homebuyers on the real estate transactions list. Many of these householders would not have been in the most recent telephone directory, because they had unlisted numbers or because they arrived at their locations after the directory was published.

For both counties, survey data were combined with objective information on the housing units (for example, size, age of the unit, sales price) from the real estate transactions data set. Table 3.3 portrays the demographic characteristics of the two samples.

The fact that the survey contained so many different demographic variables made it necessary to combine them into broader measures. We created an index to identify stage-in-life cycle groups by crosstabulating four variables: marital status, age (under 50 years, 50 years or more), presence of preschool age children, and presence of school-age children. This classificatory approach, based on McCarthy's 1976 report, identifies eight household types associated with the following percentages of homebuyers in Hamilton and New Castle counties respectively: (1) single, no children (17%, 17%); (2) young couple, no children (15%, 23%); (3) young couple, preschool children (10%, 13%); (4) young couple, school-age children (25%, 28%); (5) older couple with children (2%, 2%); (6) older couple with no children (10%, 8%); (7) older single person with no children (8%, 4%); (8) single headed household with children (13%, 5%).

We conducted a cluster analysis of the sample in four stages. First, we conducted a factor analysis of responses to the set of twenty-one items dealing with choice criteria. Factor analysis is a method for looking at the interrelationships among different variables, thereby identifying broader dimensions to represent the individual characteristics. The factor analytic results for Cincinnati identified seven factors: (1) suburban residential—overall appearance of area, style of houses, large lots, suburban setting, changes in property values; (2) childrearing—near school(s), quality of local public schools, access to child care; (3) economics—low taxes, quality of government services, safety; (4) neighborhoods—near people "like me," near friends and relatives, lived nearby before and liked it; (5) accessibility—near public transportation, near stores, near churches/synagogues; (6) urban—urban setting, near a mix of people and; (7) nonexperiential attributes—near to work, good housing prices. Six factors were identified in Wilmington:[6] (1) childrearing—near schools, near churches/synagogues, access to child care, quality of local public schools; (2) suburban residential—style of houses, large lots, overall appearance of environment/area, changes in property values; (3) economics—good housing prices, low taxes, quality of government services; (4) neighborhoods—near friends and relatives, near people "like me," lived nearby and liked it, safety; (5) urban—near public transportation, urban setting, suburban setting (inverse), a near mix of people and; (6) accessibility—close to work, near stores.

Second, we conducted a factor analysis of both samples, including all relevant background demographic and migration characteristics as well as the factor scores discussed above. Eight factors were identified in Hamilton County: (1) social rank—education, high-status white-collar job, blue-collar job (inverse), income; (2)

TABLE 3.1

Proportions of City and Suburban Respondents in Hamilton County and New Castle County Considering Various Locational Characteristics "Important" or "Very Important"[a]

Characteristic	Hamilton County			New Castle County		
	City	Suburbs	Total	City	Suburbs	Total
Overall area appearance	74%	88%	84%[b]	81%	91%	90%[b]
Good housing prices	81	74	76[b]	79	82	82
Safety	68	77	74[b]	70	69	69
Style of houses	63	70	68[b]	60	77	75
Quality of public schools	40	68	59[b]	22	48	46[b]
Lived nearby before and liked it	50	54	53	37	34	34
Suburban setting	25	61	50[b]	12	67	61[b]
Near to work	55	46	49	62	52	53
Near to friends/relatives	49	49	49	39	36	36
Change in property values	46	50	49	72	71	71

Near schools	35	54	48[b]	16	38	45[b]
Near stores	44	44	44	32	38	38[b]
Quality of government services	33	37	36	30	34	33
Low taxes	36	35	35	26	38	37[b]
Near people "like me"	36	34	34	30	29	29
Large lots	22	38	33[b]	10	44	41[b]
Near churches/synagogues	28	31	30[b]	18	18	18
Near public transportation	31	16	21[b]	21	9	10[b]
Near a mix of people	25	16	20[b]	33	17	19[b]
Urban setting	29	13	18[b]	48	12	16[b]
Access to child care	10	15	14[b]	9	13	13[b]
N=	711	1564	2275	292	2497	2789

[a]The original response categories for the above items were: (1) not important, (2) somewhat important, (3) don't know, (4) important and (5) very important. The first three categories were coded into the one group while the latter two were combined into the other one.

[b]City-suburban differences are statistically significant at least at the .05 level.
See Appendix 1 for definitions of variables.

TABLE 3.2
Homebuyers Surveys

Location	Sampling Frame	Transaction Dates	Time of Survey	Returned Surveys*
Hamilton County	5,457	1985 (Jan.–June)	Jan., Feb., 1986	2,250
	6,272	1986 (Jan.–June)	June, July 1987	1,758
	7,133	1987 (Jan.–June)	June, July 1988	2,275
New Castle County	7,500	1988 (Jan.–Dec.)	Sept.–Dec. 1989	2,789

*The analysis was restricted to homebuyers living in the dwellings that they purchased, including cases where a family rented an apartment to another family. Those purchasing for speculative purposes only—that is, residing elsewhere from the unit they purchased—were excluded from the analysis.

suburbanism—suburban residential factor score, childrearing factor score, school age children, married; (3) urbanism—urban factor score, accessibility factor score, economics factor score; (4) first time buyer—previously rented, previously resided in city, previously resided out-of-town (inverse), age (inverse); (5) starter household—two

TABLE 3.3
Demographic Characteristics of the Samples

	Hamilton County		New Castle County	
	City	Suburbs	City	Suburbs
Attended college	48%	42%a	87%	81%a
Professional workers	38%	37%	69%	66%
Blue-collar workers	30%	37%a	7%	11%a
Married	56%	72%a	48%	77%a
Children under 5	25%	34%a	12%	25%a
Children 5 to 18	29%	43%a	18%	35%a
White	86%	93%a	87%	95%a
Two or more adult workers	37%	37%	44%	48%
Household size	2.51	2.95a	2.13	2.87a
Age	38.7	38.3	37.2	37.2
Average income	$33,423	$37,852a	$46,696	$50,747a

aSignificant difference between city and suburbs at least at .05 level.

or more workers, previously resided with another family, preschool age children (inverse); (6) neighborhood orientation—child(ren) in parochial school, neighborhoods factor score; (7) nonexperiential—nonexperiential residential attributes; (8) white—white. Nine factors were identified in New Castle County: (1) social rank—high-status white-collar work, income, education, blue-collar work (inverse); (2) suburbanism—childrearing factor score, suburban residential factor score, school age children, married; (3) nonsuburban—economics factor score, neighborhoods factor score, urban factor score, accessibility factor score; (4) city orientation—moved from city, parochial school child(ren); (5) out-of-town—moved from out-of-town, previously resided with another household (inverse); (6) aging-whites—age, white; (7) two-worker household—two-worker household; (8) previously rented—previously rented; (9) preschool child(ren)—preschool child(ren).

Third, cluster analyses were conducted using the cluster feature of SPSS-X and the previously mentioned eight factors for Hamilton County and nine for New Castle County.[7] Cluster analysis is a technique for combining individuals, families, neighborhoods, and so forth, into a smaller number of subgroups based on the similarity of the individuals/census tracts with respect to variables included in the analysis. The process identified five clusters of homebuyers in Hamilton County and five in New Castle County.

Finally, the stepwise discriminant analysis feature of SPSS-X was used to identify the distinctive features of the five Hamilton County/New Castle County clusters. Discriminant analysis is a statistical technique for testing for the importance of different background characteristics in distinguishing two or more subgroups from one another—for instance, those choosing the city from those choosing the suburbs (table 3.4 and table 3.5).[8]

CHARACTERISTICS OF RECENT HOMEBUYERS

Demographic and Attitudinal Characteristics of Recent Homebuyers

Our results indicate that households in the childbearing and childrearing stages of the life cycle (the types associated with suburban living) no longer dominate the homebuyer market. That is, in both the Hamilton County and New Castle County samples, fewer than half of the buyers were couples with children (37% in Hamilton

TABLE 3.4
Group means for homebuyer clusters—Hamilton County.

Cluster[a]	Number of Households	Social Rank[b]	Suburbanism[b]	Urbanism[b]	First Time Homebuyer[b]	Starter Household[b]	Neighborhood Orientation[b]	Nonexperiential Attributes[b]	White[b]
One	61	1.08	1.17	.24	.35	-.07	.10	-.02	.17
Two	74	.93	-.14	-.47	-1.30	-.15	-.24	-.52	.33
Three	159	-.74	-.21	-.74	.05	.31	-.09	-.26	.10
Four	79	1.04	-.74	-.52	.55	.11	-.56	.15	.20
Five	183	-.51	.25	1.00	.29	-.26	.42	.48	-.41
All groups	556	.01	.02	.00	.05	-.01	.01	.03	-.02
F statistic		247.21	49.96	170.25	68.62	7.59	16.91	21.66	11.06

[a]Clusters: One, suburban middle class families; Two, executives from out of town; Three, blue collar suburbanites; Four, upwardly mobile childless households; Five, lower status urbanites.

[b]Statistically significant differences at least at the .05 level.

TABLE 3.5
Group means for homebuyer clusters—New Castle County

Cluster[a]	Number of Households	Social Rank[b]	Suburbanism[b]	Nonsuburban Attributes[b]	City Orientation[b]	Out-of-Town Orientation[b]	Aging/ White[b]	Two Workers[b]	Previously Rented[b]	Preschool Child[b]
One	69	.34	.45	1.39	-.13	-.30	-.06	.30	-.26	.08
Two	57	-1.53	.90	-.02	-.34	-.01	-.05	.24	-.11	.27
Three	157	.33	.53	-.16	.35	-.27	-.33	.06	-.27	.33
Four	187	.60	-.62	-.43	-.15	.38	.08	-.08	.33	-.17
Five	59	-1.68	-.88	.11	.05	-.33	.32	-.10	.03	-.52
All groups	529	.00	.00	-.01	.00	-.02	-.05	.04	-.01	.00
F statistic		380.51	95.99	62.05	8.21	13.91	7.84	2.78	9.84	11.41

[a] Clusters: One, suburban "urbanites"; Two, blue-collar suburbanites; Three, suburban middle-class families; Four, blue-collar suburbanites; Five, low-status empty nesters.

[b]Statistically significant at least at the .05 level.

County, 43% in New Castle County). Nearly as many households (32% and 40% respectively) were in the prechild stages of the life cycle—that is, in the stages that have been linked with city living.

Hamilton County contained somewhat smaller proportions of homebuyers in the prechild and child-oriented stages of the life cycle than New Castle County and a higher proportion of households in the postchild stages (18% versus 12%). Hamilton County also had higher proportions of single headed households with children (13% versus 5%). The latter result probably reflects the generally lower housing costs in Hamilton County. Single parents who would not be able to afford a home in New Castle County are able to afford the more modest costs in Hamilton County.

Suburban type residential values more clearly dominate the homebuyers market than stereotypical suburban type demographic characteristics. This is most clearly shown by the proportions of homebuyers seeking "suburban" versus "urban" residential characteristics. Whereas half or more of the respondents said that it was "important" or "very important" to obtain a suburban setting, less than a fifth of the respondents in the two counties said that it was important to obtain an urban setting.

The same conclusion (that is, the greater importance of suburban attributes) emerges when we examine the results dealing with attributes associated with suburban/urban living. Roughly half of the respondents in the two counties stressed the importance of living near schools or emphasized the importance of public school quality in their housing search. The proportions of homebuyers stressing the schools is somewhat greater than the proportions with children. This seeming discrepancy probably reflects the emphasis on school variables among young couples planning to have children in the near future.

A considerably smaller proportion (33%, Hamilton County; 41%, New Castle County) emphasize "large lots," a prototypical suburban attribute. This finding probably reflects the fact that many young couples cannot afford such housing now, although they may be striving for such properties as part of their housing ideal.

Urban type residential attributes were mentioned far less frequently than suburban ones. Only about a fifth of the respondents felt that it was important to live in a neighborhood with a mix of people. A similarly small proportion sought to live near public transportation.

A priori, we expected Hamilton County buyers to place a

greater stress on public school quality. As a result of Wilmington's combined city-suburban school districts, we anticipated that buyers there would perceive minimal differences between city and suburban schools. Consequently, they would not emphasize this criterion. Table 3.1 supports this expectation. A significantly higher proportion of Hamilton County than New Castle County buyers considered public school quality "important" or "very important" in their housing search (59% versus 46%).

Conversely, we expected New Castle County buyers to place a stronger stress on property value appreciation so as to counterbalance or keep up with the sharply rising housing costs in that county. The results are as expected. Whereas nearly three-quarters of the New Castle buyers stressed this factor, this was true for only half of the buyers in Hamilton County.

Our results highlight a third difference between buyers in the two counties. This one was unexpected. Hamilton County buyers were more likely to emphasize neighborhood values, such as finding a home in a community they had lived in previously or one where they would be close to friends and relatives. The lower neighborhood emphasis among New Castle buyers reflects the fact that a larger proportion are highly paid executives moving up within the homeownership stock. Such homebuyers are less likely to stress neighborhood values.

Homebuyer Clusters

Table 3.4 provides limited support for our hypothesis that both counties would contain identifiable cosmopolitan clusters. Hamilton County did contain this type of cluster (14% of the homebuyer population). However, this cluster was identifiable only with respect to the demographic characteristics mentioned in the neighborhood revitalization literature (for example, a college education, the absence of children). This cluster was not distinguishable on the basis of residential attitudes such as an interest in urban living or an interest in racially mixed neighborhoods. The reasons for this being so are discussed below.

The above conclusion—no cosmopolitan cluster in New Castle County—requires a caveat. The county does contain a cluster, "suburban urbanites," which bears a faint resemblance to the cosmopolitan stereotype. That is, these homebuyers stress urban residential criteria (strong neighborhoods, accessibility, "urban living"). In terms of these latter values, such households would ordinarily be considered "urban." However, in contrast to what might be expected, these homebuyers have the demographic and migration characteristics of family-oriented suburbanites (relatively high income, one or more young children, a previous location in the suburbs). It appears that in metropolitan areas like Wilmington, where most of the urban amenities such as shopping and restaurants are located in the suburbs, many of the more urban type households are to be found there as well.

Both Hamilton and New Castle counties contain lower status homebuyer clusters ("lower-status city dwellers" in Hamilton County and "lower-status childless households" in New Castle County). These clusters differ in several important ways (tables 3.4 and 3.5). In general, the Hamilton County households are further along in the family housing cycle than they are in New Castle County. Specifically, the former are typically households with children moving from a rental apartment into their first owned home. In contrast, the norm in New Castle County is newly formed families with no children. Furthermore, these lower-status Hamilton County buyers have far stronger links to the central city. Not only are they more likely to have moved from a location in the city, they are also more likely to stress urban locational choice criteria, including a concern for accessibility and an interest in racially mixed neighborhoods. This latter finding undoubtedly reflects the relatively large proportion (28%) of blacks in the Hamilton County cluster and the greater interest of blacks in integrated neighborhoods. In any case, the attitudinal results for Hamilton County help to explain why the "demographic urbanites" in Hamilton County were not distinguishable in terms of residential attitudes: the "lower-status city dwellers" were the ones most likely to emphasize urban residential attributes.

Hamilton and New Castle counties resemble one another with respect to the presence of three other homebuyer clusters: (1) "blue-collar suburbanites"; (2) "suburban middle-class households"; and (3) "executives from out-of-town." The distribution of homebuyers among these three clusters varies by county. Hamilton County contains a higher proportion of blue-collar suburbanites, whereas New Castle County contains a higher proportion of middle-class families and executives from out-of-town. This latter finding undoubtedly reflects the continued migration of salaried white-collar professionals into the Wilmington area to take jobs in banking and related financial concerns.

Conclusions

Cincinnati and Wilmington are representative of older, relatively densely settled cities in the northeast and upper midwest. They have both declined in population since 1960, have lost a substantial proportion of their white population, and have few, if any, areas within their borders with "suburban" attributes. The supply of upscale housing in these cities is limited—new building has occurred almost entirely in the suburbs and the bulk of the higher priced homes are found beyond the cities' boundaries. Consequently, findings from this and later chapters should be generalizable to this broad grouping of cities.

Cincinnati and Wilmington have implemented two sharply different approaches to school desegregation. Cincinnati has implemented a magnet schools program limited to the city. Wilmington is one of the only cities in the north that use metropolitan school districts to maintain integrated schools. We expected Wilmington's approach to school desegregation to have more impact on residential choices and attachments than Cincinnati's Alternative Schools strategy. As a consequence of the metropolitan school districts, families would see relatively few differences in quality (and integration) between city and suburban schools. This would promote city choices. Chapter 4 tests for the validity of this hypothesis.

The statistical profiles of recent homebuyers presented in this chapter indicates that demographic and lifestyle changes over the past several decades have had only a limited impact on the homebuyers market. While the stereotypical suburban middle-class family (a couple with children) is no longer as dominant as it was during the 1950s, 1960s, and 1970s, the childless, cosmopolitan household is not nearly as important as is suggested by the revitalization literature. Two key findings support this conclusion. First, families with suburban values *continue* to dominate the homebuyers' market. Second, neither Hamilton County, Ohio, nor New Castle County, Delaware, contains a cluster comprising upwardly mobile childless couples with cosmopolitan values.

In the next chapter we move from our aggregate profiles of homebuyer clusters to an analysis of the homebuyer decision between locating in the city or the suburbs. In this analysis we examine not only the roles of lifestyle and life cycle but also views about the schools in the city and suburbs.

PART 2

THE MOBILITY PROCESS

4

CITY-SUBURBAN CHOICES

If policymakers are to do a more effective job in developing policies to attract and hold middle-income families, this will require improved knowledge of the underlying factors affecting mobility decisions. Up to now there has been extensive research on the decision of *when* to move, but relatively little on the choice of *where* to move. Previous research by the Ohio author of this book shows policy variables having relatively little influence on cities' ability to hold middle-income families (Varady 1983). What is not known, but is of critical importance to policymakers, is why certain types of families choose particular locations, and the impact that different types of policies might have on this type of decision (Rossi and Shlay 1982). It is especially important to know the impact of concerns about public school quality, in general, and particular types of desegregation strategies in particular, on city-suburban choices. (Chapters 10 and 11 discuss in considerable detail the literature on the impact of two options—metropolitan school districts and magnet schools—on white flight.)

Addressing this gap in the literature, this chapter seeks to answer four sets of questions. First, to what extent does the emphasis on public school quality vary between householders in these two metropolitan areas, and how does this emphasis vary among other demographic subgroups? Second, to what extent do perceptions of differences in school quality between the city and the suburbs differ by metropolitan area as well as by demographic subgroup? Third, how does the likelihood of making a city or suburban choice vary by metropolitan area, by demographic subgroup, and by residential assessments (including evaluations of the public schools)? Finally, what is the relative importance of different background characteristics in influencing city-suburban choice when the interrelations among these variables are taken into account?

The first part of this chapter reviews the literature on residential decision-making, beginning with economic and ecological theories and then studies from the 1950s and 60s dealing with the underlying causes of white suburbanization. The section next discusses the more recent research from the 1970s and 80s dealing with central city revitalization—that is, Who has been moving into the cities and why? The second part of the chapter uses this literature review to: (1) develop a schematic model of the city/suburban choice that we use to guide our research and (2) to develop a set of hypotheses dealing with the factors we expect to influence city/suburban choices. The final section uses the merged Cincinnati/Wilmington data set to test these hypotheses.

ECONOMIC AND ECOLOGICAL THEORIES

Mieszkowski and Mills (1993) conclude that there are two major theories of suburbanization. The first they term the "natural evolution" theory: "when employment is concentrated at the center of the city, around a port or railhead, residential development takes place from the inside out" (136). The central city area becomes filled with businesses and residences, and development then shifts to open tracts of suburbia. High-income groups, seeking more land and larger houses, move to the periphery. Lower-income groups settle in the smaller central city properties. Economic development is tied to the residential movement.[1] Thus, "this natural working of the housing market leads to income stratified neighborhoods" (136). This theory is based on the assumption that "the middle class . . . prefers larger single family lots in the suburbs to denser multi-family residences in the central city" (136).

The second theory of suburbanization, a "flight from blight" approach, is built around the fiscal and social problems of cities, such as high tax burdens, low quality schools, and racial tensions. Affluent city residents escape from these problems by moving to the suburbs; the loss of these residents adds to the city's unattractiveness. Individuals not only prefer residing with others of similar income, race, education, and ethnicity, but "by residing in income-stratified communities, the affluent avoid local redistributive taxes" (137). One result is that the concentration of high-income, highly educated people leads to well-financed and high-achieving school districts, which become magnets for further suburbanization.[2]

It is unclear from the literature which of the two theories provides a more accurate understanding of suburbanization since the end of World War II. Mieszkowski and Mills point out that suburbanization remains a global process and that suburbanization in the United States has not accelerated during the post–World War II period despite the increased presence of urban problems. Thus, there is strong evidence that the natural evolution theory is empirically validated. On the other hand, cross-country evidence suggests that the USA has experienced more decentralization than other nations; the greater decentralization does seem to support the flight from blight thesis. The most that can therefore be said is that both theories are important.

Better understanding of the importance of the two theories will only take place when broad economic variables like "restructuring the economy" are specified so that they can be tested at the micro-level (Kephart 1991).[3] Then, individual residential choices could be examined against other factors, such as the individual's housing and neighborhood quality.

Demographers (Frey 1979, 1985; Frey and Kobrin 1982) have tested for the importance of these push-and-pull forces, using aggregated data and examining, among other things, the correlation between citywide crime rates and both the overall mobility rate and the incidence of city-to-suburban moves. Unfortunately, this type of research illustrates the ecological fallacy; it produces assertions about individuals as the unit of analysis based on the examination of groups or other aggregations. It is conceivable, for example, that those people least concerned about crime in high crime areas are the ones most likely to choose suburban locations.

Survey analysis that focuses on individual households is the appropriate analytic approach to improve understanding of mobility decisions. In recent years, social scientists concerned with intraurban migration have chosen the individual household as the unit of analysis and have conceptualized mobility as consisting of two interrelated steps: the decision to stay or to move; and the search for and selection of an alternative. They have seen the latter decision— which is the focus of this chapter—as consisting of three components:

a. Specifying criteria for evaluating vacancies. Each household establishes the range of acceptable alternatives, based on site and neighborhood characteristics.
b. Searching for vacancies. The household's limited search space is a function of its familiarity with different school districts and government units, and this familiarity, in turn, is affected by commuting and social patterns.
c. Choosing a home. "Vacancies are evaluated in terms of the weighted sum of the attributes used to delineate the aspiration region. These weights reflect the relative importance of the criteria used to specify the aspiration region and so they will vary according to the preferences and predilections of the household concerned" (Knox 1982: 128).

A MODEL OF RESIDENTIAL CHOICE[4]

The conceptual model used in this chapter (figure 4.1) draws from theoretical studies of residential mobility, especially those dealing with the search for and selection of an alternative location (Herbert 1973; Knox 1982; Moore 1972). It consists of three sets of variables: (1) background characteristics and mobility experiences; (2) the importance attached to different housing and neighborhood components combined with evaluations of these components; and (3) the city-suburban choice.

The model implies that specific background characteristics can affect the city-suburban choice indirectly or directly. That is, some factors may affect choice through their impact on the criteria used in the housing search (an indirect effect: Herbert 1973; Katzman 1980; Michelson 1977). For example, those people with higher education may place a greater emphasis on public school quality in their choice of a location and would also be more likely to hear about good places to live in the city. Other factors might affect search behavior or the ability to follow through on preferences (a direct effect: Brown and

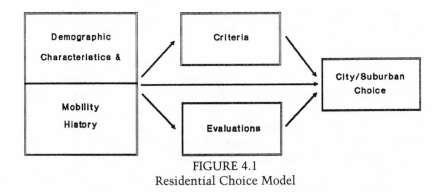

FIGURE 4.1
Residential Choice Model

Holmes 1971). The question is: What factors would be expected to influence the choice, either indirectly or directly? Our expectations, based on previous research, are discussed below.

THE INFLUENCE OF LIFE CYCLE AND LIFESTYLE

Since the 1950s many sociologists have argued that the household's life cycle position along with its lifestyle is critical in predicting whether the household will move to a city or a suburban location. Abu-Lughod and Foley (1960) assert that, as families proceed through the different stages of the life cycle—postmarriage, childbearing, childrearing, "empty nester"—they have different residential requirements, which lead to different locational choices. Bell (1958, 1968) observes that industrialization has provided families with the choice of three lifestyles, each one creating different residential needs: familism, a way of life centered around the children; careerism, in which members of the household are mainly oriented towards upward social mobility; and consumerism, an attempt to attain the "good life." Sociologists attribute the high rate of post–World War II suburbanization to the large number of families in the childbearing and childrearing stages of the life cycle seeking the larger homes and properties available in the suburbs.

Michelson (1977) notes that the childrearing-familism model fails to explain all household locational choices. Many lower-income households, including first-time owners wanting to suburbanize, are unable to do so because of high suburban housing costs. For instance, many blacks who can afford suburban housing remain in the central city because of housing discrimination (Kain 1986). Finally, some blue-collar families, called "urban villagers" by Gans (1962b), remain in the central city out of choice to maintain close and familiar social patterns.

Empirical research during the 1950s, 1960s, and early 1970s emphasized the importance of familism and family life cycle position in explaining city-versus-suburban choices. In these studies, households moving to the suburbs were usually families with children, while the smaller number of households moving to the central city were young singles or couples without children. City and suburban movers gave sharply different reasons in explaining their most recent moves. Suburban movers usually cited reasons related to the betterment of their children—a larger home or a better social environment. Those who moved to the city usually cited reasons related to consumerism or careerism, such as better access to jobs and other downtown amenities.

A Shift in Influence?

As mentioned in chapter 1, the dispersion of multifamily housing, including apartments, as well as restaurants, cinemas, and nightclubs in the suburbs may have increased the attraction of "nontraditional households" such as singles, couples without children, and gays to suburban areas. However, recent empirical research provides conflicting evidence on whether the determinants of city-suburban choice have, in fact, changed. Two studies imply that a change has occurred; they suggest that city and suburban movers did not differ either in their demographic characteristics or their reasons for choosing their current city or suburban location (Goodman 1978; Spain 1987).

On the other hand, two recent multivariate studies provide conflicting and ambiguous results. Contrary to expectations, Marshall and O'Flaherty (1987) found that respondents 33 years of age and younger were more likely to suburbanize, while marital status had no significant effect. Pollakowski and Edwards (1987), however, found that marriage greatly increased the likelihood of suburbanizing, but that the effect of having children was unclear.

Both the Marshall/O'Flaherty and Pollakowski/Edwards studies are seriously flawed. First, both were limited to families originating in the central city. Second, neither study included consideration of residential preferences or assessments. Thus, the approach used eliminated the possibility of testing for the indirect impacts of background characteristics on locational choices through preferences or assessments.

OTHER FACTORS INFLUENCING RESIDENTIAL CHOICES

In this chapter we integrate previous work by geographers on mobility patterns into the choice predictors model (Herbert 1973; Moore 1972). This research indicates that householders tend to make short-distance moves, implying that a key factor in predicting city-suburban choice is knowing where the householder is moving from. City residents tend to remain in the city; suburbanites remain outside the city limits. We intend to determine the importance of previous location over and beyond other demographic and attitudinal factors in distinguishing city versus suburban buyers.

In addition, we seek to improve existing knowledge of the importance of the public schools in explaining suburbanization. Theorists have generally asserted that school issues are important. Tiebout, in his widely cited 1956 article, asserts that families choose residential locations that offer the combination of public services and taxes that best suits their tastes and income. Armor (1980) is among the many social scientists who view suburbanization as a consequence of declines in central city public schools and, more specifically, as a response to forced integration programs. In recent years urban economists have tested Tiebout's thesis using empirical data. Lowery and Lyons (1989) using Louisville data found little support for the thesis, but Percy and Hawkins (1992) found evidence from Milwaukee. In the latter study, the four top reasons for selling a home were: housing values, schools, crime, and taxes. The second and fourth reasons refer to the tax service package, thus supporting Tiebout.

In fact, survey studies tend to deemphasize the role of school issues in affecting residential choice (Spain 1980, 1987; Tuchfarber et al. 1980), though educational issues take on greater significance when the analysis is restricted to families with children. This body of research, which relies on perceived reasons for moving or for selecting the current location, may, however, understate the importance of schools. Respondents may be unwilling to admit that their choice is based on the racial or class composition of local public schools, since this attitude may be interpreted as racist. Furthermore, studies like these, which focus on "primary" reasons for moving, neglect the possibility that schools are important in conjunction with other factors. We seek to advance existing understanding of the role of school issues by examining the extent to which the householder's evaluation of the city public school system, juxtaposed against the householder's emphasis on quality public education, influences the city-suburban choice.

HYPOTHESES

We predicted that five sets of factors influence city-suburban choice.

First, we expected that, as a result of New Castle County's city-suburban school districts, householders would perceive narrower differences between the city and suburban public schools. Consequently, New Castle County householders would be less concerned about central city public schools and would be more likely to choose city locations.[5]

Second, we assumed that despite recent changes in American metropolitan areas, such as the construction of apartments and entertainment spots in the suburbs (Gross 1991; Nemy 1991), family life cycle and familism would continue to be important in predicting city and suburban choices (Abu-Lughod and Foley 1960; Bell 1958, 1968).

Specifically, families with children, those emphasizing public school quality and concerned about the quality of central city schools, those seeking suburban-type residential attributes (for example, stylish homes, large lots, greenery), and those valuing efficient government services (Levin 1987) would be more likely to choose the suburbs. On the other hand, singles, couples without children, householders emphasizing cosmopolitan values, good housing values, and accessibility would be more likely to choose the city (Gale 1984, 1987; Goodman 1978; Spain 1987; Palen and London 1987).

Third, we anticipated that families relocating from the city would choose city locations and that those relocating from the suburbs and from out-of-town would choose suburban locations (Herbert 1973; Knox 1982; Moore 1972).

Fourth, we envisioned that blue-collar workers, families with parochial school children, and families with a neighborhood oriented life style (Gans 1962a) would be more likely to choose city locations.

Fifth, we expected higher income families to be more likely to realize their residential preferences and consequently to be more likely to relocate to the suburbs. On the other hand, as a result of housing discrimination, blacks would be less likely to consider and choose the suburbs.

METHODS

The analysis in this chapter utilizes the New Castle County survey (N=2,789) and only the third wave of the Hamilton County survey (N=2,335). We did not use the earlier two waves of Cincinnati data because these waves did not include the full set of locational choice predictors that were included in the third wave.

We conducted a factor analysis of responses to the set of housing and locational criteria. Six broader dimensions emerged from this analysis: (1) childrearing—near schools, quality of local public schools, accessibility to childcare; (2) neighborhood orientation—near friends and relatives, lived nearby before and liked it, wanted to live near people who were mostly similar to himself (herself), near churches/synagogues; (3) suburbanism—overall appearance of area, style of homes, large lots, expected changes in property values; (4) efficient government—low taxes, good housing prices, quality of government services; (5) urbanism—prefer urban area, wanted to be near a mix of people, prefer suburban area (inverse); and (6) accessibility—close to work, near stores, near public transportation.

In addition, we created three indexes to measure the importance attached to different housing and neighborhood components combined with an evaluation of the strength of the city/suburbs with respect to these components: suburban environment better; suburban schools better; and city housing prices better. Appendix 1 defines the variables in the analysis.

Table 4.1 presents the bivariate crosstabular results—the impact of particular background characteristics. Multiple regression analysis was utilized to explain variations in school-related attitudes as well as variations in the likelihood of choosing a suburban location, taking into account the relations among the variables. We ran the regression analysis in two stages: (1) the impact of background

TABLE 4.1
Crosstabular Results. Factors Influencing City-Suburban Choice:
Combined Hamilton County, New Castle County Sample

Characteristic	Proportion Choosing Suburbs
Metropolitan location	
Wilmington	90%
Cincinnati	69%[a]
Age 20 to 29 years	
No	82%
Yes	77%[a]
Age 50 years and over	
No	81%
Yes	80%
Married	
No	72%
Yes	84%[a]
Preschool child	
No	79%
Yes	85%[a]
School age child	
No	77%
Yes	87%[a]
Parochial school child	
No	81%
Yes	76%[a]
Income	
Below $45,000	78%
$45,000 and above	84%[a]
Education	
High school or less	92%
Attended college	89%[a]
High status white-collar job	
No	81%
Yes	80%
Blue-collar job	
No	80%
Yes	83%[a]
Two or more workers	
No	81%
Yes	80%

(continued)

TABLE 4.1 (continued)

Characteristic	Proportion Choosing Suburbs
White	
No	61%
Yes	82%[a]
Moved from suburbs	
No	66%
Yes	91%[a]
Moved from outside the metropolitan area	
No	79%
Yes	88%[a]
Previously owned	
No	72%
Yes	87%[a]
Newly formed household	
No	81%
Yes	79%
Neighborhood orientation	
Low	81%
High	80%
Efficient government	
Low	79%
High	82%[a]
Urbanism	
Low	93%
High	69%[a]
Accessibility	
Low	84%
High	80%[a]
Suburban environment better	
Low	68%
High	92%[a]
City housing prices better	
Low	88%
High	74%[a]
Suburban schools better	
Low	69%
High	91%[a]

[a]Statistically significant differences at least at the .05 level.
See Appendix 1 for definitions of variables.

TABLE 4.2

Comparisons between Hypotheses and Crosstabular/Regression Results

Characteristic	Hypothesis	Crosstabs	Regression
Cincinnati metropolitan area	+	−	−
Age 20–29 years	−	−	NS
Age 50 years or more	−	NS	+
Married	+	+	NS
One or more children under 6	+	+	+
One or more children 6 to 17	+	+	NS
Education	−	−	−
Income	+	+	NS
Two or more workers	−	NS	NS
Parochial school children	−	−	NS
High status white-collar worker	−	NS	NS
Blue-collar job	−	+	NS
White	+	+	+
Moved from suburban location	+	+	+
Moved from outside SMSA	+	+	+
Previously owned	+	+	+
Newly formed household	−	NS	NS
Efficient government	+	+	+
Neighborhood orientation	−	NS	−
Urbanism	−	−	−
Accessibility	−	−	−
City housing prices better	−	−	−
Suburban schools better	+	+	+
Suburban environment better	+	+	+

objective characteristics on intermediary variables such as the emphasis on suburban residential attributes; and (2) the influence of both background objective characteristics and intermediary variables on the city-suburban choice.

We used multiple linear regression analysis rather than logit analysis (a technique more obviously suited to a dichotomous variable) because only the former produces beta coefficients that can be used to prepare path diagrams. Existing research (Cleary and Angel 1984) has suggested that, when the split on the dependent variable is 25%/75% and probably even 10%/90% (Wolinsky and Johnson 1991), the results are comparable to logistic regression. In order to test for the validity of this assertion, we utilized logistic regression to determine the impact of the same set of predictors on the odds of choosing a suburban location. The logit results were, in fact, quite similar to those obtained from multiple linear regression analysis. The same three measures of previous locations were highly predictive of choosing the suburbs, and all the attitudinal orientations were related in the same direction in both analyses. The few differences were on background variables.[6]

Table 4.2 summarizes both the crosstabular and the regression results by indicating for each predictor the expected direction of the relationship (that is, whether the factor was expected to promote a city or a suburban choice) and the sign, positive or negative, of the significant result (if there was one) for the two types of analysis.

We summarized the regression results with a path diagram. The hypothesized causal relationships were indicated by unidirectional arrows extending from each determining variable to each variable depending on it. Because the large number of paths led to a cluttered diagram difficult to read and to interpret, we decided not to include it here.

Table 4.3 summarizes the information in the path diagrams by indicating the indirect, direct, and total effects of the different variables. In order to measure the indirect effects, it was necessary to compute the effects of the background characteristics through the different paths (for example, school-age children to importance of public schools to suburban choice). The results from the separate indirect paths were added to compute the total indirect effects. The total effect for each variable can be obtained by adding the direct and indirect effects.

EMPHASIS ON PUBLIC SCHOOL QUALITY

As part of the mailed questionnaire, we asked respondents about the importance of twenty-one different locational choice criteria, including public school quality. Specifically, we asked: How important was the quality of local public schools in your decision to buy this house? About half thought this factor was important, including 24 percent who considered it to be "somewhat important" and 28 percent who considered it "very important." Of the remaining half of the sample who considered schools relatively unimportant, 30 percent considered public school quality "not important at all," 16 percent considered it "somewhat unimportant," while 2 percent were "not sure."

TABLE 4.3
Direct and Indirect Relationships between Homebuyer Characteristics and
Likelihood of Choosing a Suburban Location. Combined Hamilton
County and New Castle County Sample

Characteristic	Direct and Indirect Effects
Cincinnati metropolitan area	−.130
	(.018)[1,2,5,6,7]
Age 20–29 years	—
	(.011)[1,2,7]
Age 50 years or more	.040
	(−.034)[1,2,3,4,5,6,7]
Married	—
	(.053)[1,2,3,4,6,7]
One or more children under 6	.030
	(.047)[2,3,6,7]
One or more children 6–17	—
	(.056)[2,6,7]
Education	−.040
	(−.049)[1,2,3,5,6,7]
Income	—
	(.035)[1,2,4,5,7]
Two or more workers	—
	(.002)[1]
Parochial school children	—
	(−.032)[2,4,6]
High-status white-collar worker	—
	(—)
Blue-collar job	—
	(−.011)[3]
White	.030
	(.012)[1,2,3,4,7]
Moved from suburban location	.270
	(.148)[3,4,5,6,7]
Moved from outside SMSA	.190
	(.095)[1,2,3,4,5,6,7]
Previously owned	.040
	(.091)[1,2,3,5,6,7]
Newly formed household	—
	(−.002)[2]
Efficient government	.050
	(NA)
Neighborhood orientation	−.050
	(NA)

(continued)

TABLE 4.3 (*continued*)

Characteristic	Direct and Indirect Effects
Urbanism	−.280
	(NA)
Accessibility	−.040
	(NA)
City housing prices better	−.160
	(NA)
Suburban schools better	.180
	(NA)
Suburban environment better	.130
	(NA)

Note: Indirect relationship via: 1 = efficient government, 2 = neighborhood orientation, 3 = urbanism, 4 = accessibility, 5 = housing prices, 6 = suburban schools, 7 = suburban residential environment
See Appendix 1 for definition of variables.

We anticipated that middle-class families in the childbearing and childrearing stages of the family life cycle would be the ones most likely to emphasize public school quality. The results (not presented here) generally support the importance of family life cycle position. Having one or more preschool or school-aged children was the most important predictor of interest. Marital status (married) and age (inversely) contributed to this type of emphasis. Not surprisingly, those with one or more children in parochial schools tended not to emphasize public school quality.

In direct contrast to what had been predicted, socio-economic status did not lead to a stress on public school quality. A college education promoted decreased interest once other factors were controlled. Two other indicators of middle-class status (income, high-status white-collar work) did not play a significant explanatory role in the analysis.

A priori, there was no reason to expect metropolitan location to affect the degree of emphasis on public school quality. However, Hamilton County homebuyers were significantly more likely to emphasize public school quality than those in New Castle County even when other factors were controlled (beta=.21). The existence of the combined city-suburban school districts in New Castle County may have caused buyers there to downplay the issue of school quality in the housing search.

The family's migration history was also a significant predictor of the degree of emphasis on public school issues. Those moving from the suburbs and from out-of-town (probably from the suburbs of other metropolitan areas) were more likely to emphasize public school quality (even when the presence or absence of children and other life cycle indicators were controlled). Those moving from the city were less likely to have such an emphasis. These findings reflect the fact that those in the suburbs tend to emphasize a family oriented lifestyle, which includes a stress on public school quality.

ASSESSING CITY AND SUBURBAN PUBLIC SCHOOL QUALITY

Elsewhere on the survey respondents were asked to evaluate the public schools in Cincinnati and Wilmington: Generally speaking, how would you compare the quality of education in the Cincinnati/Wilmington public schools as compared to Hamilton County's/New Castle County's suburban school districts? More than half (54%) considered the suburban schools to be superior, while a little over two-fifths (44%) considered the city and suburban schools to be about equal. Only 2 percent thought the city schools were superior.

Because of New Castle County's city-suburban school districts, we expected Wilmington area homebuyers to be less likely to perceive differences in quality between the city and suburban schools. The findings are as expected. A far higher proportion of New Castle County (57%) than Hamilton County buyers (28%) perceived city and suburban schools to be about equal in quality, whereas a far higher proportion of Hamilton County (69%) than New Castle County (43%) buyers perceived the suburban schools to be better. There existed slight differences between the counties (less than 1% in New Castle County, 3% in Hamilton County) in the proportion that considered the city schools to be superior.[7]

Metropolitan location remained important in predicting evaluations even when other background characteristics were taken into account. That is, Cincinnati area homebuyers were significantly more likely to consider suburban schools superior (beta=.26). In addition, several other personal characteristics played an important role in predicting the school assessments. In general, those for whom school issues were most salient (families with young children), those emphasizing social mobility (higher income families), and those already choosing suburban services (that is, those relocating from suburban locations) were the ones most likely to consider suburban schools superior. Whites were also more likely to feel that schools were superior in the suburbs. Whether they felt this way because of the racial makeup of the city schools, lower test scores, safety problems, or some other issues is impossible to say from the data at hand. Chapter 11 discusses perceived weaknesses of Cincinnati's public schools.

What Types of Households Make City and Suburban Choices?

Overall, the bivariate results (table 4.1) refute our hypothesis regarding the impact of metropolitan location on city-suburban choice. That is, in contrast to what was expected, Hamilton County movers were more likely than their counterparts in New Castle County to choose central city locations. About 30 percent of Hamilton County homebuyers chose the city as compared to 10 percent of buyers in New Castle County.

The preceding is probably a reflection of the fact that Cincinnati is larger than Wilmington and contains a more diverse selection of middle-class neighborhoods. This greater diversity of options may have contributed to an increased likelihood of locating within the city limits.

Alternatively, the finding may be due to the fact that Wilmington comprises a smaller percentage of the metropolitan area than does Cincinnati. Consequently, the probability of selecting the city of Wilmington is smaller because fewer homes exist.

Finally, it is possible that, while New Castle County homebuyers perceived minimal differences between the city and suburban public schools, they were reluctant to locate in the city, because this decision would result in their child(ren) being bused for nine of twelve school years. With the limited data gathered on the homebuyer surveys, it is not possible to test for the validity of these three alternative explanations.[8]

As was expected on the basis of previous geographical studies, a key predictor was the location from which the family moved. People originating in the city tended to remain there; suburban movers remained outside the city boundary. Out-of-town movers were almost as likely to choose the suburbs as those moving from suburban locations.

As expected, families in the childbearing and the childrearing stages of the life cycle were more likely to suburbanize. As shown in table 4.1, married couples and families with young children were more likely to be concerned about public school quality and were more likely to prefer a suburban residential environment. Consequently, they were more likely to choose suburban locations.

Our results provide mixed evidence of specific age groups being "city-directed." As expected, those in their twenties were more likely to buy in the city. However, older householders—those fifty and over—were no more likely than others to buy city homes. A separate analysis limited to Hamilton County buyers (Varady 1990a) showed that suburban "empty nesters" were as likely to choose the suburbs as the central city. This reflects the fact that: "Once in place, the elderly seldom move, because of their limited financial means . . . their sentimental attachment to place, and the great expenditure in time and energy associated with moving" (Fitzpatrick and Logan 1985: 107). When suburban elderly do move, they make short-distance moves to facilitate maintenance of social relations. Apparently, they are able to find nearby housing that meets their needs for less space.

The results support the hypothesized importance of the family mobility cycle in influencing city-suburban choice. As expected, those "moving up" within the homeownership stock (that is, those who had previously owned) were most likely to locate in the suburbs. Conversely, first-time buyers (that is, previous renters) were the ones most likely to make city choices.

In general, the results for the socio-economic variables were as expected. College-educated buyers were more likely to choose the city. However, occupational type (high-status white-collar work) did not promote city choices. The fact that two-earner households were not, as expected, more likely to locate in the city is probably due to the fact that this variable is a poor indicator of careerism. That is, in many households, the second earner works out of necessity rather than choice.

One of the two indicators of a neighborhood oriented lifestyle— having a child in parochial school—did, as expected, promote city choices. However, in direct contrast to what had been predicted, blue-collar workers were more likely to choose suburban than city locations. This finding may reflect the fact that, as manufacturing jobs have shifted to the suburbs, blue-collar workers have looked to the suburbs to be closer to their jobs.

We expected higher income families to be more likely to realize their residential preferences. Table 4.1 supports this expectation. Those with incomes above $45,000 were more likely to make suburban choices than those with incomes below this level.

As expected, race affected city choices. Blacks were significantly less likely to relocate to the suburbs than whites (62% versus 81%). The fact that three-fifths of black homebuyers were purchasing in the suburbs is noteworthy. The notion of nearly all white suburbs surrounding black central cities is clearly an oversimplification that is no longer real.

The results for the subjective measures provide additional evidence of the importance of both life cycle and lifestyle in distinguishing city from suburban buyers. As expected, suburban choices were promoted by the locational criteria and neighborhood assessments associated with childrearing—a concern for suburban type residential attributes (for instance, large properties, stylish homes, greenery) and a concern about central city public schools. Conversely, city buyers were influenced by the quest for urban residential attributes (for instance, neighborhood diversity) as well as a desire to preserve neighborhood social relations.

The findings related to money-related criteria were unsurprising. On the one hand, the quest for good housing prices and accessibility to work contributed to city choices. On the other hand, buyers who stressed efficient government services were more likely to choose the suburbs.

UNDERLYING CAUSES OF CITY AND SUBURBAN CHOICES

When we controlled for other background characteristics, Hamilton County buyers were still less likely to make suburban choices. This is indicated by the negative beta coefficient (–.13) between a Hamilton County location and choosing the suburbs. As mentioned earlier, this finding probably reflects the greater choice of middle-class neighborhoods in Cincinnati than Wilmington.

The multivariate results also highlight the importance of geographical variables. That is, the family's previous location remains a statistically important predictor in the regression model. In fact, the dummy variable identifying families who previously moved from the suburbs was the most important predictor of a suburban choice (beta=.27).

Two key aspects of a family-oriented lifestyle important in the crosstabular analysis (marital status, young children) are unimportant when background characteristics are controlled in the regression analysis. Thus both play a meaningful role in location decision-making but it is an indirect one. That is, married couples and families with young children were more likely to be concerned with public school quality and were more likely to prefer a suburban environment. The two latter attitudes promoted suburban choices.

The results for particular age subgroups change somewhat between the crosstabular and regression analyses. Youth (households 20 to 29 years) drops out as an important predictor of city choices once the interrelations between it and other variables are taken into account. On the other hand, age (households 50 years and older) becomes statistically significant, promoting *suburban* choices.

The results for the indicators of a neighborhood oriented lifestyle also change somewhat. First, having one or more children in parochial school vanishes as a statistically significant predictor. The path model results (not presented here) show, however, that this variable does promote city choices, albeit indirectly. Second, the variable indicating blue-collar work also drops out as a determinant of suburban choices. This variable is shown to promote city choices in the path model, but the overall effects for this variable are much smaller than for the parochial school one.

Although we had expected income to have a strong direct impact on locational choices by affecting the family's ability to implement its locational choices, this was not the case. A high income did promote a suburban choice, but this was due to the indirect paths of influence. Specifically, family income promoted suburbanization through a greater emphasis on suburban residential attributes.

In the previous section we saw that blacks were more likely to choose city locations than whites. This could have been because blacks were more likely to live in the city or because they tended to have lower incomes. In fact, race (white) had a direct impact on suburban choices even when other factors such as income and previous location were controlled. At first glance, this finding appears to provide implicit evidence of racial discrimination in the housing markets of these two metropolitan areas. That is, blacks were less likely than whites to consider suburban locations because they anticipated experiencing discrimination. However, it is plausible that some black home seekers focused their search within the city to live near other blacks or to be accessible to social institutions such as black churches.

With one exception, the crosstabular and regression runs for residential attitudes produced similar results. The exception has to do with the extent to which the household had a neighborhood orientation. Although a neighborhood orientation did not prove significant in the crosstabular runs, it did prove to be a significant predictor of city choices in the regression runs.

Conclusions

In order to improve existing understanding of city-suburban choices, this chapter has focused on four issues: (1) the extent to which different background demographic characteristics and metropolitan location influence householder emphasis on public school quality; (2) the extent to which different background demographic characteristics and metropolitan location affect perceived differences in public school quality between the city and the suburbs; (3) the extent to which different background demographic and mobility characteristics, residential assessments, and metropolitan location influence city-suburban choices; and (4) the impact of background characteristics and metropolitan location on city-suburban choices, once the interrelations among these factors are controlled.

Our findings can be summarized as follows. First, as we had expected, families with children were more likely to be concerned about public school quality. However, in contrast to our expectations, both a college education and a New Castle County location promoted a lack of concern about public school quality.

Second, as anticipated, those householders for whom public school quality was a more salient issue (for example, those with children) were more likely to believe suburban schools were superior. Also as expected, New Castle County buyers were far less likely than those in Hamilton County to perceive differences in public school quality on both sides of the city-suburban boundary. Thus, New Castle County's metropolitan school districts are having some impact on the assessments made by homebuyers.

Third, despite recent changes in metropolitan areas, such as the construction of apartments in suburbia, family life cycle position and lifestyle (familial versus cosmopolitan) remain important in explaining the choice between the city and suburban locations. On the one hand, families with children, families seeking suburban attributes such as large lots, and families concerned about inadequate central city schools were more likely to buy suburban homes. On the other hand, college-educated householders, householders without children, and householders emphasizing urban residential attributes, including accessibility to employment, were most likely to purchase in the city.

Family life cycle position provides an incomplete explanation for choices, however. Several other factors played an important role in the bivariate analysis in distinguishing those buying in the city from those purchasing in the suburbs. Black households, low income households, those with children in parochial schools, those emphasizing good housing prices, those moving from a city location, and those in Hamilton County were most likely to locate in the city. Those moving up within the homeownership stock tended to choose suburban sites.

Our analysis revealed the importance of family migration history in understanding locational choices. In general, homebuyers made short-distance moves, with city residents remaining in the city and suburban ones remaining outside the city boundary. Those moving from beyond the metropolitan area were distinctive in their tendency to choose suburban locations.

Fourth, while the regression results generally were similar to the crosstabular ones, there was one important exception. The emphasis on neighborhood social relations emerged as an important predictor of city choices when other factors were controlled. The regression results also helped to explain the findings dealing with metropolitan location. Living in New Castle County promoted city choices indirectly. That is, homebuyers in the Wilmington area were less likely to perceive differences in school quality between the city and the suburbs; this promoted city choices. However, Hamilton County buyers were more likely to choose city locations than their counterparts in New Castle County even when other factors were held constant. This direct impact more than counterbalanced the indirect one. Additional research is needed to determine whether the greater propensity to make city choices in Cincinnati was because of the greater diversity of middle-class neighborhoods in Cincinnati, as compared to Wilmington, or whether it reflected a reluctance among buyers in Wilmington to purchase in the central city and then have their children bused for nine of twelve years.

One promising strategy for cities like Cincinnati and Wilmington to attract greater numbers of middle-income families is to try to identify "market niches" where the city already has a competitive advantage and to develop programs to attract and hold a larger share of these subpopulations. We have identified two such subgroups: highly educated cosmopolites without children and neighborhood-oriented middle-income families.[9] Later chapters of this book discuss housing, schooling, and other programs that could be used to draw these families. However, before discussing those programs, it is first important to examine the patterns of residential attachments of these and other population subgroups.

5

MOVING PLANS

If policymakers are to be successful in stabilizing the tax base of central cities, they will need to hold as well as attract middle-income families. Retention is especially difficult. Historically, families have moved outward during successive stages of their "housing careers" as they strive for their ideal of a new, large, detached suburban home (Michelson 1977; Simmons 1968; Wald 1986).

Neighborhood revitalization experts offer a glimmer of hope to retention efforts by pointing to the growing proportion of highly educated white-collar workers with a strong taste for central city living. It is possible that these householders who have purchased in gentrifying neighborhoods will desire to "stay put" as they age because their residential environment is congruent with their preferences and lifestyle. On the other hand, it is equally likely that these cosmopolites will develop a taste for suburban living (more space, better public schools) as they move into the childbearing stages of the life cycle. In fact, some journalists have argued that the quest for suburbia is just as strong today for recently married couples as it was for their parents thirty years ago (Adler 1986; Kowinski 1980).

Clearly there is a need for a better understanding of the determinants of mobility for different population groups including but not limited to cosmopolites. This chapter addresses this gap in the literature through an analysis of the determinants of moving plans of recent homebuyers. We are also interested in examining the impact of Cincinnati's and Wilmington's desegregation strategies on mobility intentions. Earlier we noted that, as a result of New Castle County's metropolitan school districts, perceptions of quality differences between city and suburban schools are minimized. The last chapter showed that this strategy does not necessarily help to attract middle-income families to the city. The question that we explore in this chapter is: Does this approach to school desegregation help to hold families in the city once they move there?

More specifically, this chapter seeks answers to two sets of questions. First, what types of recent homebuyers—identified based on demographic, locational, housing, and attitudinal characteristics—tend to develop the most rapid moving plans? Second, what is the importance of these different background characteristics, once the interrelations among them are taken into account?

The next section of this chapter develops a conceptual model of the mobility process as well as a set of hypotheses to guide our research. These hypotheses are tested using the merged Cincinnati-Wilmington data set.

A key limitation of this chapter should be noted. That is, we examine the determinants of moving plans rather than the influences on mobility behavior. Since previous research has shown only a modest association between plans and behavior (Van Arsdol et al. 1968), we utilize plans more as an indicator of attachment to the current location rather than as a predictor of behavior. Our analysis based on plans should offer insights into the underlying causes of behavior. Because of the modest link between plans and behavior, the findings should be used cautiously.[1]

Our main argument in this chapter is that the higher mobility propensity of recent city homebuyers is mostly, but not exclusively, due to the demographic characteristics of city buyers, for example, the higher proportion of city buyers who are single or who are young couples without children. This high mobility propensity even extends to city buyers with a taste for urban living. As these households move on to later stages of the life cycle, and as many choose to have children, they will seek residential features more readily available in the suburbs. However, even if cities can attract more of these households "temporarily," this can benefit the tax base and in other ways promote economic and social viability.

A MOBILITY MODEL

Speare et al.'s mobility model (1974) provides the theoretical framework for this chapter. Moving is conceptualized as consisting of three stages: the development of a desire to move; the selection of an alternative location; and the decision to move or stay. The desire to move occurs when the level of stress exceeds the threshold level. Stress may arise from a change in the household or a change in the residential environment. Stress does not, however, necessarily lead to moving. Some households adapt by altering the home; others lower their housing aspirations and expectations. The final decision, whether to move, is dependent on the level of stress from the current location, the expected level of utility at alternative locations, and the cost of moving.

Drawing upon Speare's work, the conceptual model for this chapter consists of three sets of variables: background demographic, locational, and housing characteristics; residential assessments and perceived progress towards the householder's housing ideal; and moving plans.[2]

This chapter makes two contributions to the mobility literature. First, we examine in greater detail than has been the case previously the role of contextual variables in explaining city-suburban differences in mobility propensity. We theorize that moving plans are influenced by the degree of congruence between the residential preferences/lifestyle of householders and their residential location. Among homebuyers living in the central city, those who have a taste for urban living (a cosmopolitan lifestyle) would be disinclined to move. Conversely, city buyers who are oriented toward suburban living (that is, those pursuing a familial lifestyle) would be expected to plan to move, other factors holding constant.

Secondly, this chapter contributes to the limited research that is available on the determinants of mobility among metropolitan families who purchased homes during the mid-1980s. As Kendig (1984) notes, the motives of these families for purchasing and possibly for moving are probably dissimilar from those who arrived earlier when housing market conditions were different. Analysis of the determinants of moving plans of this recently arrived group can inform policymakers of the attachments and motives of those who are currently choosing central city locations.[3]

We attempt to build upon Apgar and Pollakowski's 1986 study of the determinants of mobility behavior within a national sample of recent buyers. Our analysis differs from theirs by focusing more directly on the impact of lifestyles and residential preferences on moving plans. Whereas Apgar and Pollakowski relied upon demographic characteristics as proxies for lifestyles, we utilize residential preferences and assessments.

Hypotheses

First, we assumed that suburban buyers would be less inclined to move. This would be due to compositional differences between the city and suburban populations (for example, the suburbs contain a larger proportion of families with children). When these demographic characteristics are controlled, we expect the impact of city-suburban location to disappear.

Second, we expected that, as a result of New Castle County's metropolitan school districts, homebuyers in the city would not be able to flee integrated schools by relocating to the suburbs. Consequently, they would intend to stay put. Therefore, among city homebuyers, a New Castle County location would contribute to an increased likelihood of planning to remain. A priori, there was no reason to expect a New Castle County location to promote stability in an analysis limited to suburban buyers.[4]

Third, we expected families in the childbearing stages of the life cycle would be inclined to remain. Specifically, the following characteristics would promote plans to stay: age, marital status (married), preschool and school-age children, and the fact that the family previously owned.

Fourth, those advancing or likely to advance in their occupational careers would have rapid moving plans. Specifically, education and a high-status white-collar job would promote moving plans. Since those moving from out-of-town are often middle-level managers in large corporations who shift positions frequently, we expected them to have especially rapid moving plans.

Fifth, we expected indicators of a neighborhood-oriented lifestyle (children in a parochial school, a blue-collar job) to be correlated with intentions of remaining.

Sixth, we expected income and race to influence the ability to translate moving desires into plans. As a result, we expected high-income families and whites to have more rapid moving plans.

Seventh, we expected homebuyers achieving congruence between their preferences and their actual housing situation to be most inclined to stay. Specifically, the following variables would promote the intention to remain: having a taste for central city living and living within the central city, emphasizing neighborhood social relations while living in the central city, seeking suburban residential attributes while living in the suburbs, emphasizing high-quality public schools while living in the suburbs, and emphasizing good housing prices while living in the city.

Finally, those householders furthest along toward their own housing ideal would be most inclined to remain. This would include homebuyers who perceived that they had made great progress toward their ideal home, as well as those who lived in large and expensive units.

METHODS

The preceding hypotheses are tested through analysis of the merged data set discussed earlier. As in chapter 4, we use only the wave 3 (1987) Hamilton County data (along with the New Castle County information), because only the third wave contained information on all of the predictor variables included in the mobility model. Appendix 1 defines the independent and dependent variables included in the analysis.

In order to measure moving plans, we asked respondents: How long do you expect to live in your current home? The six response categories ranged from "one year or less" to "more than five years." Since the results were highly skewed toward the latter category, we decided to recode the variable into two groups—those who intended to stay (that is, to remain five years or more, 56% of the total) and those who intended to move (that is, to remain less than five years, 44%).

Both crosstabular analysis (table 5.1) and regression analysis are used to examine the determinants of moving plans. The regression runs were completed in two stages: (1) the impact of background characteristics on residential preferences/assessments and on progress towards the respondent's "ideal" home, and (2) the impact of

TABLE 5.1

Crosstabular Results. Impact of Background Demographic, Housing and
Attitudinal Characteristics on Moving Plans among Recent Hamilton
County and New Castle County Homebuyers (Proportions Planning to
Move Within the Next Five Years.)

Characteristic	City	Suburbs
Hamilton County location		
No	65%[a]	48%[a]
Yes	42%	36%
Age 20–29 years		
No	41%[a]	39%[a]
Yes	66%	57%
Age 50–59 years		
No	52%[a]	46%[a]
Yes	26%	26%
Married		
No	54%[a]	51%[a]
Yes	45%	41%
Preschool age children		
No	50%[a]	43%
Yes	44%	42%
School-age children		
No	51%[a]	41%[a]
Yes	40%	33%
Parochial school children		
No	50%[a]	44%[a]
Yes	36%	30%
Income		
Below $45,000	49%	42%
$45,000 and above	48%	44%
Education		
Below bachelor's degree	39%[a]	37%[a]
Bachelor's degree or higher	56%	48%
High status white-collar job		
No	39%[a]	37%[a]
Yes	53%	46%
Blue-collar job		
No	51%[a]	45%[a]
Yes	35%	34%
Two or more workers		
No	50%	44%
Yes	47%	42%

(continued)

TABLE 5.1 (continued)

Characteristic	City	Suburbs
White		
No	46%	43%
Yes	49%	43%
Moved from suburbs		
No	46%[a]	48%[a]
Yes	54%	41%
Moved from outside the metropolitan area		
No	47%[a]	40%[a]
Yes	60%	57%
Previously owned		
No	55%[a]	52%[a]
Yes	36%	36%
Newly formed household		
No	47%[a]	42%[a]
Yes	61%	52%
Neighborhood orientation		
Low	55%[a]	51%[a]
High	44%	36%
Urbanism		
Low	42%[a]	41%[a]
High	50%	45%
Suburban environment better		
Low	49%	50%[a]
High	46%	38%
City housing prices better		
Low	49%	43%
High	48%	43%
Suburban schools better		
Low	50%	48%[a]
High	44%	40%
Housing progress		
Little	62%[a]	58%[a]
Great	24%	27%
Number of bedrooms		
Below 4	51%[a]	46%[a]
4 or more	42%	38%
Housing prices		
Under $70,000	51%	48%[a]
$70,000 or more	47%	40%

[a]Statistically significant differences at least at the .05 level.
See Appendix 1 for definition of variables

background characteristics, residential preferences, and perceived housing progress on moving plans. Each of these runs was conducted separately for city and suburban homebuyers in order to assess properly the impact of contextual variables.[5] For example, we only expected the interest in urbanism to promote perceived housing progress and residential stability in the regression run limited to central city homebuyers. Table 5.2 summarizes the results dealing with direct effects and indirect effects (that is, influences through residential attitudes).

WHAT TYPES OF HOUSEHOLDS PLAN TO MOVE?

As predicted, city homebuyers across the two metropolitan areas had a statistically significant higher propensity to move than did suburban ones. Whereas 48 percent of city homebuyers planned to move within five years, only 43 percent of those in the suburbs planned to move that quickly. (Among New Castle County homebuyers, the gap was much greater, 65% versus 48%.)

The results refute our hypothesis that among city homebuyers, those in New Castle County would be less likely to move. Whereas approximately two-fifths of Hamilton County city buyers planned to move within the next five years, more than three-fifths of the New Castle County buyers planned to move this quickly. Thus, the crosstabular results provide no evidence that Wilmington's metropolitan school districts were helping to hold families in the city.

Nevertheless, we still need to account for the surprising results regarding intermetropolitan differences in mobility propensity. Why did Hamilton County buyers have stronger attachments to their locations? Perhaps, because the city of Cincinnati contains a wider diversity of housing and neighborhoods than the city of Wilmington, this greater variety may have contributed to plans to remain. On the other hand, the results may reflect an especially high mobility propensity among New Castle County buyers. This could be due to the fact that many of the New Castle County respondents are employed by large corporations like DuPont. These employees may have assumed that they would be moved for job advancement purposes in the near future. Alternatively, the housing and economic boom in the county in the late 1980s may have led homebuyers to think that they would be able to purchase move-up housing relatively rapidly.

TABLE 5.2

Direct and Indirect Relationships between Homebuyer Characteristics and Moving Plans for City and Suburban Homebuyers. Combined Hamilton County and New Castle County Sample.

Characteristic	City	Suburbs
Cincinnati metropolitan area	−.140	−.090
	(−.040)[2,4,5]	(−.014)[1,2,3]
Age	−.200	−.150
	(−.057)[2,4,5]	(−.041)[1,2,3]
Married	—	−.060
	(.000)[3,4]	(−.015)[2,3]
One or more children	—	—
	(—)	(−.011)[1]
One or more children 6–17	—	−.090
	(.003)[4]	(−.010)[2,3]
Parochial school children	—	—
	(−.009)[1,3]	(−.001)[1]
Income	—	.090
	(−.050)[2,5]	(.033)[1,2,3]
Education	.100	.060
	(−.006)[1,2,4]	(.002)[2]
High-status white-collar job	—	—
	(—)	(.001)[1]
Blue-collar job	—	—
	(—)	(—)
White	—	—
	(.003)[3]	(.003)[2]
Newly formed household	—	—
	(—)	(−.001)[1]
Moved from suburbs	—	—
	(.010)[1,2,3]	(−.001)[1]
Moved from outside metropolitan area	—	.130
	(.004)[1]	(.027)[1,2,3]
Previously owned	—	−.050
	(−.067)[1,4,5]	(−.043)[1,2,3]
Housing prices	—	—
	(−.026)[5]	(−.025)[3]
Number of bedrooms	−.090	−.050
	(—)	(—)
Neighborhood orientation	−.080	−.070
	(−.038)[5]	(−.014)[3]
Urbanism	—	—
	(−.044)[5]	(—)

(continued)

TABLE 5.2 *(continued)*

Characteristic	City	Suburbs
Suburban environment better	—	–.040
	(–.023)[5]	(–.041)[3]
Suburban schools better	—	—
	(.020)	(—)
Housing progress	.290	.230
	(NA)	(NA)

Notes:
City buyers, indirect through: (1) neighborhood orientation, (2) urbanism, (3) suburban environment better, (4) suburban schools better, and (5) housing progress.
Suburban buyers, indirect through: (1) neighborhood orientation, (2) suburban environment better, and (3) progress toward housing ideal.

In general, the results support the hypothesized importance of family life cycle position and position in the family mobility cycle in influencing mobility plans. Younger couples, as well as newly formed households, were most likely to have rapid moving plans. On the other hand, married couples, those with young children as well as those moving up within the ownership stock (that is, those who had previously moved), were most likely to plan to remain.

The results also support our assertion that those households experiencing (or likely to experience) social mobility would have the most rapid moving plans. That is, recent buyers who had completed college or who had high-status white-collar jobs tended to be the most mobile. The high mobility propensity among buyers coming from out-of-town was expected, since these are frequently middle-level managers in large corporations who experience frequent job shifts.

As anticipated, indicators of a neighborhood-oriented lifestyle did promote residential stability. Having a blue-collar job or having a child (or children) in a parochial school promoted plans to remain.

The bivariate crosstabular results do not support our hypotheses dealing with income and race. Contrary to expectations, there were insignificant associations between moving plans and both of these demographic variables.

The results for the contextual variables are mixed and deserve a more extended discussion. Our assumption that city buyers with a taste for urban living would be inclined to remain is not supported.

In fact, those scoring high on the urbanism index had stronger moving intentions. We did find that city buyers who emphasized a neighborhood orientation were more likely to plan to remain, but this was true for suburbanites as well. In contrast to what had been expected, the perception that housing values were better in the city did not promote plans to remain among city buyers.

Table 5.1 shows that suburban-oriented families living in the city did not have especially rapid moving plans. That is, neither of two indexes (an emphasis on suburban schools while living in the city, an emphasis on suburban neighborhoods while living in the city) were associated significantly with moving plans.

Finally, there is strong evidence to support the hypothesized importance of progress towards family housing goals in explaining variations in mobility plans. As anticipated, those who perceived that they had made great progress or had attained their housing ideal were far less likely to move than those who thought that they had made little progress. The results dealing with housing conditions are similar. Those living in large, expensive homes, the types sought after by most Americans, expected to stay put.

UNDERLYING CAUSES OF MOBILITY

We included city-suburban location in a regression run along with other background demographic, housing, and attitudinal characteristics. The results (not included here but available from the authors) show that city-suburban location remains an important predictor even when variables are controlled. This means that city-suburban variations in mobility propensity are not exclusively due to compositional differences. A city location likely promoted moving, in part, due to higher crime rates, higher population density, and other environmental conditions. The higher propensity to move in the city also reflects supply characteristics (more starter homes, fewer planned subdivisions, fewer upscale homes). Other factors being equal, families in the city trying to improve their housing situation are less likely to find the types of homes they want. This makes them want to move.

The results dealing with metropolitan location remain unchanged in the regression analysis. That is, among city buyers, a New Castle County location promotes mobility plans, rather than stability as had been assumed.

Indicators of family life cycle and position in the mobility cycle remain important, although the impact of particular variables changes. Age is the most important objective predictor of residential stability. Two other indicators of life cycle position—marital status and the presence of school-age children—promote stability but for suburban families only. The fact that a family had previously owned continues to play an important role, but the variable identifying newly formed households drops out as important.

As was the case for the crosstabulations, the regression equations highlight the importance of education in predicting moving plans. White-collar work drops out as important, because it is intercorrelated with education. Out-of-town movers remain a highly mobile group, but only in the suburban sample. This may reflect the fact that middle-level managers tend to be referred to suburban locations from which they can, if necessary, move quickly to their next position.

The indicators of a neighborhood oriented lifestyle decline in importance. The presence of children in parochial schools no longer plays a meaningful role in the analysis. Having a blue-collar job promotes plans to remain, but only among city buyers. This may reflect the strong attachments of some working-class families to their city locations.

Race remains unimportant in explaining variations in mobility plans. Income, however, becomes more important once we take into account the interrelations among the predictors. The direction of influence for income varies between the city and suburban samples. In the suburbs we find the expected relationship; high incomes promote mobility plans. Just the opposite is true in the city. This probably reflects the fact a small subgroup within the more well-to-do population looks for and is able to find the type of housing it wants in the city. In Cincinnati this includes but is not limited to neighborhoods with views over the Ohio River. Chapter 6 contains a more detailed discussion of this subject.

The regression results provide greater support for the contextual variables than was true for the crosstabular results. Living in the city and having a taste for urban living, or emphasizing city housing prices, promotes plans to remain. Residing in the city and emphasizing high quality public schools promotes moving. In all three cases the effects of the indexes are indirect; consequently the magnitude of the overall effects are quite modest.

How can we interpret both the crosstabular and regression findings? For example, what does it mean that city dwellers with an urban orientation are more likely to move in the crosstabular analysis but that this characteristic (urbanism) promotes stability in the path model? To understand these findings, one needs to remember that individual buyers have a number of traits. While urbanism appears to promote residential stability, other traits of cosmopolites (youth, a college education, the absence of children) promote mobility. Taking all their traits together, cosmopolites have weak attachments to their locations.

Finally, there is little difference between the crosstabular and regression results in the importance of progress towards housing goals in explaining variations in mobility plans. Homebuyers making substantial progress are the ones most likely to stay put.

Conclusions

Most of our hypotheses dealing with the determinants of moving plans of recent homebuyers were supported. First, city buyers had more rapid moving plans than those in the suburbs. The gap was largely but not exclusively due to differences in the composition of the two populations. Second, indicators of family life cycle, family mobility cycle, social mobility, a neighborhood orientation, and progress towards the family's housing ideal played key roles in explaining variations in mobility plans.

The results suggest that, even if cities are able to attract increasing numbers of "cosmopolitan" homebuyers, it may be difficult to hold them through later stages of the family life cycle. In contrast to what we had expected, city buyers with a strong taste for urbanism had more rapid moving plans than those without an urban orientation. However, assuming cities were only successful in attracting and holding cosmopolitan homebuyers for the prechild stages of the life cycle, such attraction/retention would be helpful in stabilizing the tax base and maintaining a diverse population.

Our analysis provides no basis for optimism concerning the ability to hold middle-class families in cities through the use of metropolitan school districts. In contrast to what we had anticipated, Wilmington city buyers had more rapid moving plans than otherwise comparable families in Hamilton County.

6

SEGMENTATION OF THE HOMEBUYER MARKET

In the two previous chapters, we discussed the underlying causes of mobility decisions of recent homebuyers—that is, the factors that cause them to choose city or suburban locations and the characteristics that predispose them to remain at or move from particular locations. It is now appropriate to examine the spatial consequences of these decisions: how these recent homebuyers are distributed within the Cincinnati and Wilmington metropolitan areas.

The subject of residential patterning is of more than academic interest. Two of the most promising approaches that have been suggested to attract and hold middle-income families in central cities are: (1) to utilize "neighborhood specific" marketing, emphasizing the advantages of particular areas to specific subgroups, and (2) to design "specialized neighborhoods to recruit residents selectively" (Lowry 1980: 32). Unfortunately, the development and implementation of these strategies requires more detailed information on the segmentation of city and suburban housing markets than is currently available. More specifically, planners possess inadequate knowledge on the extent to which central cities have a competitive advantage over the suburbs in addressing certain market niches, such as neighborhoods for cosmopolitan type households. Such information could help in developing neighborhood-specific marketing strategies.

Addressing this lack of information on housing market segmentation, we seek to answer two questions in this chapter. First, to what extent is it possible to identify in statistical terms groupings of communities that are distinctive based on the demographic, housing, and attitudinal characteristics of recent homebuyers? Second, to what degree is it feasible to map these statistical results to show the degree to which similar communities adjoin one another? Furthermore, to what degree does such mapping support the concentric zone and sector models developed by human ecologists?

APPROACHES TO STUDYING HOMEBUYER MARKETS

This chapter attempts to build upon two bodies of research. The first body of literature identifies the boundaries of homogeneous communities statistically.[1] Social area analysis operationalizes three constructs using census measures: social rank (that is, education, rent); family status (that is, fertility, women at work); and ethnic status (that is, neighborhood proportion black). Next, census tracts are classified in social space with respect to the three constructs.

Maloney (1974) used this approach to classify Cincinnati census tracts. Specifically, he used social area analysis to classify Cincinnati census tracts into four quartiles based on social rank. Maloney's study differs from Shevky and Bell's seminal 1955 work in its emphasis on social rank as the sole basis for differentiation, rather than on the combination of social rank, urbanization, and ethnic status. Furthermore, Maloney combined a wider variety of census variables into his social rank measure (income, education, occupation, overcrowding, household composition) than did Shevky and Bell.

In contrast to social area analysis, which utilizes deductive reasoning, studies of factor ecology derive "factors," the equivalent of constructs, by a statistical procedure that examines the interrelations among the census measures. Factor ecologies of North American cities typically identify the same three factors—social rank, family status, and ethnic status—as are identified by social area analysis.

The second body of literature consists of ecological models used to predict how the homogeneous clusters mentioned above are distributed in space. The concentric zone model assumes that land uses are organized in a series of rings around a central point. The sector model is based on a central business district with a series of pie-shaped wedges emanating from it. The highest grade residential areas occupy the most desirable spaces, typically away from manufacturing uses. The Real Estate Research Corporation used a variation of this model in a 1973 working paper for the city of Cincinnati. The report highlighted the importance of Cincinnati's sectors in distinguishing four neighborhood types: "Hill-Newer" (suburbs within the city), "Valley-Established," "Basin-Old Town," and "Transition-Dynamic."

The multiple nuclei model asserts that the central business district is not the single focal point for cities. Since this latter model does not hypothesize the existence of a generalized spatial form, it is not utilized in this chapter.

This chapter combines the preceding aspatial and spatial approaches to study homebuyer markets. We attempt to make four specific contributions to the literature.

First, this is one of the first studies to use cluster analysis to study the segmentation of homebuying markets from both an aspatial and spatial perspective. This procedure begins with a relatively large number of measures for a set of geographical units such as census tracts. At each step, the procedure joins together the census tracts or other geographical units based on their similarity. As the analysis proceeds, distinctive clusters emerge that are labeled and mapped. Both cluster analysis and studies using factorial ecology analysis can be used to identify neighborhood types. However, with cluster analysis, the finer differentiation that exists within these areas can be discerned more clearly (Knox 1982: 89). In an earlier study, Hanz (1971) used cluster analysis to examine the Cincinnati homebuyers' market but only from an aspatial perspective.

Second, we attempt to correct for the overreliance on census measures that has occurred in previous studies in which social area analysis or factorial ecology analysis was used. Since the census offers little information on the lifestyles of householders (neighborhood, cosmopolitan, familial), these latter studies overlook much of the complex differentiation of contemporary metropolitan areas. This chapter includes attitudinal measures of lifestyle orientation as well as the traditional objective census indicators.

Third, we seek to determine the utility of the concentric zone and sector models in describing urban spatial patterns, taking into account recent patterns of central city revitalization. Schwab's 1987 study of neighborhood change in Cincinnati merely hints at the importance of gentrification in modifying the predictive value of the sector model. Given Cincinnati's unique topography (the Ohio River, hills to the east and west of downtown, an industrial valley extending to the north), Schwab had anticipated that the sectoral model would be particularly useful in explaining Cincinnati's spatial structure. Some of the results were as anticipated (for example, housing prices rose most rapidly in the historically high-status eastern sector of the city and the suburbs). One finding was, however, unexpected based on the sector model: a key factor predicting price increases was the availability of large, vacant, single-family homes. Since the latter type of housing is typically found in older neighborhoods near the central business district (CBD), the results therefore provide indirect evidence of gentrification. The latter trend is, however, inconsistent with sector theory that presumes rising values with increased distance from the CBD.

Schwab's study, while useful, lacks a geographical orientation. He did not identify the number of communities that were meaningfully affected by gentrification, nor did he indicate whether there existed a contiguous grouping of gentrifying communities. This chapter addresses these and related issues.

Finally, in contrast to earlier studies of homebuyer markets, this one will compare the structure of the homebuyer markets in two metropolitan areas: Cincinnati and Wilmington.

To summarize, we will be testing three hypotheses. First, we expect that combinations of three broad sets of factors—social rank, lifestyle, and ethnicity—will define, aspatially, clusters of community areas homogeneous with respect to the characteristics of recent homebuyers. We do not, however, anticipate that all of the possible clusters (that is, combinations from the above three factors) will emerge from the analysis (see Abu-Lughod and Foley 1960). For example, if housing discrimination severely limits housing opportunities for upwardly mobile black families, working-class and middle-class blacks would live in the same cluster. Figure 6.1 lists the seven clusters we expect to exist.

Life Style

		Cosmopolitan		Familial	
		Black	White	Black	White
Social Rank	Low	N/A	N/A	3	5
	Medium	N/A	1	4	6
	High	N/A	2	N/A	7

Legend

1. **Middle Class Cosmopolitan**
2. **Upper Middle Class Cosmopolitan**
3. **Black Working Class**
4. **Black Middle Class**
5. **White Working Class**
6. **White Middle Class**
7. **White Upper Middle Class**

FIGURE 6.1
Hypothesized Market Segments

Second, we expect that the spatial distribution of these clusters will reflect both the sector model as well as recent patterns of neighborhood revitalization. Based on Schwab's Cincinnati's research, we predict that clusters one and two (cosmopolitan) will be close to downtown. Clusters three and four (black) will be located in the northern sector, while clusters five and six (white working and middle class) will be in the western sector. Finally, the seventh cluster (upper middle class) will be heavily concentrated in the eastern and northeastern sectors.

Third, we expect that the cosmopolitan cluster will be more prominent in Cincinnati than Wilmington; that is, it will comprise a larger proportion of the communities in the city. This reflects Cincinnati's more viable downtown, the parks and cultural institutions close to downtown, and the physical setting of many of the inner-city communities, overlooking the Ohio River.

HOMEBUYER MARKET TYPOLOGIES

Using the Hamilton County and New Castle County home-buyer data sets described in chapter 3, we conducted the cluster analysis in five stages. First, we used the Aggregate feature of SPSS-X to create 26 summary measures for the 71 city and suburban communities in Hamilton County, and 28 measures for the 65 communities in New Castle County (see Appendix 2 for definitions of these community variables):

(a) demographic characteristics (for example, average income);
(b) locational preferences/lifestyle (for example, average factor score, suburbanism);
(c) migration/mobility characteristics (for example, percentage of first-time homebuyers); and
(d) housing characteristics (for example, average home price).

Second, we conducted a factor analysis of the Hamilton County and the New Castle County community characteristics. We identified the following factors in Hamilton County (see Appendix 2 for more detailed definitions): (1) social rank—house size, income, college, white-collar, home prices, rooms, blue-collar (inverse); (2) suburban lifestyle—dwelling unit age (inverse), city (inverse), married, new home, urbanism (inverse), suburbanism (for example, large lots), out-of-town; (3) familistic lifestyle—children, childrearing (for example, near schools), family size, single parent; (4) nonexperiential—nonexperiential (for example, accessibility to work), own, newly formed household, plan to move; (5) economic criteria—age, black, accessibility (that is, to stores, public transportation, churches), economics (for example, low taxes); (6) neighborhood orientation—neighborhood (for example, near friends), two or more workers (inverse), and (7) parochial school children—parochial school children. The factors identified in New Castle County were similar: (1) social rank—age, income, college, white-collar, blue-collar (inverse), own, out-of-town, economics (inverse), home size, home price, rooms, newly formed household (inverse); (2) familistic lifestyle—family size, married, children, childrearing; (3) suburbanism—city (inverse), suburbanism, urbanism (inverse), new home, dwelling unit age; (4) residential mobility—plan to move, black; (5) neighborhood orientation—neighborhoods, accessibility; (6) single parent household—single parent household, and (7) parochial school—parochial school children, two or more workers. We then created composite scales for each of these seven dimensions by summing the scores for all of the items encompassed in the factor.

Third, we conducted a cluster analysis using the Cluster feature of SPSS-X and the above seven factors (see Norusis 1985: 181). Eight groupings of Hamilton County communities and seven groupings of New Castle County communities (discussed below) emerged from the cluster analysis.

Fourth, we utilized the stepwise discriminant analysis feature of SPSS-X to identify the distinctive features of each of the eight clusters. Tables 6.1 and 6.2 present the detailed statistical findings.[2] Figures 6.2 and 6.3 are typologies of the actual market segments.

The fifth and final stage was to map the results using the Atlas mapping software. Adjacent similar communities are given the same shading. Figures 6.4 and 6.5 are the mapped results for Hamilton and New Castle counties respectively.

Homebuyer Market Typologies

Figures 6.2 and 6.3 show that, as expected, lifestyle (for example, whether households who were oriented to a familistic way of life predominate) and social rank (income, housing prices) played a key role in defining the clusters. The critical role of lifestyle in the analysis highlights the importance of including attitudinal measures in studies like this.

In contrast to what had been expected, neighborhood racial composition played a far smaller role in defining the clusters than had been expected. In Hamilton County, the insignificant results for race reflect the diversity among the racially mixed housing markets with respect to social rank, mobility, and other demographic and housing characteristics. The clustering statistical routine recognized this diversity and distributed these racially mixed submarkets relatively evenly among the eight cluster types. In New Castle County, on the other hand, racial composition played an insignificant role

TABLE 6.1

Standardized Group Means for Hamilton County Homebuyer Clusters

Cluster[a]	Number of Communities	Social Rank[b]	Suburbanism[b]	Familism[b]	Nonexperiential Attributes[b]	Economics	Neighborhoods	Parochial School Children[b]
One	5	-1.42	-1.33	1.82	1.50	.14	-.14	-.93
Two	10	1.25	-.76	-1.19	.15	-.52	-.43	-.42
Three	10	-.47	-.63	-.51	.42	.53	-.22	-.79
Four	13	-.60	-.14	-.10	.10	-.08	-.16	.16
Five	8	-.33	.16	.16	.16	.40	.28	1.30
Six	4	-.43	-.82	.08	.10	.66	.40	2.88
Seven	16	.17	1.05	.30	-.57	-.16	.44	-.37
Eight	5	1.76	1.53	.59	-1.41	-.60	.31	-.27
All groups	71	.00	.00	.00	.00	.00	.00	.00
F statistic		22.75	24.11	10.02	6.27	1.67	1.09	70.88

[a]Clusters: (1) poor inner city, (2) cosmopolitan, (3) baseline, (4) suburban working class, (5) urban middle class, (6) urban working class, (7) suburban middle class, (8) suburban ideal.

[b]Statistically significant differences at least at the .001 level.

TABLE 6.2
Standardized Group Means for New Castle County Homebuyer Clusters

Cluster[a]	Number of Communities	Social Rank[b]	Familism[b]	Suburbanism[b]	Residential Mobility[b]	Neighborhoods	Single Parents[b]	Parochial School Children[b]
One	8	.46	-1.38	-1.56	1.07	-.02	-.42	-.66
Two	3	-.58	-.93	-1.90	1.51	-1.62	2.29	-.05
Three	13	-.57	-.32	.18	-.17	-.09	.37	.19
Four	12	-1.23	-.11	-.43	.04	.08	.16	.19
Five	15	-.01	.61	.61	-.21	-.09	-.42	.49
Six	10	1.03	.76	.79	-.45	.51	-.25	-.27
Seven	4	2.47	.64	.98	-.95	.38	-.38	-.96
All groups	65	.00	.00	.00	.00	.00	.00	.00
F statistic		150.32	10.00	31.05	3.79	2.09	5.47	2.38

[a]Clusters: (1) cosmopolitan, (2) poor inner city, (3) modest middle class, (4) baseline, (5) nicer middle class, (6) upper middle class, (7) suburban ideal

[b]Statistically significant differences at least at the .001 level.

Life-Style

| | Child-Oriented | | | | Nonchild-Oriented | |
City/sub. Location	Lower Class	Working Class	Middle Class	Suburban Ideal	Baseline	Cosmopolitan
City	1	4	6	N/A	3	2
Suburbs	N/A	5	7	8	N/A	N/A

Legend

1. Poor Inner City 5. Suburban Working Class
2. Cosmopolitan 6. Urban Middle Class
3. Baseline 7. Suburban Middle Class
4. Urban Working Class 8. Suburban Ideal

FIGURE 6.2
Actual Market Segments: Hamilton County

Life-Style

| | Child-Oriented | | | | | Nonchild-Oriented | |
City/sub. Location	Lower Class	Modest Middle Class	Nicer Middle Class	Upper Middle Class	Suburban Ideal	Baseline	Cosmopolitan
City	1	N/A	N/A	N/A	N/A	N/A	2
Suburbs	N/A	4	5	6	7	3	N/A

Legend

1. Poor Inner City 5. Nicer Middle Class
2. Cosmopolitan 6. Upper Middle Class
3. Baseline 7. Suburban Ideal
4. Modest Middle Class

FIGURE 6.3
Actual Market Segments: New Castle County

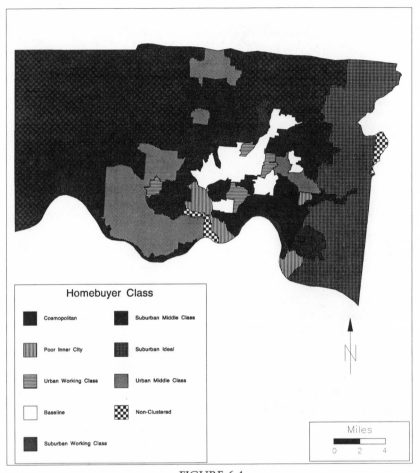

FIGURE 6.4
Segmentation of Hamilton County Homebuyers Market. *Source:* Ed
Ratledge, Center for Applied Demography and Survey Research,
University of Delaware

because there were so few black homebuyers. This does not mean
that race is irrelevant in the Cincinnati homebuyer market. A separate analysis of black suburbanization (Varady 1989) indicates that
black homebuyers are concentrated in a relatively small number of
city and suburban communities, implying that both racial
discrimination and racial preferences play an important role in locational choices.

Figure 6.2 shows that geography has played an unexpectedly

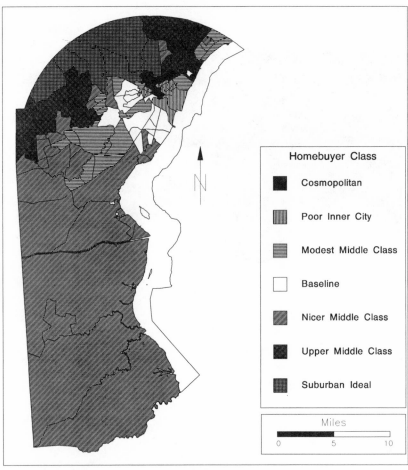

FIGURE 6.5
Segmentation of New Castle County Homebuyers Market. *Source:* Ed
Ratledge, Center for Applied Demography and Survey Research,
University of Delaware

important role in defining the clusters. Five of the eight Hamilton
County clusters consist exclusively or primarily of city communities, while the remaining three encompass suburban communities. Five of the seven types of clusters in New Castle County
consist primarily or exclusively of suburban communities. The city
of Wilmington consists almost exclusively of either cosmopolitan or
poor inner-city homebuyer clusters.

Figures 6.2 and 6.3 highlight two key differences in the residential patterns in these two counties. Hamilton County demonstrates a higher degree of differentiation with respect to working-class communities in that it contains distinct urban and suburban working-class clusters. On the other hand, New Castle County demonstrates a greater degree of differentiation with respect to middle-class clusters. It contains three distinct middle-class groupings: modest, nicer, and upper middle-class.

Figure 6.4 provides fairly strong support for our predictions regarding the spatial patterning of the clusters in Hamilton County. As predicted from the sector model, middle-class homebuyer markets are heavily concentrated in the western sector of the county and the suburbs, whereas upper middle-class communities (that is, the suburban ideal cluster) are heavily concentrated in the eastern and northeastern sections of the county. The northern sector of the city and the suburbs contain a diverse grouping of communities with respect to social rank and lifestyle.

The map also supports our predictions regarding the importance of recent patterns of neighborhood revitalization. Some of the most affluent markets in Hamilton County are located in a band of communities close to downtown. These results refute the sector model but are fully consistent with recent writings on neighborhood revitalization and gentrification.

A discussion of the eight Hamilton County and seven New Castle County clusters follows.

DISTINGUISHING FEATURES OF THE CLUSTERS

The two counties differ with respect to the number of homebuyer clusters: eight in Hamilton County and seven in New Castle County. Furthermore, some of the clusters common to both counties (for example, poor inner-city) vary in meaningful ways.

Poor Inner-City

The poor inner-city cluster corresponds closely to the stereotypical image of a depressed inner-city housing market. This grouping of five communities in Hamilton County and three in New Castle County is characterized by the poorest homebuyers (average income = $23,764 and $33,951 respectively), the oldest housing units (average age = 79 years and 67 years), the lowest housing prices (average price

= $23,234 and $51,484) and a high proportion of black homebuyers (37% and 24%).

There is a much larger gap in socio-economic status between the poor inner-city cluster and others in Hamilton County than in New Castle County. For example, in Hamilton County both the average income and the average home price are 18 percent of what they are in the suburban ideal cluster. The corresponding figures for New Castle County are 47 percent and 24 percent, respectively. This probably reflects the fact that, because of the inflated housing prices in New Castle County, many low-income buyers have been priced out of the homebuyer market, even in the inner city. In addition, the high housing prices throughout the county may have induced some middle-income families to purchase in the inner city. Both of these trends lead to a reduction in differences between the poorest and most affluent homebuyer clusters.

The inflated housing market has not only resulted in a narrowing of differences with respect to socio-economic characteristics, but has also narrowed differences in family composition. Specifically, in comparison to the poor inner-city cluster of Cincinnati, Wilmington's contains a far lower proportion of single parents (51% versus 21%) and a far smaller proportion of households with children (83% versus 38%). Not surprisingly, given the wider differences in Hamilton County, homebuyers in the Wilmington cluster had the second lowest average on the index measuring the importance of residential attributes connected to childrearing, whereas the Cincinnati poor inner-city cluster had the highest average of the eight clusters. These findings for Wilmington apparently reflect the movement of middle-income single people, as well as couples without children, into this cluster.

The locations of the Cincinnati and Wilmington poor inner-city clusters generally conform to previous ecological writings. Of the five in the Cincinnati cluster, one (the Over-the-Rhine/West End area) is a port-of-entry community immediately adjacent to the central business district, two others are located nearby in the industrial Mill Valley, a fourth is a poor white community along the Ohio River east of downtown, while a fifth is a blue-collar community, statistically allocated to this cluster because of its unusually low housing prices. All of the communities in Wilmington's poor inner-city cluster are located immediately adjacent to the downtown business district.

Cosmopolitan

The cosmopolitan cluster in Hamilton County consists primarily of an almost unbroken swath of ten communities extending from north of downtown east to the Ohio River. The Wilmington cluster of eight communities is located northeast of the central business district.

The cosmopolitan clusters in these two cities are the ones that have benefitted most from the increased interest in urban living among young, upwardly mobile householders. The statistical results highlight the high socio-economic levels. The Cincinnati cosmopolitan cluster contains the highest proportion (85%) who have attended college, and (with the suburban ideal cluster) the highest proportion with high-status white-collar jobs (about two-thirds). While the socio-economic level in the Wilmington cosmopolitan cluster is also high, its standing vis-à-vis the other clusters is not as high as is the case for Cincinnati's cosmopolitan cluster. On most indicators of social rank, the Wilmington cluster ranks third behind both the suburban ideal and upper middle-class clusters. In contrast, Cincinnati's cosmopolitan resembles the suburban ideal cluster and surpasses the suburban middle-class cluster on most social rank indicators.

The Hamilton County cosmopolitan cluster and the two most affluent suburban clusters do differ, however, with respect to other housing, demographic, and attitudinal characteristics. Consistent with the literature on gentrification and neighborhood revitalization (Gale 1984; Palen and London 1984) most (65%, Cincinnati; 77%, Wilmington) cosmopolitan cluster buyers do not have children, and nearly half are single (51% and 52%, respectively).

As might be expected, the typical cosmopolitan cluster buyer has a strong taste for urban living and is indifferent to public school quality. This is shown by the fact that in both cities the cosmopolitan cluster has, by far, the highest scores on the urbanism index and the lowest scores on the index measuring concern for residential attributes related to childrearing.

In contrast to the stereotype implied by the phrase "return to the city," these homebuyers were not relocating from suburban homes. In fact, consistent with other intramigration studies (for example, Tuchfarber et al. 1980), the overwhelming majority in Cincinnati, two-thirds (66%), were first-time homeowners, and a similar proportion (63%) were moving from another city location; less than 1 percent were relocating from out-of-town. In Wilmington, a slightly lower proportion (56%) were first-time homebuyers, and 46 percent had moved from another city location. An additional 14 percent had moved to their current location from out-of-town. Thus, in both cities, two-fifths or less of the cosmopolitan cluster home-buyers had relocated from a suburban location.

Cosmopolitan buyers are distinctive in their lack of attach-ment to their current location. Two-thirds of the Wilmington cos-mopolitan cluster buyers and nearly half (45%) in Cincinnati planned to move within five years. This is a far higher anticipated mobility rate than in any other cluster in the two counties. It appears that, for many of the young couples moving into this cluster, the taste for city living is a temporary phenomenon related to the postmarriage stage of the life cycle (Gans 1962b). This finding is consistent with our results in chapter 5. Apparently, some of the homebuyers moving into this cluster who anticipate raising a family expect to move to a suburban environment more conducive to childrearing.

Despite the overall similarities within the Cincinnati cos-mopolitan cluster, this is actually a surprisingly diverse grouping of communities. Included are several well-known gentrifying com-munities (for example, Mt. Adams), a number of high-status com-munities that have never experienced decline (Clifton, Hyde Park), a stable, racially integrated community (North Avondale), and a his-torically working-class one (Fairview), which adjoins the University of Cincinnati and which has attracted recent graduates. The statisti-cal results highlight this diversity. The standard deviation for hous-ing prices ($21,311) is larger than for any of the other seven clusters.

The physical characteristics of these communities are consis-tent with those described in the literature on neighborhood revital-ization. First, most of these communities in both cities are close to downtown and other employment centers. In Cincinnati, these com-munities are also highly accessible to major parks and cultural in-stitutions, and several have impressive views of the Ohio River. Secondly, several of the Cincinnati communities contain large older homes dating back to the Victorian period. In fact, the average num-ber of rooms per home in the Cincinnati cosmopolitan cluster (7.13) is the highest of any of the clusters, and the average building size (1,880 square feet) is second only to the suburban ideal cluster. The corresponding results for the Wilmington cosmopolitan cluster (6.66

and 1,701) are not nearly as impressive, compared either to Cincinnati or to the other clusters in New Castle County.

Baseline

The Cincinnati baseline cluster consists of ten older communities located in a sector north of downtown. (Technically, two of these community areas, Norwood and St. Bernard/Elmwood Place, are suburbs that are legally distinct from Cincinnati; they are, however, fully enclosed by the city.) The 12 communities comprising the baseline cluster in New Castle County form an almost continuous band south of the city.

This grouping provides affordable housing (average price = $40,736, Cincinnati; $64,102, Wilmington; second-lowest in both counties) for householders starting their housing and occupational careers. The two baseline clusters rank second-highest (after the poor inner-city cluster) with respect to the proportion of first-time home-buyers (72% and 68%) and rank second lowest, after the poor inner-city cluster with respect to income ($30,098 and $36,722).

One of the most distinctive aspects of this cluster is the relative absence of children, which indicates that it is composed of couples beginning the family mobility cycle (Michelson 1977). Only about two-fifths had one or more children 18 and younger (42%, 38%). Reflecting the low incidence of children and the fact that couples buying in this cluster are just beginning their housing careers, Hamilton County (but not New Castle County) baseline cluster buyers tend to deemphasize suburban residential attributes and public school quality. In both counties, baseline buyers seem to have chosen their homes primarily on the basis of economics, with the two clusters scoring highest on the economics index. As these households move into the childbearing and childrearing stages of the family mobility cycle, they are more likely to stress suburban attributes.

Working-Class

While Hamilton County contains two identifiable working-class clusters, New Castle County contains none. The escalating housing costs in New Castle County during the mid-1980s may have prevented moderate-income blue-collar families from purchasing their first home or limited them from moving up within the home ownership stock.

The urban working-class cluster in Hamilton County is composed of four noncontiguous communities on both the east and west sides of Cincinnati. The suburban working-class cluster (13 communities), in contrast, is concentrated in a band of contiguous communities to the north and west of the city.

The urban and suburban working-class clusters resemble one another in terms of the proportion of blue-collar workers (almost half), income levels (average = approximately $30,000), housing prices (average = approximately $45,000). Four results point to the more distinctively *urban* character of the former cluster: (1) the higher proportion of black homebuyers [40% versus 12%]; (2) the higher proportion of single-parent households [25% versus 15%]; (3) the higher proportion moving from a city location [77% versus 51%]; and (4) the older housing stock [average dwelling unit age = 65 years versus 54 years].

Buyers in the urban working-class cluster also are more likely to have a "localistic orientation," as indicated by the highest scores on the neighborhood index. This result means that homebuyers in this cluster are more likely to have looked for homes close to friends/relatives or to a familiar church. They are also more likely to concentrate their search in neighborhoods where they have previously lived. Another indication of the strong localistic orientation in the urban working-class cluster is the relatively large proportion (34% versus 11% in the suburban working-class cluster) who send their children to a parochial school. Many of these buyers are probably Catholic families seeking to remain in the parish in which they were raised and to send their children to the same Catholic school that they attended. In any case, having a child in the local Catholic school undoubtedly reinforces their already strong ties to the surrounding area.

Middle-Class

Hamilton County and New Castle County present us with different patterns of similarities and differences with respect to their middle-class clusters. Hence, we will discuss them separately.

The breakdown of middle-class clusters in Hamilton County is partly related to geography. Four of the eight communities in the urban middle-class cluster are in the city of Cincinnati and a majority (51%) of the buyers in this cluster moved from a city location. These four do not, however, constitute a clearly defined spatial grouping. In contrast, all 16 communities in the suburban middle-class cluster are located in the suburbs, and only one-fifth (21%) of the buyers relocated from the city. This cluster comprises much of the northern and western parts of Hamilton County.

These two clusters resemble one another in family composition. A little more than two-thirds (68% and 70%, respectively) of the homebuyers are married, and a majority (56% and 55%) have children. They differ, however, in socio-economic, mobility, and housing characteristics.

Homebuyers in the suburban middle-class cluster tend to have higher incomes, are more likely to hold high-status white-collar jobs, are more likely to be moving up within the homeownership portion of the housing stock (and not to be first-time homebuyers), tend to live in newer and more expensive homes, and are more likely to value suburban residential attributes such as large lots, as well as high-quality public schools.

The three middle-class clusters in New Castle County can be distinguished based on combinations of life cycle stage and socio-economic status. New Castle County's modest middle-class cluster, located to the southwest of the city, contains homebuyers in the earlier stages of the life cycle. The average age (33.8) is lowest among the three middle-class clusters, and this cluster contains the highest proportion of single homebuyers (36%) among the three. These are households at the beginning of their housing careers; 56 percent are first-time homebuyers.

The nicer middle-class cluster consists of 15 contiguous communities in the semirural southern part of the county. This cluster resembles the modest middle-class one with respect to socio-economic characteristics (average income, proportion completing college). However, buyers in this cluster have progressed further along in the life cycle (as indicated by the higher proportion who are married and who have children, 80% versus 64%, 52% versus 37%) and who have been able to purchase larger and more expensive homes. The stronger familial orientation is also shown in the attitudinal results. Buyers in the nicer middle-class cluster are more likely to emphasize public school quality and "suburban" type residential attributes.

The upper middle-class cluster (a grouping of ten communities to the west of Wilmington) resembles the nicer middle-class cluster with respect to life cycle position and family mobility stage. However, buyers in this cluster clearly have been more successful in their occupational careers as reflected in their higher incomes ($57,818 versus $47,650) and their living in larger, newer, more expensive homes.

Suburban Ideal

The suburban ideal cluster (concentrated in the eastern and northeastern suburbs of Hamilton County and in the northern suburbs of New Castle County) contains the type of community to which most middle-class families aspire, but that only a minority with the financial means are able to attain. This cluster in both Hamilton County and New Castle County stands out from all of the others on income (average = $54,575 and $71,961), house price (average = $129,674 and $213,930), and house size (average = 2,094 square feet and 2,847 square feet). On other measures such as education, this and the cosmopolitan cluster are quite similar in Hamilton County; this is less true in New Castle County.

This cluster is distinctive on the basis of lifestyle. Buyers in this cluster place a stronger emphasis than buyers in any other grouping do on suburban-type features such as large lots, and they place a relatively high importance on public school quality.

These differences were anticipated, based on social rank and lifestyle. However, differences based on migration history were not expected. In fact, the proportion of buyers who relocated to their current location from outside the Cincinnati or Wilmington metropolitan areas (31% and 34%) was far higher than for any other cluster in either county. This finding may reflect the desire of some upper middle-class households to try to replicate the type of suburban environment they left behind in another metropolitan area (Knox 1982). Furthermore, the pattern may be the result of realtors and relocation staff directing high-level managers and professionals to particular communities.

It seems reasonable to suppose that, since these homebuyers have attained their housing ideal (or are close to achieving it), they are more likely to plan to stay put. This was, in fact, the case. Only about a third (31%) expected to move in the next five years. This was, by far, the lowest mobility propensity of any of the seven clusters in New Castle County (average = 49%). A similar proportion in Hamilton County (30%) planned to move relatively quickly. This figure was, however, near the average (32%) for Hamilton County.

CONCLUSIONS

In general, our results are consistent with previous studies of urban spatial patterns. Social rank and lifestyle (for example, whether child-oriented households predominate) played the expected important roles in identifying eight relatively homogeneous clusters in Hamilton County and seven in New Castle County. While community racial composition played less of a differentiating role than was expected, geography played a more important role, especially in Hamilton County.

Second, as expected, similar communities did tend to form contiguous clusters. The spatial patterning of these clusters reflects both the sector model and recent patterns of neighborhood revitalization. The concentration of the suburban ideal cluster in the northeastern and eastern sectors of Hamilton County (and in the northern sector of New Castle County) highlights the continued value of the sector model. The existence of a band of cosmopolitan communities adjacent to downtown Cincinnati and downtown Wilmington reflects the revitalization occurring in central cities throughout the United States.

Finally, as expected, the cosmopolitan cluster was more "prominent" in Cincinnati than in Wilmington. Prominence was demonstrated by the standing of the cosmopolitan cluster relative to others, rather than the proportion of Cincinnati's communities placed in this category. In Cincinnati, the cosmopolitan cluster resembled the suburban ideal cluster with respect to such socio-economic indicators as education, occupation, and house size. In Wilmington, the cosmopolitan cluster ranked behind the suburban ideal and upper middle-class clusters with respect to these indicators. As a result of Cincinnati's relatively vibrant downtown and attractive, older, inner-city neighborhoods, the city is better able to attract college-educated white-collar workers with a taste for city living.

The results, therefore, provide some basis for optimism regarding efforts by cities like Cincinnati and Wilmington to attract and hold middle-income families. The cities contain two clusters of neighborhoods—cosmopolitan and baseline communities—that do not exist in the suburbs. Chapter 12 discusses strategies cities might follow to strengthen these types of communities to reinforce their competitive advantage.

PART 3

DEVELOPING PROGRAMS TO ATTRACT MIDDLE-INCOME FAMILIES

7

Local Housing Plans

In previous chapters we have argued that cities need to address middle-income housing needs if they are to remain financially viable. However, at the same time cities are experiencing an increase in the incidence of low-income housing problems, such as homelessness. With the growing claims for funding for both market- and below market-rate housing programs, it is increasingly important for cities to develop housing strategies to guide allocative decisions. The question is: Is it possible to address both types of needs, or are middle-class policies so controversial that they are likely to be ignored in these planning efforts?

We will argue that it is possible for cities to address both market-rate and below market-rate housing issues. One possible venue is the Community Housing Affordability Strategy (CHAS), required by the federal government for cities interested in receiving Community Development Block Grants (CDBG). However, there are other possible venues besides the CHAS available for this purpose, including task force reports (such as Cincinnati's Housing Blueprint discussed in this chapter), plans prepared in-house by local governmental agencies (for example, Habiter Montréal, city of

Montreal 1989; the Hartford's Housing Component, city of Hartford, Commission on the City Plan 1986) and studies prepared by outside consultants (for example, Sternlieb and Listokin's housing report, part of the Municipal Priorities Project, Brecher and Horton 1985).[1]

This chapter is divided into two parts. In the first part, we provide an overview of local housing planning efforts over the last thirty years, looking at the role of the federal and state governments as well as local task forces.

Our review shows that virtually all the plans that have been prepared, regardless of the auspices, focus exclusively on low-income housing needs. However, the three exceptions (Hartford, New York City, Montreal) show that it is possible, without too much controversy, to develop a plan addressing both middle- and low-income issues.

The second section of the chapter is a case study of Cincinnati's Housing Blueprint. We draw from an analysis of minutes of meetings and other materials prepared for committees, as well as participant observation. The Ohio author of this book served as a consultant to and a member of the Housing Blueprint Technical Working Group (TWG). This insider's perspective allows us to identify and discuss some of the reasons why the Blueprint was able to address both types of housing needs, but was not able to address another important issue, geography.

Changes in Local Housing Plans During the Past Thirty Years

In 1974 the Community Development Block Grant (CDBG) Program became the principal mechanism for allocating federal housing funds. The act consolidated Urban Renewal, Model Cities, neighborhood facilities, water and sewer, open space, and public facilities programs, which had been administered by HUD. In order to coordinate housing and community development undertakings, the act required each participating local government to prepare a Housing Assistance Plan (HAP). It surveyed the condition of the housing stock in the community and assessed the housing assistance needs of lower-income persons, specified an annual goal for the number of dwelling units or persons to be assisted, and indicated the general locations of proposed housing for lower-income persons.

Congress had high expectations for the HAP concept when it

was introduced as part of the Community Development Act in 1974. It was seen as a way to link housing assistance programs and community development activities and also as a way to improve the quality of local housing planning. Unfortunately, research on HAPs has shown them to be a failure; "[HAP] seemed no more than a paper exercise and indeed many localities treated it as no more than a minor obstacle to be overcome in the struggle for federal funds" (Christensen and Teitz 1980: 194). Reasons for the lack of success include: (1) the fact that cities lacked data of sufficient quality to complete the HAP forms, (2) the absence of technical assistance to local officials on how to use census data and American Housing Survey data (a large-scale survey of housing conditions carried out for HUD by the U.S. Bureau of Census), and (3) the fact that local planners rarely used the HAP as a strategic planning instrument—that is, to set priorities and to guide program implementation.

During the 1980s federal housing funds dried up. States and localities attempted to make up for these losses. Between 1982/83 and 1986/87, state and local funding for housing and community development rose by 38 percent. City governments spent just under 5 percent of their budgets for housing and community development, which was a higher figure than for states (Nenno 1989).

Stegman and Holden (1987) distinguish two types of municipal responses. One group of cities has tapped a variety of local revenue sources for housing assistance (for example, general obligation bonds). Another group, "second-tier localities," have not yet used general revenues for housing programs, but have responded to the federal housing cutbacks by appointing "blue ribbon panels" to study the problem.

New York City currently has by far the boldest locally funded housing initiative. In 1986 Mayor Koch announced his ten-year $4.2 billion housing plan to "produce, preserve, and upgrade" 252,000 units of housing in the city. The city is spending 3.7 times more for housing than the next fifty cities combined (Berenyi 1989; see also Lubasch 1989; Finder 1990a, 1990b).

The expanded city efforts that occurred in housing during the 1980s were due in part to decreased federal funding and in part to two increasingly serious housing problems—the growing numbers of homeless households and the "expiring use" problem in these communities. The latter refers to the privately owned, federally subsidized housing units whose low-income use restrictions or subsidy contracts are due to end.

State governments have set the agenda for local housing planning efforts (National Conference of State Legislatures 1988). California and Oregon have two of the most important state-guided housing planning efforts.

In California a state agency determines how much of the total state need is to be met by each region. A regional agency (the council of governments) identifies how much of this need each local government is responsible for. The final number is negotiated by the local government, the regional agency, and the state. Baer (1988) sees the law as an innovative and sophisticated approach to metropolitan planning in that it combines elements of "top down" and "bottom up" planning. Whether the law will be effective is highly uncertain because of three unresolved tensions: the lack of funding for housing programs by the state; the conflict between state-imposed rational planning and local home rule (for example, growth controls); and the fact that success is dependent on factors over which localities have little control, such as interest rates and the private market decisions of developers.

In New Jersey the courts, rather than the state legislature, have been the key actors in setting the agenda for local governments. The Mt. Laurel decisions require the state's 567 communities to provide zoning for low-income housing and to meet a quota established by the New Jersey Supreme Court. In 1985 a Council on Affordable Housing was created to resolve zoning disputes and to assign quotas to municipalities. A recently enacted state rule allows municipalities to pay to trade away half of their Mt. Laurel subsidized unit quota. Several suburban municipalities have paid to have the subsidized units originally allocated to them built in older central cities like Newark. Thus, the original goal of the Mt. Laurel decisions— dispersing low-income housing—has been watered down because of political considerations.

In 1990 the role of the federal government changed with the passage of the National Affordable Housing Act. The section of the proposed legislation most relevant to this chapter is the requirement that participating jurisdictions prepare acceptable Comprehensive Housing Affordability Strategies (CHAS).

The requirements for these strategies go beyond what was expected for the Housing Assistance Plans. Participating localities must describe the jurisdiction's housing market, not just the low-income sector; explain how the cost of housing is affected by public policies such as zoning, and propose ways to modify these policies;

describe the institutional structure through which the jurisdiction's housing strategy would be implemented; indicate how public and private resources would be combined to achieve the goals of the act; indicate priorities for allocating investments, both geographically within the jurisdiction and among different activities; and describe the coordination and cooperation to take place between different units of local government, as well as with the state government.

A recent HUD report (Hoben and Richardson 1992) indicates that, based on the first year of CHAS submissions, cities had made a significant effort to follow CHAS guidelines. However, there was no evidence that the cities had used CHAS as an opportunity to examine market-rate as well as below market-rate issues. Whether this will happen once cities get used to the guidelines remains to be seen.

CINCINNATI'S HOUSING BLUEPRINT

The Housing Blueprint is actually Cincinnati's fourth citywide housing strategy. In 1971 the Real Estate Research Corporation was retained to prepare a housing strategy for the city. Locally, a 28-member Working Review Committee was created, comprised of business, finance, and community representatives. It met bimonthly during the entire three-year life of the project. A development officer with the Department of Buildings and Inspections, Housing Division, was appointed executive secretary of the committee, providing local leadership as well as serving as staff.

The strategy document, which cost about $500,000, emphasized the importance of both meeting the housing needs of low- and moderate-income families and improving the city's ability to retain and attract middle- and upper-income families (Real Estate Research Corporation 1972). A key element of the strategy was the classification of every Cincinnati community into one of five types. According to the strategy, funding priority would be given to those communities beginning to experience decline, where program funding could make the difference between viability and further deterioration.

The housing strategy was officially adopted in November 1974, but has had a minimal impact. The neighborhood classification scheme has not been utilized. In the politically charged atmosphere of Cincinnati's neighborhoods, with many neighborhoods competing for limited funds, it probably was unrealistic to expect politicians and "public-spirited citizens" to withhold funds from some communities categorized as nonviable.

Cincinnati's second effort, the Housing Allocation Policy (HALP), was created in 1978, adopted in 1980, and amended in 1985. HALP provided guidelines for dispersing subsidized housing opportunities and thus was similar to other fair-share plans developed during the 1970s (Listokin 1976). HALP has had little impact in recent years because the types of housing that it was to regulate at that time (new construction and substantial rehabilitation of low-income units) are the ones no longer funded by the federal government.

The third effort, Cincinnati's Housing Agenda, was adopted by city council in 1983. It included a set of ordinances targeted to the housing needs of low- and moderate-income families along with others, promoting a strong economic base through the attraction and retention of middle-income households. Housing Agenda recommendations included the streamlining of certain regulations to speed up and secure the development process and the offer of tax abatements and attractive financing to encourage new development. The Agenda's primary significance today lies in the fact that it was the first time the city recognized the need to identify specific ways to link housing and economic development, a subject picked up again in the Housing Blueprint.

Cincinnati's Housing Blueprint originated in a memorandum from the city manager to the city council dated March 4, 1987. The manager noted that, although the city had developed an impressive array of housing programs, city leaders remained uncertain "as to how much good we have done, how much work remains to be done, how we should do it, how much it will cost, and how we will raise the money to do it" (1). The manager proposed a three-step planning process: the definition of the housing market segments that were "underserved"; product development and pricing; and the presentation of the draft Housing Blueprint to the city council by August 1987 and its adoption by September of that year. As we shall see, the timetable was overoptimistic. These tasks were to be completed by a Technical Working Group (TWG) put together by the department of neighborhood housing and conservation (NHC) but officially appointed by the city manager. The 27 members appointed included bankers, developers (profit and nonprofit), realtors, and low-income housing advocates.

From the beginning, the Blueprint was run by the director of the department of NHC, assisted by two NHC staff and two others from the department of city planning. In the summer, NHC hired the Institute for Policy Research, University of Cincinnati, to carry out the analysis of housing and population data from the census and the American Housing Survey. The three UC researchers served a dual role as consultants and as members of the Technical Working Group. The TWG met twice in September to establish the list of seven underserved market groups and then broke up into three subcommittees that worked independently on their parts of the Housing Blueprint (housing for low-income householders, housing for "special populations" such as the homeless, and market-rate housing). The TWG reassembled in the spring of 1989 to review and synthesize the three reports.

The Blueprint, released in December 1989 and subsequently approved by city council, proposed a $235 million program over eleven years to address the city's low- and middle-income housing needs (Housing Blueprint Technical Working Group 1989). Because of space limitations, we will focus on the section of the Blueprint dealing with market-rate housing; table 7.1 summarizes the Blueprint's production targets.

To stabilize the city's population, NHC was to act as the residential development packager by identifying sites, assisting with acquisition, expediting zoning changes, funding engineering analysis and site preparation, and selecting developers. Once developers were attracted to sites, the city would utilize a combination of city-financed, below market-rate construction loans and city-financed, below market-rate mortgages to homebuyers to ensure the projects were feasible. The below market-rate mortgage loan programs were to be financed by "enterprise funds," fees the city collects from parks, stadium use, and other operations that normally are invested in regular bank accounts. The cost to the city would be the interest not received through the normal investing of funds.

An early draft of the Blueprint included a proposal to use tax abatements to stimulate market-rate housing production. A union representative on the TWG objected to this recommendation, because he felt that it would result in a loss of tax revenue for the city schools. As a result, the proposal was dropped.

In general, the proposed economic incentives for middle-income families were not controversial. TWG members, including low-income housing advocates, thought that middle-income subsidies were sensible in order to stabilize the city's population and tax

TABLE 7.1
Cincinnati Housing Blueprint: Needs Estimates and Production Targets

Target Group	Existing Unmet Needs	Production Targets
1. Homeless	800 homeless individuals	150 transitional dwelling units[1] 223 supervised housing units 236 SRO units 90 shelter beds 101 very low-income housing units
2. Low-income renters	19,620 in "inadequate" homes[2]	1,237 units annually[3]
3. Frail elderly/ handicapped	4,028 have trouble functioning independently, lack home modification	Develop a 30-unit senior citizen demonstration housing project
4. Single family substandard housing units	6,850 substandard units valued at less than $40,000	Assist 1,000 single-family dwelling units annually
5. Market-rate rental	No unmet need[4]	Capture at least 20% of market rents $600/month+
6. Market-rate homeownership	Virtually no new housing production is occurring	Capture at least 24% of the market

[1]The production targets for the homeless population are over a five-year time period. For the other segments, production would occur over a ten-year period.
[2]Households in need suffer from one or more of the following: substandard conditions, severe rent burden, or overcrowding.
[3]Seventy-six percent of the production is in the form of housing rehabilitation.
[4]The city is already capturing more than half of the market for luxury rental housing. Cincinnati possesses a number of marketplace advantages for this segment; therefore, the goal is to capture as large a share of the market as possible.

base. The fact that the middle-income programs were considered in the abstract, and not in dollars that could be devoted to low-income housing needs, deflected controversy, as did the fact that most committee members thought that enterprise funds would only be available for middle-income housing programs.

The task force approach per se did not affect arguing over equity issues, because middle-class housing subsidies generally were not controversial in the first place. The task force approach was helpful in other ways, however. It resulted in an increased awareness of housing needs through the data provided by various agency representatives as well as in increased political support for the final Housing Blueprint document.

A major weakness of the Blueprint was the avoidance of geographical concerns. For example, there is no statement in the document regarding the extent to which the Blueprint should follow the city's own housing dispersal policy, the Housing Allocation Policy mentioned earlier. This was deliberate. When the TWG began its work, members agreed to avoid controversial neighborhood issues. Most members had in mind subsidized low-income housing in middle-income areas; they had little inkling that proposals for middle-income housing in established low-income areas like the city's East End (see chapter 9) could be almost as controversial.

This issue—whether the city should follow its own dispersal policy—emerged again in August 1991. At that time Housing Opportunities Made Equal (HOME, the Cincinnati metropolitan area's fair housing agency) issued a report criticizing the city's policy of concentrating low-income assisted housing in one or a few low-income predominantly black neighborhoods (Housing Opportunities Made Equal 1991). About the same time, a lawsuit was filed by property owners in the Over-the-Rhine neighborhood (a low-income neighborhood just north of downtown), challenging the city's policy of concentrating low-income housing in the area. The suit, if upheld, would have suspended the city's eligibility for federal low-income tax credits. Although the court declined to issue an injunction that would have halted the city's expenditure of funds to purchase low-income housing properties, the fact that there was a suit at all highlights the seriousness of this locational issue. The lawsuit is still pending and may be picked up again in the future. Thus, although this aspect of geography was put aside in the Blueprint process, it did not, and probably will not, go away.

The one exception to avoiding geographical issues in the Blueprint had to do with proposals for additional market-rate housing along the Ohio riverfront: "We are . . . convinced that the River presents a housing amenity that certain housing markets should be able to exploit to the City's advantage" (52).

It is easy to see why an exception was made to the principle of avoiding neighborhood issues in the case of riverfront development.

First, it was important for TWG to establish that there were, in fact, locations in the city with sufficient land for market-rate development. The riverfront, both to the east and west of downtown, does contain such developable land. Second, TWG members thought that additional housing along the riverfront would not be controversial, because residential displacement would be minimal.

Another weakness of the Housing Blueprint was a lack of attention to school issues, even though, as we have seen in this book, school-related concerns are important in influencing the city-suburban choices of middle-class families with children. The one paragraph in the Housing Blueprint devoted to school issues emphasized the positive aspects of the city public schools (the existence of specialized "magnet" public schools) and the existence of high-quality private and parochial schools. The market-rate housing subcommittee decided not to deal with the public school problems in any detail for two reasons. First, school-related problems tend to be highly controversial. TWG made a deliberate effort to avoid controversy. Second, the city has little direct leverage over educational policy. The weak coordination between the city and the school board is reflected in the fact that the board was invited to participate in the Housing Blueprint process, but declined to do so.

CONCLUSIONS

This chapter provides some basis for optimism concerning the feasibility of addressing both market-rate and below market-rate housing needs in citywide housing strategies. In the first place, the guidelines for local housing plans required for federal housing funding have become broader as HUD has replaced the Housing Assistance Plans (HAP) with Comprehensive Housing Affordability Strategies (CHAS). Cities must now take a look at the entire housing market, not only the low-income part, and must also examine the linkage between the public and private sectors. Whether or not officials will broaden the scope of the CHAS document to address middle-income housing needs is uncertain.

The discussion of middle-class housing policies need not be controversial. Low-income housing advocates (and others) tend to support these programs once they become informed about the need to deal with problems such as population decline and a weakened tax base. Before they support middle-income housing policies, however, low-income advocates need to become convinced that cities are simultaneously addressing low-income needs.

In addition to being broad in scope, local housing plans also need to address geographical issues such as the types of revitalization strategies appropriate in different areas. Furthermore, far more attention than in the past should be given to the linkage between housing and nonhousing programs. This linkage includes better coordination of housing and social services for the frail elderly and the homeless, as well as strategies for linking housing and schooling policies in efforts to attract middle-income families.

8

MIDDLE-INCOME HOUSING PROGRAMS

In this book we have argued that cities need to attract more middle-class families in order to remain viable, economically, socially, and politically. To do this, they need to stimulate middle-income housing production by offering incentives such as tax abatements and subsidized below market-rate mortgage loans, by providing assistance to developers (for example, selling land to them at a nominal cost) and marketing cities as an attractive place to live (Byrum 1992; Peirce 1993; Rusk 1993).[1]

Incentives such as subsidized mortgages make sense economically. An analysis for Cincinnati's Housing Blueprint, a citywide housing strategy, indicated that a below market-rate mortgage program would pay for itself within eight years through higher revenues for the city (Housing Blueprint Technical Working Group 1989; for additional information on this mortgage product, see table 8.1).[2] However, such programs could become so controversial, because they help middle-income rather than low-income people at a time that there are large unmet below market-rate housing needs, that politicians might refrain from implementing them.[3]

TABLE 8.1
Cincinnati's Proposed Below Market-rate Mortgage Program

The Housing Blueprint Technical Working group proposed an adjustable rate mortgage or permanent mortgage product implemented through local banks, with financing at 1 percent to 1.75 percent below market rates.

The market objective of this program was to maintain a 24 percent share of the owner-occupied housing market of houses with values in excess of $50,000. This means that during an average year when 3,000 new owner-occupied dwelling units are built, 720 of the dwellings should be built in the city.

The state of Ohio's linked deposit program provides a model for this below market-rate financing. The city of Cincinnati's enterprise funds treasury operation (monies it receives for the operations of the stadium, golf and tennis courts, and so forth) is currently designed to achieve the maximum amount of interest earnings on deposits. An alternative to achieving maximum earnings could be established by the bank in which the deposit is made, a below market-rate mortgage pool, whereby deposits are applied to new home construction in the city.

For example, to create a five-year adjustable rate mortgage pool of $20 million at 1 percent below market interest rates would require a deposit of $1,150,000 for 5 years at zero percent interest as a compensating balance. The cost to the city would be the interest lost on the deposit. If the city earns 10 percent interest on its deposits, the cost would be $115,000 a year for five years, or $575,000. For that investment the city could receive $25 million in new housing. At current property tax rates, $25 million produces $517,800 in annual property taxes for Hamilton County (which includes Cincinnati and some of its suburbs), the Cincinnati school district (roughly coterminous with the city) and the city of Cincinnati. This represents slightly greater than a one-year payback period when all the taxing authorities are considered together. The city of Cincinnati would receive approximately $88,000 of the total property taxes in the example, which would represent a 7.6-year payback period.

The Technical Working Group recommended that this product not be used "across the board" on every newly constructed owner-occupied dwelling unit in the city, but did not specify how the program would be targeted. Furthermore, the working group suggested that different rate reductions be used for different market segments, with the highest reduction for the lowest housing price category ($50,000 to under $90,000, 1.75 percent), a lower reduction for the middle category ($90,000 to under $125,000, 1.25 percent), and the lowest reduction for the highest price group ($125,000 and up, 1.00 percent).

The above description is drawn from pages 50 to 52 of the Blueprint.

It is likely that the recent emphasis on "equity planning" (Krumholz 1982; Krumholz and Forester 1990) within the planning profession is making the implementation of middle-income housing programs even more difficult. The term *equity planning* (Keating and Krumholz 1991) was first used to describe the work of Norman Krumholz as planning director in Cleveland between 1969 and 1975. This type of planning seeks to provide a wider range of choices for residents with few options. Equity planners argue that where limited funds are available—a situation typifying many American cities— most or all should go to low-income communities rather than to downtown redevelopment or middle-income housing. As planning director, Krumholz fought public subsidies for a private downtown Cleveland development and more recently, as a professor at Cleveland State University, has objected to the city's program of tax abatements and below market-rate mortgages for middle-class families.

Because Krumholz's views have been so widely disseminated and because he is held in such high esteem within the planning profession[4], we believed that his disciples in Cleveland and elsewhere (in conjunction with minority politicians and community activists) would actively resist middle-income housing programs. As we shall see, our expectations were not borne out.

Up to now, little has been written on the political acceptability of these programs. This chapter addresses this gap in the literature. More specifically, it examines the middle-income housing strategies that have been developed and implemented in seven U.S. and Canadian cities: Baltimore, Maryland; Cleveland, Ohio; Montreal, Quebec; New York City, New York; St. Louis, Missouri; St. Paul, Minnesota; and Wilmington, Delaware.

These seven cities were selected on the basis of three criteria: (1) to include cities that began programs as early as the 1970s as well as cities that developed them more recently; (2) to cover the range of middle-income housing initiatives that have been implemented in recent years (tax abatements, subsidized mortgages for new construction, subsidized loans for home improvements); and (3) to include at least one Canadian city to add a comparative dimension.[5] The cities were identified through a literature review and through informant interviews with national housing experts. The list of seven is sufficiently representative of cities with recently developed programs so as to offer useful insights into their operation.[6]

This chapter addresses a larger debate about the value of government programs for middle-income families. Historically, there is much basis for skepticism about the desirability of these efforts. Urban renewal is probably the best known example of a well-intentioned program promoting the return of the middle-class that hurt the poor. The "city as polity" perspective described in chapter 1, argues that corporations can be involved in redevelopment in ways that promote the broader public interest, that advance the welfare of lower-income residents, and that further their own profits. The seven case studies in this chapter provide some support for this latter viewpoint. We show why it is possible to develop housing policies that help both middle- as well as lower-income families.

Several other issues related to abatements and subsidized loans are not addressed in this chapter: whether they are legal in different states and provinces; whether they are inequitable, providing disproportionately large benefits to middle-income families; and the extent to which the two options are cost-efficient, providing sufficient revenues in the long run to counterbalance the short-term costs of the program.

Although our primary focus is on demand-side economic incentives such as tax abatements, we also discuss in some detail complementary efforts to publicize central city living to prospective home-buyers and supply-side strategies to make land available to developers at a nominal cost. Our interest is in the different approaches the cities have taken toward the provision of incentives, the stated goals of the programs, their sources of financing, the number of families that have been assisted thus far, and the extent to which these efforts have been controversial. The chapter draws upon published materials, interviews with project officials, and site visits. Table 8.2 summarizes the characteristics and level of effort for the middle-income programs in these seven cities.

SEVEN CITIES AND
THEIR MIDDLE-INCOME HOUSING PROGRAMS

New York. The improvement of New York City's economy during the mid-1980s resulted in a cutback in incentives and abatements. At that time the city had three tax abatement programs that were administered "as of right" and that sought to get construction going.

First, under the J-51 program, participants were eligible for full abatements on the rehabilitation of multifamily unit housing—that

TABLE 8.2

Summary of Characteristics and Level of Effort for Different Middle-Income Housing Programs

City/Program	Description	Level of Effort
New York		
J-51	Tax abatements for rehabilitation of multifamily unit housing.	"Very small" today; 5000 units/year in 1980s
421a	Exemption on increased taxes on improvements, multifamily unit buildings	"Couple of hundred" since 1977
421b	Exemption on taxes on improvements for construction of single-family houses	n.a.
St. Louis, Missouri		
Chapter 353	Private corporations are loaned power of eminent domain and tax abatements	Between 1985–91 329 properties had rehabilitation or new construction
Cleveland, Ohio		
Cleveland Action to Support Housing (CASH)	Below market-rate rehabilitation and construction loans	360 since 1978
Cleveland Land Bank	City sells vacant land parcels for $100	n.a.
Tax abatements	10 years for scattered sites, 15 years for planned development	n.a.
"Soft second" loans	Loans forgiven if the homebuyer remains	n.a.
Living in Cleveland Center Inc.	Variety of citywide and regionwide marketing programs	—
St. Paul, Minnesota		
Middle-Income Fund	Below market-rate renovation loans in spotlight neighborhoods	500 loans available; high level of demand

(*continued*)

TABLE 8.2 *(continued)*

City/Program	Description	Level of Effort
Montreal, Quebec		
Homeownership Assistance Program	5-year decreasing municipal tax credit	1200 to 1500 families
Habiter Montréal	City-owned land made available to developers	25,000 units
Baltimore, Maryland		
Vacant House Loan Program	Market-rate loans to acquire and repair vacant buildings	3 loans
Settlement Expense Program	Loans to pay for settlement costs, buildings priced $60,000 to $100,000	n.a.
Wilmington, Delaware		
Wilmington Partnership "soft second" loans	Second mortgage loan does not have to be repaid if the family remains	194 units assisted
Wilmington Homeownership Corporation (WHOC)	Agency rehabilitates and constructs homes in selected neighborhoods	321 units
Wilmington City Housing Corp. (WCHC)	zero % loans to builders	10 loans

is, on both the land and improvements—for up to thirty years. With this type of "deep abatement," owners could wipe out their taxes to 100 percent of the tax bill.

Sternlieb and Listokin (1985: 384–85) cite evidence indicating that the program paid for itself within a relatively short period. However, the program was widely abused in that it became the source of windfalls for many owners who would have renovated their housing anyway. Because of the resulting controversy, the program was amended in the late 1980s to limit the prices of properties that were eligible, so that the program was not available for luxury housing. When the program was amended, price ceilings were added, and the program was geographically restricted so as to exclude luxury areas. However, if the property receives substantial governmental assistance, it can still receive an abatement. (This also applies to the 421 programs discussed below.) Today the private sector program is very small compared to the early 1980s, when 5,000 units per year were being assisted. Eligible properties are capped at $30,000 assessed valuation before renovation. Utilization of the J-51 program is expected to increase when New York City's housing market rebounds.

The 421a program for new construction of multiunit buildings (rentals, cooperatives, condominiums) is not technically an abatement. Properties are granted an exemption from increases in taxes on improvements, but people pay taxes on the underlying real estate. The abatements are for an original period of ten years, but can in some cases be extended to fifteen or twenty-five years. It is estimated that the average abatement is worth about $30,000, present value.

The original 421a program was amended because it was providing subsidies for upscale families. As modified, the program is targeted to particular areas of the city. If developers want to use it on a noneligible site, they either have to provide (on-site or off-site) 20 percent of the units for low-income families or provide a payment equivalent to what it costs to achieve that goal. Since the program was amended in 1987, it has only helped to produce several hundred units.

The 421b program provides a ten-year exemption of taxes on improvements for the construction of single-family homes. For the first two years the buyer pays no taxes, the second two years, only 20 percent, and so forth. This abatement program has experienced few difficulties since it was introduced.

Currently, New York City has an enormous presence in the area of middle-income housing programs. This includes the Mitchell Lama cooperative housing program, rent regulation (which disproportionately benefits middle-class families), and New York City's ten-year housing plan. Of the 50,000 units to be produced under the plan, roughly a third are to go to middle-income families.

The Housing Partnership New Homes Program, administered by the New York City Housing Partnership (a private nonprofit agency) along with the New York City Department of Housing, Preservation, and Development, is of particular relevance to this chapter, since it is similar, in many respects, to programs developed in other cities (see New York City Housing Partnership 1992). Under the program, the city contributes land targeted toward middle-income homeownership (condominiums, fee simple) and $10,000 per unit toward infrastructure costs. The Housing Partnership selects the builders, packages the financing (using below market-rate interest mortgages available from the New York State Housing Finance Agency), and supervises the marketing along with community-based organizations. Since 1983 this program has helped to produce 8,000 homes.

This program has not been as controversial as earlier ones in New York City for five reasons. First, the program provides an opportunity for public review whereas in earlier programs developers operated "as of right." Now plans are discussed at community planning boards and the city council.

Second, a strong constituency has developed in the minority and immigrant communities for this program. These groups have limited homeownership opportunities, both in the city and in the inner suburbs; this type of program provides them with the ownership break that they want. The Partnership's Project director, Katherine Wylde, notes that the social justice argument against middle-income housing programs has become marginalized because of the emergence of such a minority middle-class: "If you want us [the minority middle-class] to stay [in the city], there has to be a product. The private market cannot deliver the product without assistance."[7]

Third, this program addresses a gap in the building production process that had existed previously—that is, a way to get land to private developers without providing a public benefit to a private entity. The Partnership releases the land *but with restrictions.* To be eligible for the program, household income cannot exceed 165 percent of the median, or $63,000. The income breakoff identifies where the private market starts functioning in New York City. The city is therefore focusing on income categories where the private market is not working.

Fourth, the program is helping to bring in private financing. Eighty percent of the financing in this program is private.

Finally, features have been built into the program to limit profit, to provide close oversight, and to prevent speculation. All of these features help to defuse criticism.

While there is currently minimal public debate about New York City's middle-income programs, there has been some criticism of these programs from within the academic community. Peter Salins, of Hunter College, complains that there is no clear definition of where the middle class starts and where it ends: "[the middle class] is in the eyes of the beholder."[8] As a result, this type of program often helps those in the higher portions of the middle-income bracket—families who do not need or do not deserve help. In addition, this type of effort often leads to "boondoggles," help to developers who produce overpriced units in areas with already high vacancy levels. Among New York's middle-income housing efforts, Salins is least critical of the Partnership program because it is directed toward lower middle-income families, because the subsidies are not that great, and because the program is "trying to lubricate the process"[9]—that is, create a housing industry in areas where the housing market is not working.

St. Louis, Missouri. St. Louis has been in the forefront of efforts to attract middle-income families. Chapter 353, Missouri's Urban Redevelopment Law, enacted in 1949, permits private corporations to organize limited profit corporations to develop plans for clearing areas and eliminating blight. These private development corporations are loaned the power of eminent domain as well as tax abatement. The program has been effective in attracting firms to the central business district. Since 1971 an increasing proportion of the activity under the statute has been in residential neighborhoods away from the central business district. In these more recent developments, tax abatements are passed on to homebuyers in order to encourage rehabilitation. Typically, the pass-through feature is used when the redevelopment corporation is not interested in purchasing the building and doing the renovation. Instead, the homebuyer sells the property to the redevelopment corporation, which immediately sells it back to the owner, who is allowed the tax abatement on the pass-through from the Chapter 353 corporation.

Mandelker et al. (1979) cite conflicting evidence on the impact of the tax abatements in attracting business firms to the CBD. There has, however, been no comparable research in St. Louis examining the effectiveness of tax abatements in attracting homebuyers to neighborhoods where Chapter 353 corporations operate.

In the mid-1970s there was a great deal of controversy in St. Louis about the use of public funds to aid private developers. A consulting firm, Team 4, argued that private developers could not be expected to go into inner-city areas unless city government did things for them, such as allow them (the developers) to carry out projects under the Chapter 353 statute. Team 4 also recommended that limited city funds for infrastructure improvements be focused on redevelopment areas with market strengths. This is the triage approach promoted by Anthony Downs (1980), among others.

Critics also complained about the use of public funds to subsidize projects where the primary beneficiaries would be private investors. They objected that most of the redevelopment funds would be used in the central corridor of St. Louis, thereby largely bypassing predominantly black North St. Louis.

There was some conflict related to the use of abatements in the late 1970s and early 1980s when displacement occurred. The displacement problem was most pronounced in the Pershing-Waterman area (see Monti 1990). However, with the decline in residential investment in the St. Louis inner city during the late 1980s, there has been a lot less controversy concerning displacement.

One institution that continues to be worried about tax abatement is the St. Louis School Board. The public schools are more dependent on property taxes than is city government, which also relies on earnings, sales, and utilities taxes; only 10 to 12 percent of the city's revenues come from the property tax.

In general, however, there is less debate about tax abatements today than there was ten years ago. One reason is that demand for housing is so weak. Consequently, there is a feeling: "Whatever it takes [to attract the middle class] so be it."[10] A second reason for the lowered level of controversy has to do with the way tax abatements are provided. In the early 1980s the community development agency devoted a great deal of time to fine tuning the abatements to conform to the pro formas of developers—that is, to make sure that the amount of the abatement was what was necessary to make the project successful. While there was haggling about the specific level of abatement, there were also extended public hearings (both at the level of the development commission and at the board of aldermen) where opponents of tax abatements were able to raise the equity issue. Now tax abatements are an accepted part of the development process. If an area is to be redeveloped, there will be an "automatic" ten years of abatement. Thus, the forum for squabbling about abatements has been removed.

The third reason for declining controversy over abatements in recent years has been that the eligibility requirements and monitoring of CDBG funds have been tightened considerably, making it more difficult to underwrite middle-income housing programs. Tax abatement has taken on increased importance because it is one of the few middle-income housing tools left. St. Louis has been fighting hard for its share of middle-income families, but has achieved limited success because of the weak market for middle-income housing in the city. The task was made even more difficult when the City Living Program, which attempted to market the city better towards middle-class families, lost its funding. It had been funded under the Community Development Block Grant program, but after a long debate the federal government said that it was an ineligible expense. HUD did not mind the concept of marketing, but disagreed with its being funded by CDBG funds.[11]

The history of tax abatements in St. Louis shows that they can be implemented effectively through private corporations. However, the long-term effectiveness of the strategy is limited by broader demographic and housing trends as well as constraints imposed by the federal government.

Cleveland, Ohio. Cleveland Action to Support Housing (CASH) was incorporated in 1978 and for the first four years offered direct low-interest rate loans for low-income buyers. In 1982 CASH was restructured to service moderate-income and middle-income homeowners. The purpose of the program is to create a partnership with Cleveland area banks in order to generate low-interest loans for middle-income families. More generally, CASH is seeking to make banks and other financial institutions more attentive to doing business in the city.

Although CASH offers both below market-rate rehabilitation and new construction loans, we will focus on the latter here. In the spring of 1992 CASH offered loans with an interest rate of 7.25%, whereas market-rate loans were 9.2%. Thus, there was a 2-point subsidy. These market-rate loans are linked to twenty-year deposits by the city in banks to compensate the banks for the costs of providing these loans.

CASH mortgages are typically provided with three other types of subsidies. First, through its land bank, Cleveland sells land parcels to the buyer for $100. The only requirement is that the buyer have an adequate plan for the site. Second, tax abatements are available on construction: ten years in the case of scattered site units and fifteen years in the case of planned developments. Third, Cleveland utilizes discretionary Community Development Block Grant (CDBG) funds to provide "soft-second" or "deferred" zero percent nonpayment loans. Homebuyers do not have to repay the loan as long as they remain at the location. The loans are addressed to the appraisal gap, the difference between actual construction costs and the relatively low appraisals in the neighborhoods around the newly constructed homes. The four subsidies taken together represent one-third of the cost of the homes. Nonprofit community organizations are responsible for obtaining construction loans for builders and for selling the homes through extensive marketing. The city of Cleveland has set up a new construction department to deal with land assembly, subdivision development, and cooperation with neighborhoods on infrastructure issues.

A key aspect of the CASH program is that anyone, regardless of income, is eligible in the target area (areas of slum and blight). Federal Community Development Block Grant funds can be used for middle-income families under the CASH program because the effort is aimed at correcting slums and blight. Most of the new construction has taken place on the East Side of Cleveland, where vacant land has been made available as a result of demolitions carried out by the city's building department. Efficient development requires at least six units per site, and almost all of the developments have been this big.

The CASH program is being implemented just east of the central business district, where modest detached homes are being built on blocks that either have been cleared or have only a few substandard homes. In addition, a cluster development of about forty Cape Cod type homes was built in the densely developed Glenville area near the eastern edge of the city, where riots took place in 1968. Finally, about a dozen prototypically upper middle-class suburban type homes have been constructed on large plots of land (about 3/4 of an acre) in a number of east side locations.

Thus far, CASH has provided $18 million in loans for 360 homes. This is small for a city of roughly 100 square miles with 200,000 housing units, where about 2,000 are abandoned each year. There is, however, evidence of impact beyond the small number of housing units that have been built. Banks now want to lend in Cleveland outside the CASH program. A few years ago, they would have been unwilling to lend in these areas. They are even willing to provide mortgages in what might otherwise be considered "impossible" situations (for example, helping to finance new homes costing $125,000 in Hough on blocks where existing homes are valued at about $20,000). Finally, the fact that some suburban families are now willing to consider living in the city of Cleveland, whereas they probably would not have done so a few years ago without the program, can be considered a meaningful accomplishment (Bell 1992; Chatman 1993; Lubinger 1992).

At present, the program's middle-income thrust is not controversial, in part, because most of the city's Community Development Block Grant funds are used for low-income families. Furthermore, elected officials, including the black mayor, Michael R. White, have become more enthusiastic toward the CASH program over the last ten years.[12] Local politicians see these developments as important in creating a new future for their wards. They can point to these developments with pride and say that their ward is not only for poor people.

However, Norman Krumholz has criticized CASH and other programs helping middle- to upper middle-income families. Describing one site which had been assembled from seven parcels and sold to a city policeman for over $200,000, he noted that this was not what the city intended when it set up the program; its actual intention had been to provide affordable housing.[13] Krumholz's criticism is part of an ongoing debate about the desirability of providing subsidies for housing, retail, and office development in and around downtown Cleveland. Krumholz argues that these subsidies would be better used to assist low-income people.

Central city advocates such as Richard Shatten, director of Cleveland Tomorrow, a downtown business group, reply by pointing out that, without the subsidies, Cleveland's already visible downtown revitalization would not have occurred (Krumholz and Shatten 1992).[14] Other middle-income housing advocates such as Tom Bier (Urban Studies Center, Cleveland State University) go further and ask: How will it be possible to revitalize cities like Cleveland unless additional middle-income families are attracted? He argues that if incentives are provided to help middle-income families locate in the suburbs (through funding for new highways and federal tax treatment of capital gains, which encourages movement to larger and more expensive homes), what is wrong with subsidies to encourage some middle-income families to consider living in central cities?[15]

Like St. Louis, Cleveland has initiated a public relations program, Living in Cleveland Center, Inc., to market the city to moderate- and middle-income families. Anda Cook, project director, points out that it is necessary to change homebuyers' perceptions before they will purchase in the city of Cleveland: " 'Build it and they will come,' does not apply. People have concerns and anxieties that need to be dealt with."[16]

The Living in Cleveland Center runs a variety of citywide and regionwide programs: prepurchase counseling in connection with the Community Reinvestment Act, which seeks to increase loan availability in the city; preparation and dissemination of advertisements, news releases, and informational documents; ongoing, for-credit courses for realtors; a "major event" to publicize restored and rehabilitated homes in the city; and a bureau of speakers to go to major agencies and companies to make luncheon presentations on the subject of city living opportunities. The center is also involved in a neighborhood stabilization project in the Collinwood area, which involves both community organizing and the implementation of an affirmative marketing program (including below market-rate loans for down payments and settlement costs) aimed at attracting white families to the area.

Unlike St. Louis's marketing program, the one in Cleveland remains open and active.[17] The Living in Cleveland Center has an annual budget of about $150,000. The largest revenue source, CDBG ($45,000) is used for prepurchase counseling. Since these are moderate-income families, this is an eligible activity under CDBG. The project director must spend a significant portion of her time raising funds for the middle-income components of the center. Currently, the remainder of the budget is funded from an allocation from the Cleveland Human Relations Board and grants from two foundations and from tuition charges from the real estate courses.

Cleveland's strategy of focusing on downtown revitalization and subsidized middle-income housing is beginning to pay off. The much publicized construction of downtown offices, a shopping mall, a sports complex, and a rock and roll museum have earned Cleveland the nickname "Comeback City." Business and political leaders in other Ohio cities who, as recently as ten years ago told Cleveland jokes, now travel to that city to learn about its successful regeneration efforts (DiLonardo 1993a, 1993b). Whether these much heralded improvements will slow population decline and alleviate social problems remains to be seen.

St. Paul, Minnesota. The Middle-Income Housing Fund (MIHF), begun in February 1992, has been termed the nation's first (Jossi 1992). St. Paul provides 7.55 percent loans, which are 1 percent below market-interest rates. The city is making $20 million of loans available for 500 families and individuals with incomes from $30,000 to $55,000 (with exceptions to $75,000). The loans may be applied to homes with values up to $150,000. St. Paul, like other cities, has had below market-rate mortgage loan programs previously. Unlike those earlier programs, however, this one will not be available exclusively for first-time homebuyers.

St. Paul created the program by refinancing bonds from pre-1980 federal legislation. In 1980 federal tax reforms (the "Ullman legislation," see Rogers and Zucker 1989) hurt local efforts by restricting the issuing and marketing of tax-exempt bonds. Under the revised code, these bonds (1) have to be used by first-time home-buyers, (2) are restricted to families with low incomes as defined by the regulations, and (3) are restricted on the basis of home purchase price "caps."

The Middle-Income Housing Fund is seeking to stem population loss, especially of growing middle-class families. City officials are also attempting to maintain the diversity of the city with respect to age, social class, and families with or without children (McClure 1991). The city is especially interested in attracting and holding "baby boomers." These households are at a stage in the life cycle when they want to buy a second home, and they think of moving to the suburbs first. The program provides them with an economic incentive to look at the city. The Middle-Income Housing Fund also addresses the fact that families often want to remain where they are, but do not have enough space. In St. Paul much of the housing that is available is too small for middle-class families. Consequently, program funds can be used either to move to a larger home or to renovate and rehabilitate buildings.

The program also seeks to promote neighborhood improvement. In contrast to Cleveland, which has focused on new construction on vacant blocks, St. Paul emphasizes rehabilitation and renovation on settled blocks. This difference in programmatic emphasis reflects the generally better neighborhood conditions in St. Paul. The Middle-Income Housing Fund is targeted to "spotlight" neighborhoods where homeownership is at least 50 percent and where housing is beginning to deteriorate. These areas cover roughly one-third of the city. As Gloria Bostrum, deputy director for housing of the city's planning and economic development department, asserts, "These are areas where, if we address [deterioration] now, we're going to be able to make a difference" (McAuliffe 1991). It is assumed that, when people in these spotlight neighborhoods see improvements on one house, they will then go ahead and make improvements on their own homes (Davis 1992: 8A). Neighborhood preservation is especially critical in St. Paul, where a large proportion of the tax base is concentrated in residential properties. In contrast, in Minneapolis the tax base is concentrated in downtown commercial properties.

When the Middle-Income Housing Fund was first announced in February 1992, demand for the loans exceeded expectations. The St. Paul Department of Economic Development received 3,700 calls in the first five days of the program. Four area lenders were deluged with a thousand calls the first day the program became available. The mayor appeared on television to discuss the program and was approached by officials from other cities for information about it. City officials, including the mayor, felt that this was a model that could be used elsewhere: "Other cities have the opportunity to duplicate our financing and our housing fund. . . . Low-interest, middle-income housing programs have been long overlooked by governments and foundations because of their attention to low-income, first-time buyer programs."[18]

There was some political risk-taking involved in the development of St. Paul's program. Although the mayor felt it important to stabilize the city's population of middle-income homeowners (as well as to provide affordable housing), he needed convincing early on in order to go ahead with the strategy. Now there is near universal backing for the program. One reason for the support is that the city has a relatively strong track record vis-à-vis low-income housing issues. In the 1980s St. Paul helped to fund 3,000 moderate/low income housing units, provided a total of $170 million in mortgage loans, and implemented nine low- and moderate-income home improvement and homeownership programs. A second reason for the program's popularity is that the Middle-Income Fund does not draw financial support away from low-income housing programs. While the former relies on state and federal grants, the latter uses special bonds.

The program has not completely escaped criticism, however. In a report that was broadcast on Minnesota Public Radio in early February 1992, Edward Goetz, University of Minnesota, and George Garnett, West Bank Community Development Corporation, Minneapolis, complained that the middle class did not need help and that, instead of trying to attract and retain middle-class families, the city should try to create a "new" middle class.[19]

Statutory changes would be required for the city to raise more than the current $20 million for the Middle-Income Housing Fund. Specifically, it would be necessary to revise bond financing legislation. Recognizing this problem, the city of St. Paul has proposed that the current federal tax law be amended to authorize a qualified Middle-Income Housing Opportunities (MIHO) initiative. The initiative would amend the Internal Revenue Code to allow the use of tax-exempt bonds for such middle-income mortgages. These loans could only be offered by issuers working in areas with older houses (some low-income) and with existing minority populations. As of summer 1993, the U.S. Conference of Mayors had endorsed this strategy, and both the National League of Cities and the Association of Local Housing Finance Agencies were considering it.[20]

Montreal, Quebec. Montreal—similar to many large northeastern metropolitan areas like Boston and Philadelphia—has experienced the transition from an industrial and manufacturing center based on a port to a service-based economy.[21] In addition, for the last four decades, Montreal has experienced demographic trends comparable to U.S. metropolitan areas. The city of Montreal's population dropped by 200,000 during the 1970s while the remainder of the Montreal urban community (the other municipalities on Montreal Island, equivalent to the inner suburbs in the U.S.) expanded in population. In another parallel to U.S. cities, jobs have decentralized away from the city of Montreal, first to other localities on Montreal Island and then to off-island suburban cities.[22]

Montreal is well known for its urban redevelopment of the 1960s and 70s, which revolved around the "grand projects" of Mayor Jean Drapeau, including the 1967 World's Fair and the 1976 Olympic Games. The grand projects were important for establishing Montreal's reputation as a world-class city. However, one of the main disadvantages of the strategy was the lack of attention to social needs. Most importantly, the city did not develop public housing programs at a scale comparable to other Canadian cities.

The city of Montreal's middle-income housing strategy is in response to the flight of middle-class Quebecers to the suburbs, which has reduced the proportion of inner-city residents speaking French as a first language to barely half (Burns 1992). Native residents who have moved out have been replaced by immigrants, many unemployed. About one-quarter of those on welfare are immigrants, and many of these are blacks from Haiti.[23]

The explicit aims of Montreal's middle-income policies are to make the city more competitive with its suburbs in attracting young moderate-income families who are purchasing their first home, to address Montreal's shrinking population, and to achieve a more balanced social mix—that is, more families with children (Hulchanski et al. 1990: 101). To achieve this goal, Montreal has implemented two middle-income housing programs: a Homeownership Assistance Program, aimed at the demand-side; and "Operation Habiter Montréal," aimed at the supply-side.

The Homeownership Assistance Program consists of a five-year decreasing municipal tax credit, which can amount to a maximum of $5,000 in assistance. Annual tax credits of up to $1,000 for five years are allotted to participating citizens. The tax credit is based on the value of the home, excluding land value. To be eligible, the family must live in a new house or condominium. The program has been relatively successful. As of December 1991, the program had assisted a thousand families. The figure stood at between 1,200 and 1,500 in June 1992.

Operation Habiter Montréal is the successor to Operation 10,000 Houses (1978), which was expanded in 1982 to become Operation 20,000 Houses. The latter program achieved its goal of 20,000 housing units between 1979 and 1986. When the program again required changes in 1986, it was replaced with Operation Habiter Montréal. Under this program, the city makes municipal land available at market or below market prices to housing developers who build projects in compliance with a development program prepared by the city for the property. The program includes identification of target groups as well as the development of architectural design criteria and specific requirements. Approximately 25,000 units have been built under the program. In general, it has had more impact than the Homeownership Assistance Program. Its selling point is that it stimulates demand which, in the future, will presumably generate additional tax income for the city. A city housing department official claimed that the program would pay for itself through increased tax revenue within seven years.[24]

Montreal's two middle-income programs have not been controversial. One reason for this is that the Homeownership Assistance Program is implemented in conjunction with Quebec's Downpayment Assistance Program. In other words, Montreal's program has been seen to be successful in leveraging outside funds. Second, the middle-income programs are endorsed because they promote two widely supported goals in addition to those already mentioned: job creation and additional housing production.

However, as was the case in Cleveland and St. Paul, Montreal's middle-income effort has been criticized by some scholars. For example, Leveilee and Whelan (1990) complain that Montreal's housing strategy has too much of a middle-income focus:

> Public money is so restricted that it seems almost impossible to do two things at the same time; that is, to implement programs that could attract middle-class people, and to finance new pro-

grams of social housing. So little has been done in public housing in the past that substantial action in the field of social
housing is like acting anew. Moreover, due to the increasing
rate of unemployment and poverty over the past 10 years, the
needs for social housing are higher than ever. (165)

Finally, Montreal officials recognize the need to increase demand for central city living to make these two programs effective. To
do this, they have developed a communications plan and a series of
press releases emphasizing the benefits to living "in town," including the lower transportation costs (Piche-Cyr 1990). Because of the
concentration of public facilities and cultural institutions downtown, Montreal's public relations effort probably has a greater potential for success than the communications strategy being used in
cities south of the Canadian border.

Baltimore, Maryland. Baltimore is noted for its downtown renewal program, including such projects as Charles Center, Harbor
Place, the National Aquarium, new hotels, a convention center, and,
most recently, a new baseball stadium (Oriole Park at Camden
Yards). Supply-side subsidies have been directed to some of the upscale condominiums in the Inner Harbor.[25]
    There has been some debate about the merits of this downtown
revitalization strategy. Optimists (including former Baltimore
mayor and now Maryland governor, William Donald Schaefer) point
to the city's comeback, both physically and psychologically.[26]
Critics such as Szanton (1986) question the benefits of downtown
improvement for the bulk of the city's population. There has, in fact,
been little evidence of spillover benefits from redevelopment
projects to poor, minority areas away from downtown.
    Baltimore has the second oldest urban homesteading program
in the country (after Wilmington, Delaware) and one that is widely
considered the most successful. Under the program, initiated in the
early 1970s, a vacant house (often no more than a shell) is sold to a
homesteading family for a dollar, with the proviso that the family
fixes it and lives in it. The city provides low-interest loans, makes
infrastructure improvements such as parks, and, in some cases, constructs in-fill housing on vacant lots.
    Otterbein, immediately adjacent to the Inner Harbor, is Bal-
timore's most successful homesteading area. Over time, Otterbein
has remained middle-income, while other homesteading areas have
tended to attract lower- and moderate-income families. Further-

more, the Otterbein project has had a positive impact on downtown—for example, helping to keep nearby restaurants open.

At the present time, one of the city's most important middle-income housing efforts is the Vacant House Loan Program administered by the Baltimore Community Development Finance Corporation (CDFC), a quasi-governmental agency. Announced in August 1992, the program has made available $4 million in market-rate loans for buyers willing to acquire and repair vacant buildings owned by private individuals. The program has no income guidelines.

The goals of the program are not only to provide safe and affordable housing but also to stabilize communities:

> Currently, there are about 5,000 vacant houses in Baltimore City, eighty-six percent of which are privately owned. Almost all of the properties share common walls with occupied buildings: as the vacant [one] deteriorates, the adjoining buildings are damaged both structurally and in terms of market value. (Baltimore Community Development Financing Corporation no date)

Thus, by saving these vacant buildings the program could help to make neighborhood conservation feasible.

The Vacant House Loan Program does not offer the types of economic incentives provided by cities like Cleveland, Montreal, and St. Paul. The main advantage of the Baltimore program for middle-income buyers is the CDFC flexible guidelines. That is, the city is providing loans that banks would not ordinarily provide because of the appraisal gap described above—that the value of the loan after renovation exceeds the worth of the property because of low neighborhood housing prices. In other words, the city is hoping that, by making loans available, it will be successful in attracting additional middle-income families.

As of February 1992, three loans had been made available under the Vacant House Loan Program, and eight additional loans were expected to be approved soon. Reggie Stanfield, the project director, felt that the program was almost on track in terms of the number of loans that had been, and were likely to be, approved.[27] Because of the high costs of renovation, only middle-income families had been able to take advantage of the program.

When the program was initiated, it was hoped that the city would be responsible for the first stage (providing acquisition and construction loans) but that the private sector would step in for the second stage (offering permanent financing to homebuyers). However, as the program has evolved, the city is responsible for both stages. As a result, payback is slower, and funds will be recycled more slowly.

The program has not been controversial.[28] The representative of the Maryland Alliance for Responsible Investment (an organization attuned to low-income housing issues), who sits on the board of CDFC, has not criticized middle-income eligibility for the program. One reason for the lack of controversy is that the program promotes neighborhood heterogeneity. Furthermore, as the project director points out, Baltimore's housing programs have neglected middle-income families, and there is a need to redress this imbalance: "These are people paying taxes, whose choices are slightly limited. They cannot go to expensive locations in the suburbs and get the same value."[29] Whether a program like this, lacking substantial economic incentives, can attract meaningful numbers of middle-income families to the city, remains to be seen.

In February 1993 Baltimore initiated a second middle-income program, the Settlement Expense Program. The program is designed to assist first-time homebuyers and existing homeowners who "move up" to homes in the $60,000 to $100,000 price range. Under the program, which has no income guidelines, families receive loans of up to $5,000 for ten years at 10 percent interest. Families apply for the settlement loan (as well as a regular mortgage loan) at one of five participating banks. Taxable bonds are being used as the funding source.

The rationale for the program is that many families do not have the cash to pay for settlement costs (covering title transfer fees and taxes), which amount to 8 percent of the costs in Maryland. It is hoped that, by making this loan available, some middle-income families (who otherwise would not do so) will consider the city.

Baltimore is beginning to develop a marketing program (in conjunction with a consultant) to better market its neighborhoods to middle-income families. Project officials expect to model the effort based on Pittsburgh's already established program. Not too much emphasis has been devoted to marketing in Baltimore during the last ten to twelve years, since the Institute on Living Council, a consortium of neighborhoods advising the city, produced a major brochure.

Once Baltimore chooses a marketing strategy, the challenge will be to find a funding source for its implementation. Mayor Kurt L. Schmoke has indicated that general funds are quite limited. Further, as is the case in Cleveland and St. Louis, this type of program is not considered eligible for CDBG funds with its low/moderate-income dictates. The city could use taxable municipal bonds for funding such a marketing effort, but it is unclear whether voters would approve of their use.

Wilmington, Delaware. The Wilmington Homeownership Corporation (WHOC) seeks to recapture the city's tax base and to stabilize neighborhoods by rehabilitating and constructing homes in selected neighborhoods. Covering about half of the city, these target areas contain blocks that are generally in good condition but that usually contain a few substandard units.

To be eligible for assistance, families must have between 80 and 120 percent of the median income for the Wilmington area—that is, $16,500 to $33,000. A program official contacted in connection with this research insisted that this was a low- and moderate-income program. Technically, she is correct, based on federal definitions. In reality, the program *is* serving some middle-income families, albeit ones towards the bottom of the middle-income category.

The program is marketed to city employees and public housing residents. The rationale for seeking public housing residents is that, if these relatively mobile householders become homeowners, this will free up units for poorer families.

WHOC was originally funded by a $1 million state grant; the agency is now sustained financially by loan repayments. Like Baltimore's Community Development Finance Corporation, WHOC is a 501-C3 non-profit organization. Its quasi-governmental, nonprofit status makes it possible for the agency to service loans and provides greater flexibility than would be possible for a regular city department.

WHOC works in conjunction with two other, similar nonprofit agencies. The Wilmington Partnership offers "deferred" or "soft" second mortgages. A bank or savings and loan institution provides a regular mortgage for 75 percent of the cost of the home. The partnership provides a loan for the remaining 25 percent as well as for settlement costs. If the family stays in the home for ten years, the loan is forgiven. The Wilmington City Housing Corporation (WCHC) offers zero percent loans to builders, with the savings in interest costs passed on to home purchasers.

In addition, the city of Wilmington provides a tax abatement on improvements. Thus, if a family puts $60,000 into repairs, it does not have to pay higher taxes based on the renovation. The effect of all of these subsidies is that a house that WHOC sells to a middle-income family for $68,000 in the city would cost $104,000 to $117,000 in the suburbs.

A key aspect of the WHOC program is that families buy the houses after repairs are made. The rationale is that working couples do not have the time to make the repairs; "when you are trying to save a city where 80 percent of the homes are absentee owned in some of the neighborhoods, you have to stabilize and anchor the neighborhoods."[30] Neighborhood conservation requires decisive action from an agency like WHOC.

As of February 1993 WHOC had constructed or rehabilitated (or was in the process of completing) 321 units; the WHOC original plan was to construct/rehabilitate and sell 600 units. The partnership had assisted 194 units, while WCHC had provided 10 loans. (In some cases, individual homes received two or more types of assistance.) Overall, the number of homes assisted is large for a city of Wilmington's size.

According to Alan Matas, former director of WHOC, Wilmington's programs are beginning to turn around particular blocks.[31] Decay has stopped, and homeowners are calling police when they would not previously have done so as tenants. In addition, other developers are beginning to come into these areas. WHOC has just completed two houses on the East Side of Wilmington. Houses in the surrounding area were appraised at $68,000. Five years ago, they would have been worth about $20,000.

WHOC is now expanding its role to become a for-profit developer and to focus on a more clearly defined middle-income market. In such market-rate developments, WHOC does everything from buying the property to bringing in the contractors, thereby eliminating several layers of profit. This for-profit effort has not been contested by developers because they usually do not go into these neighborhoods.

WHOC's middle-income focus has not been an issue because the program helps lower-income people as well. The fact that WHOC is now doing for-profit development in order to generate funds for lower-income housing could help to defuse the "social justice issue" if it emerges in the future. The money that is used by WHOC to help middle-income people could conceivably go to lower-income people. However, such a scenario is highly unlikely. If a low-income family was provided with sufficient subsidies to become a homeowner, the family might still find it difficult to afford the cost of fixing a broken window or repairing a furnace.

Furthermore, the fact that WHOC technically is a low- and moderate-income housing program also helps to prevent conflict. The federal government provides a precise definition of what constitutes a moderate-income family (between $16,500 and $33,000 in Wilmington). In contrast, "middle-income" is one of the most ambiguous terms in our vocabulary. (As Peter Salins mentioned earlier, "What constitutes middle-income is in the eyes of the beholder.") There is little question, however, that, many householders with incomes in the high $20s and low $30s consider themselves middle-income regardless of how the government classifies them, and there is no reason to question their self-classification. The ambiguity surrounding the term "moderate-income" works to the benefit of agencies like WHOC. Housing advocates who might criticize helping middle-income families generally will not quarrel about assisting moderate-income ones. Thus, as long as agency officials use the term "moderate income," they can have it both ways. They can see themselves and be viewed by others as focusing on those in need (moderate-income families) while they are in reality helping some in the middle-income grouping.

INTEREST IN TAX ABATEMENTS AND BELOW MARKET-RATE MORTGAGE LOANS

As we have just seen, middle-income housing programs are politically acceptable in cities as diverse as New York, Cleveland, St. Paul, and Montreal. Before we can conclude that the option is feasible, we need to see whether there is sufficient interest among buyers to justify the costs of development and implementation. To address this issue, we turn to the combined Cincinnati/Wilmington data set. For an earlier analysis of this subject based solely on the Cincinnati data set see Varady (1990b).

Demand for Abatements and Loans

We measured interest in tax abatements and below market-rate mortgages by the following set of questions (see table 8.3):

Some cities are considering providing financial incentives to attract homebuyers. We are interested in knowing what impact

TABLE 8.3
Respondent Interest in Different Types of Economic Incentives

Program	Not Too Likely	Somewhat Likely	Unsure	Very Likely	Extremely Likely
Tax Abatements					
Worth $500/year	38%	33%	7%	15%	7%
Worth $1,000/year	26%	28%	7%	22%	17%
Government Subsidized Mortgage Loans					
1% below market	31%	32%	7%	21%	9%
2% below market	22%	24%	6%	22%	26%

these programs might have had on choosing your current community. How likely would you have been to buy a comparable house in another city or township if that locality had offered: (1) tax abatement ($500 a year reduction in property taxes for the first five years); (2) tax abatement ($1,000 a year reduction in taxes for the first five years); (3) home financing at 1 percent below market rates (worth about $500 a year); or (4) home financing at 2 percent below market rates (worth about $1,000 a year)?

In each case, respondents were asked whether they would have been "not too likely," "somewhat likely," "very likely," or "extremely likely" to have widened their housing search.

We considered but decided against specifying that the city of Cincinnati/Wilmington would offer these financial incentives. Had we done so, the question would have been irrelevant to the one-third of the sample located in the city. Two separate composite scales were developed to measure interest in tax abatements/loans by summing the component items. However, prior to summing the items, we recoded the variables so that "don't know's" and "no answer's" would be the middle or third category. In the first version of the scales, scores ranged from 2 (high interest) to 10 (low interest). We decided to transform the scale so that high scores represented high interest. To do this, we subtracted the original scale scores from 10. The new scale scores ranged from 0 (low) to 8 (high). For the crosstabular analysis that follows the results for this scale were recoded into two groups: (1) people scoring between 0 and 3—that is, with a relatively low level of interest—about one-half of the total and (2) those scoring between 4 and 8, those with a relatively high degree of enthusiasm.

Our results indicate a fairly high degree of interest in both tax abatements and below market-rate loans among Hamilton County and New Castle County homebuyers. Demand for loans is greater than for tax abatements. If we look at the most popular option (2 percent below market-rate mortgages), nearly one-half (48%) of the respondents said that they would have seriously considered a comparable home in another municipality or township had the municipality offered this type of financial incentive.

In general, we can see that the level of interest among respondents was dependent on the level of benefit provided. For example, while nearly half of the respondents were interested in a 2 percent below market-rate loan worth $1,000 a year for five years, a little less than a third (30%) were interested in an otherwise comparable program offering loans 1 percent below market rates worth $500 a year.

What Types of Households are Interested in Loans and Abatements?

Both crosstabular analysis (table 8.4) and stepwise regression analysis (table 8.5) are used to test for the importance of different background characteristics in explaining variations in interest in tax abatements and below market-rate mortgage loans. We utilize regression analysis in order to determine the influence of particular background characteristics in predicting interest, taking into account the interrelationships between those factors and all others.

A key premise of this chapter is that background characteristics indirectly influence interest in these two program options. That is, variables like age and income influence residential attitudes like perceived housing progress, which are in turn linked with interest. In order to examine these indirect patterns of influence, the regression analysis was conducted in three stages: (1) background objective characteristics influencing locational assessments and preferences; (2) background characteristics influencing interest in tax abatements and government loans; and (3) background characteristics *and* locational preferences influencing interest. These regression results were represented by path diagrams whose results are summarized in table 8.5. Appendix 1 defines all of the variables in the analysis.

As we had expected, interest in tax abatements and government loans was a function of the extent to which the household was

TABLE 8.4
Factors Influencing Interest in Tax Abatements and Government-Financed
Below-Market-Rate Loans

| | Program | |
Characteristic	Tax Abatements	Government Loans
City		
Wilmington	46%	54%
Cincinnati	48%	53%
Age 20 to 29		
No	45%[a]	51%[a]
Yes	53%	64%
Age 50 and above		
No	47%	55%[a]
Yes	45%	44%
Married		
No	54%[a]	62%[a]
Yes	44%	51%
Child under 6 years		
No	48%[a]	54%
Yes	44%	54%
Child 6 to 17 years		
No	49%[a]	56%[a]
Yes	43%	50%
Parochial school child		
No	47%[a]	54%
Yes	43%	52%
Income		
Below $45,000	52%[a]	60%[a]
$45,000 and higher	41%	48%
Education		
No college	48%	56%
Some college	45%	52%
High-status white-collar job		
No	49%[a]	55%
Yes	45%	53%
Low-status white-collar		
No	46%[a]	53%
Yes	51%	56%

(continued)

TABLE 8.4 *(continued)*

Characteristic	Program	
	Tax Abatements	Government Loans
Blue-collar job		
No	46%	54%
Yes	46%	54%
Two adult workers		
No	46%	54%
Yes	46%	53%
White		
No	58%[a]	65%[a]
Yes	46%	53%
Moved from suburbs		
No	49%[a]	56%
Yes	45%	53%
Moved from out-of-town		
No	46%	54%
Yes	47%	55%
Previously owned		
No	51%[a]	60%[a]
Yes	42%	48%
Newly formed family		
No	46%[a]	53%[a]
Yes	52%	62%
Efficient government		
Low	40%[a]	48%[a]
High	52%	59%
Neighborhood orientation		
Low	47%	56%[a]
High	46%	52%
Urbanism		
Low	43%[a]	51%[a]
High	50%	57%
Accessibility		
Low	44%	50%[a]
High	48%	56%
Housing progress		
Modest	53%[a]	62%[a]
Great	39%	45%

[a]Statistically significant differences at least at the .05 level
See Appendix 1 for definition of variables.

TABLE 8.5

Direct and Indirect Relationships between Background Characteristics and Interest in Tax Abatements and Government-Financed Low-Interest Loans

Characteristic	Tax Abatements	Government Loans
Cincinnati metropolitan area	.060	—
	(−.041)[1,2,4]	(−.041)[1,2,4]
Age	−.080	−.140
	(−.013)[1,2,3,4]	(−.013)[1,2,3,4]
Married	−.040	(−.050
	(.000)[1,2,3,4]	(.000)[1,2,3,4]
Children under 6 years	—	—
	(−.007)[2,3]	(−.006)[2]
Children 6–17 years	—	—
	(−.005)[4]	(−.005)[4]
Parochial school children	—	—
	(.008)[2]	(−.009)[2,3]
Income	−.050	−.060
	(−.050)[1,2,4]	(−.050)[1,2,3,4]
Education	—	—
	(−.012)[1,2,3]	(−.014)[1,2]
High-status white-collar job	—	—
	(—)	(—)
Low-status white-collar job	—	—
	(—)	(—)
Two adult workers	—	—
	(.007)[1]	(.007)[1]
White	−.050	−.050
	(−.017)[1,2,3]	(.015)[1,2,3]
Moved from suburbs	—	−.030
	(−.008)[3]	(−.003)[3]
Moved from outside SMSA	—	—
	(.021)[1,2,3,4]	(.024)[1,2,3,4]
Previously owned	—	—
	(−.047)[1,2,3,4]	(−.045)[1,2,4]
Newly formed household	—	—
	(−.004)[2]	(−.004)[2]
Neighborhood orientation	.070	.090
	(NA)	(NA)
Efficient government	.180	.160
	(NA)	(NA)
Urbanism	.030	—
	(NA)	(NA)

(continued)

TABLE 8.5 (*continued*)

Characteristic	Tax Abatements	Government Loans
Accessibility	—	.030
	(NA)	(NA)
Housing progress	–.120	–.110
	(NA)	(NA)

Notes:
Tax abatements, indirect relationships via: (1) efficient government, (2) neighborhood orientation, (3) accessibility, and (4) housing progress.
Government loans, indirect relationships via: (1) efficient government, (2) neighborhood orientation, (3) urbanism, and (4) housing progress.
See Appendix 1 for definition of variables.

predisposed toward city or suburban living. Table 8.4 shows that those who had made the most progress toward their housing ideal (presumably a large single-family home in the suburbs) were least likely to be interested in these incentives. For example, while less than half (45%) of those who had made great progress towards their housing ideal were interested in these loans, almost two-thirds (62%) of those who had made modest progress were interested.

As we had hypothesized, those homebuyers who emphasized urbanism, accessibility to work, and economic criteria such as good housing prices were interested in tax abatements and loans (table 8.4). Nearly three-fifths of those who emphasized urbanism were interested in government mortgage loans, but this was true for only a little over half of those who downplayed urbanism. Furthermore, those who stressed efficient government services, typically families who emphasized good housing values, were also the ones most likely to be interested in utilizing these economic incentives.

However, householders with a strong neighborhood orientation (who normally would be expected to be predisposed toward city living) were not more likely to be interested in these economic incentives. In fact, those stressing neighborhood life were less likely to be interested in government loans. Those with a neighborhood orientation would be less likely to seek a home in another jurisdiction because they feel tied to their current location. It is also possible that these "rooted" homebuyers might have been concerned that these loans would be used by lower-income buyers to purchase in their area. In their eyes, this migration would pose a threat to neighborhood viability. With the data at hand it is impossible to test for the validity for these alternative explanations.

In general, table 8.4 supports our hypothesis that those in the earliest stages of the life cycle and in the baseline stage of the family mobility cycle were most likely to be interested. More specifically, those in their twenties, singles, newly formed households, and households without young children tended to be most interested in these options.

We had assumed that the parents of parochial school children would have a strong neighborhood orientation, which would lead to an interest in abatements and loans. The results refute this hypothesis but are consistent with our findings discussed above concerning neighborhood orientation. Parents with parochial school children were significantly less likely to be interested in tax abatements. There is another possible explanation for this finding beyond the possibility that these householders might have feared neighborhood change. That is, the results may simply reflect the fact that these households were in the childrearing stage of the life cycle when families seek suburban locations. A suburban emphasis would decrease interest in these economic incentives.

As expected, demand for these market incentives was a function of available financial resources. Lower-income buyers were significantly more interested in abatements and loans than were high-income buyers. For example, whereas three-fifths of those with incomes below $45,000 were interested in government loans, only half of those with higher incomes were interested.

The results provide little evidence that households emphasizing careerism (college-educated householders, white-collar workers, and two-worker households) would be especially interested in tax abatements and below market-rate loans. There were insignificant associations between interest levels on the one hand and both education and the presence of two workers on the other. Furthermore, high-status white-collar workers were less, rather than more, likely to be interested in tax abatements.

There were two reasons why we had expected blacks to be more interested in these incentives than whites. First, on the whole, blacks would be poorer, and the lack of financial resources would promote interest. Second, because of housing discrimination in the suburbs, blacks would be more likely to look for housing in the central city. As a result, tax abatements and loans would be viewed as helpful in purchasing within the city. Table 8.4 supports the hypothesized impact of race. Blacks were more interested in these options than any other demographic subgroup. For example, nearly two-thirds (65%) of the black buyers in the sample were interested in government loans, as compared to only 53 percent of the whites.

Table 8.4 confirms our hypothesis that interest is a function of migration history. Those moving from city locations, as well as first-time buyers (indicated by families who previously rented) were significantly more likely to be interested in tax abatements. The opposite was true for those moving up within the homeownership stock.

We had assumed that out-of-town movers would be more likely to stress nonexperiential attributes, such as good housing prices, and, as a result, would be especially interested in city locations and tax abatements. Table 8.4 provides no support for this hypothesis; out-of-town movers were no more interested in these options than others.

Finally, our expectation was supported that there would not be statistically significant differences in interest between Hamilton County and New Castle County.

Underlying Causes of Interest

The path diagrams (not included here) provide little support for our hypothesis that background characteristics only affect interest levels indirectly—that is, by first influencing locational preferences and assessments, which, in turn, affect interest. In fact, there are many background characteristics that influence interest indirectly as well as directly, while some have only direct impacts.

To a large degree, the regression results parallel the bivariate crosstabular findings. That is, in general, characteristics that predispose homebuyers towards city living (an emphasis on urbanism or accessibility, an early stage of the life cycle or family mobility cycle, low-income or a concern for economics, race) also fostered interest in tax abatements and government loans.

Several factors do drop out as important between the crosstabular and regression runs: the presence of young children, high-status white-collar work, moving up within the homeownership stock, and newly formed households. The three most important predictors of interest were age (inversely), an emphasis on economics, and progress towards one's own housing ideal (inversely).

The results dealing with household metropolitan location (Hamilton or New Castle counties) are complex and rather difficult to explain. This factor was not important in the crosstabular analysis. The direct impact in the path model for tax abatements means that living in the Cincinnati area contributed to interest even when other background characteristics and residential attitudes were controlled. The result probably reflects the fact that Hamilton County buyers have a greater variety of neighborhood options available to them within Cincinnati's boundaries than is true for the New Castle County buyers considering neighborhoods in the Wilmington. This greater variety makes Hamilton County buyers more likely to be interested in tax abatements.

However, the positive direct impact (.06) was almost entirely counterbalanced by the negative indirect effects (-.041). Cincinnati buyers were more likely, all other factors controlled, to have made progress towards their housing ideal and to have a strong neighborhood orientation. Both of these latter attitudes promoted disinterest in tax abatements. Taking into account the positive direct and the negative indirect effects, the total effect was minimally positive.

In contrast, the metropolitan location variable did not have a significant direct impact on interest in subsidized government mortgages. Given the same indirect negative effects that were true for tax abatements, the total effect is negative. There is no obvious explanation why the results for the metropolitan location variable varied by program type.

CONCLUSIONS

Cities need to attract more middle-income families in order to remain viable, economically, socially, and politically. One way to do this is to stimulate middle-income housing production by offering tax abatements, below market-rate mortgages, or other types of financial incentives. These programs make sense economically; they may be so controversial, however, because they help middle-income people, that they may be impractical. In order to test this hypothesis concerning political impracticality, we conducted case studies of seven North American cities where middle-income programs have been implemented: Baltimore, Cleveland, Montreal, New York City, St. Louis, St. Paul, and Wilmington.

The first generation of middle-income programs implemented in the 1970s (tax abatements in New York and St. Louis) was plagued by abuses and was controversial, but policymakers were able to modify the programs in order to deal with these problems. The new generation of programs implemented in the 1980s and 90s contain a greater diversity of approaches (below market-rate mortgages, tax credits, "deferred" mortgages), are more closely linked to supply initiatives and city marketing programs, and rely more on semi-public nonprofit corporations for flexibility.

Although these more recent programs have not been able to reverse patterns of central city decline (because they do not address "macro" forces such as continued construction on the metropolitan fringe), they have achieved some notable successes. In Cleveland, banks are providing more mortgage loans in the city, and a middle-class presence is now apparent in previously abandoned neighborhoods on the city's East Side. In Wilmington, anecdotal evidence indicates that the system of middle-income programs is leading to both higher confidence levels and higher housing prices in some areas that had been undergoing decline.

In contrast to what we had expected, these middle-income housing programs have not been controversial. There are six reasons for this. First, most of the cities have a good track record in helping low-income families. Second, the focus on moderate-income families in cities like Wilmington minimizes criticism from low-income housing advocates while allowing assistance to lower middle-income families. Third, these programs support desired citywide goals such as a stronger tax base, population stabilization, greater social diversity, increased housing production, job creation, and attraction of skilled white-collar workers. Fourth, middle-income programs are usually financed by special local or state funding sources and do not compete with low-income housing programs for federal dollars. Fifth, the middle-income programs have been able to leverage additional public and private sector funds, thereby increasing their popularity. Finally, these programs are endorsed by politicians (including black mayors, such as White in Cleveland and Schmoke in Baltimore) because they are an important part of neighborhood stabilization efforts.

Recent writings on inner-city poverty (see, for example, Wilson 1987, 1989b) highlight the key role that middle-income housing programs could play in future inner-city revitalization efforts. In the last decade the migration of black middle-class families from the inner city has accelerated, increasing the social isolation of the most needy families. Middle-income housing programs offer the prospect of attracting more families who could serve as role models for the underclass. To put it more graphically, kids from poverty families, who are familiar with middle-income homes, would probably feel a greater sense of worth than if all the homes around them were for the poor. Furthermore, these middle-income housing programs would provide middle-income blacks with choices regarding new housing that they generally do not have. Finally, these programs could be implemented in conjunction with community development corporations (CDCs), such as the Bedford Stuyvesant Restoration Corporation in Brooklyn, New York, which have established a successful track record in producing new housing units in the inner city and which stress income and tenure mixing.[32]

Not only are these middle-income housing programs politically acceptable, they are also practical from a demand point of view. Nearly one-half of the merged sample of Cincinnati and Wilmington respondents said that they would have considered comparable housing in another locality had it offered tax abatements or below market-rate loans.

Interest in these programs was, however, concentrated among those predisposed towards central city living. That is, demand for the options was particularly high among singles and young couples without children; lower-income families; newly formed households; those stressing urbanism, accessibility, and good housing values; and those who had only made modest progress towards their housing goals.

Thus, while cities could use tax abatements and below market-rate loans to attract lower middle-income families early in their housing careers, these programs would not be of much help in attracting families at later stages when such families attempt to move up within the homeownership stock and when they usually relocate to the suburbs. However, even if cities are only able to achieve the first goal, this would be an important accomplishment.

Finances, politics, and mindsets at the national level are the main obstacles to the expansion of middle-income housing programs. Michael White of Cleveland and other big city mayors understand the need for a middle-income policy, but many U.S. Department of Housing and Urban Development (HUD) officials do not. Through required local housing plans called Community Housing Affordability Strategies (CHASs), HUD could, but has not yet chosen to, encourage local officials to think regionally and to devise ways to attract and hold the middle class.

At present, federal housing and taxation policies hurt such efforts. HUD officials refused to allow St. Louis to use Community Development Block Grant funds to develop a series of brochures marketing neighborhoods; the final compromise that was reached (plan summaries) will be less effective as a marketing tool than the city's original approach. Although St. Paul's innovative Middle Income Housing Fund could serve as a model for other cities, its funding stems from federal tax policies prior to 1980. To create a similar program today would require changes in the tax law. St. Paul has proposed such changes, but their prospects are highly uncertain.

Urban scholars can play an important role in developing these middle-income programs. Improved knowledge is needed on (1) the level of interest in different types of financial incentives other than those discussed in this chapter and the extent to which they can influence locational choices,[33] (2) the rate of return on different types of middle-income programs, (3) the impact that middle-income migration can play in inner-city revitalization efforts, and (4) the degree to which cities have been successful in coordinating demand, supply, and marketing initiatives. However, for academics to participate in this way, they need to take a step beyond equity planning, recognizing the need to maintain a solid middle-income population base, while at the same time improving the quality of life for all city residents.

9

OVERCOMING RESISTANCE TO MIDDLE-INCOME HOUSING IN LOW-INCOME COMMUNITIES

Chapter 8 examined the feasibility of city efforts to develop and implement economic incentives like tax abatements and below market-rate mortgages. This chapter presents a case study that examines the practicality of municipal efforts to facilitate the construction of this housing, whether these incentives are used or not.

In recent years it has become increasingly difficult for cities to promote the construction of market-rate housing in established lower-income areas. For example, in the mid-1980s, the residents of the working-class Federal Hill neighborhood in Baltimore objected to a proposal for condominium apartments on Baltimore's harborfront (Wessel and Reich 1992). Throughout the country, lower-income residents are opposing not only market-rate housing but a variety of public improvements including college dormitories and subway stops (Fainstein 1990). Thus, the tendency to oppose unwanted public projects—the so called not-in-my-backyard (NIMBY) syndrome—previously limited to middle-class communities, is now found in lower-income communities as well.

Owners fight such developments fearing that their homes will be taken through eminent domain for public improvements such as parks. Renters resist, citing fears that area improvement will lead to higher rents, thereby forcing them to move. Both owners and renters fight such plans asking what good these projects do for them.

Well thought out neighborhood plans offer the prospect of overcoming community resistance to market-rate projects (Fainstein 1990). Such plans can provide accurate information to residents on what is being planned in the area. In addition, neighborhood planning offers a mechanism for coordinating different public bureaucracies. Finally, the decentralization, of which neighborhood planning is part, offers the opportunity for greater cooperation between community groups and private investors. Specifically, through such planning efforts community councils are able to achieve compromises with developers so that development is linked with improved housing for existing low-income residents (Marcuse 1990).

Wessel and Reich's 1992 case study of Baltimore's HarborView redevelopment offers four general lessons for planners regarding how to carry out such a neighborhood planning process: (1) involve the public early in the planning process; (2) take an early, comprehensive look at the issues (including the long-range and regional implications of the project); (3) develop appropriate linkage projects that compensate the city and possibly nearby communities for the impact that the project imposes; and (4) know the "bottom line" (that is, understand and track the financial feasibility of projects to avoid giving the developer the upper hand in negotiations).

This chapter's case study of Cincinnati's East End Riverfront Community Development Plan and Guidelines attempts to build upon Wessel and Reich's work. Members of a Cincinnati housing task force working on a separate citywide plan (the Housing Blueprint, see chapter 7) thought that this community was the ideal location for additional market-rate housing. However, they greatly underestimated the opposition of residents to proposals for medium (six story) high-rise condominium apartments.

Why did residents resist these proposals and how was the city able to overcome the resistance? Had city officials followed Wessel and Reich's suggestions, the process might have gone much more smoothly. Beyond their suggestions, our case study emphasizes: (1) the value of advocate planners (outside experts who bolster the tech-

TABLE 9.1
Chronology of the Planning Process in the East End

10/86	Councilman S. Chabot introduces a motion to form a team to promote substantial housing development in the East End.
11/87	Lead planning activities are transferred from the Department of Neighborhood Housing and Conservation to the Department of City Planning and the Riverfront Advisory Council. Draft Eastern Riverfront Concept Plan is developed.
3–4/88	The Riverfront Advisory Council Plan group assembles to guide the Eastern Riverfront Plan development.
11/88	Land Design/Research (LDR), Inc. is awarded the contract for phase 1.
12/88	A revised concept plan is completed by RAC and community representatives.
12/89	City Planning Department, Riverfront Advisory Council, and LDR complete phase 2 and present the results to the city manager.
10/90	Contract finalized with EDAW, Inc. to prepare the urban design plan.
1/91	The East End Community Report, prepared by Michael Maloney and Associates and Applied Information Resources, is released.
2/91	Urban Design Advisory Group (consisting of the RAC Plan Group, city staff, Ohio-Kentucky-Indiana Regional Council of Governments and neighborhood residents) reviews draft outline for EDAW design plan.
4/91	The East End Area Council submits "Recipe for Success" for the Eastern Riverfront Plan outlining seven points the community would like to see incorporated into the plan.
6/91	Plan is revised by EDAW, Inc.
9/91	Arnold Bellow is assigned to be project manager for the East End.
5/92	Both the city planning commission and the city council approve the East End Riverfront Community Development Plan and Guidelines, along with the accompanying zoning regulations, including the Environmental Quality/Community Revitalization district.

nical proficiency of community councils); (2) the importance of personality and planning styles in affecting planning outcomes; (3) the need to keep citywide issues in clear focus while at the same time providing for the needs of local residents; and (4) the importance of coordinating the efforts of different city agencies.

The following discussion is a detailed account of the history of the East End plan. By exposing readers to the social, economic, political, bureaucratic, and personality variables that influenced the course of the planning effort, we hope to show the complexities of the case. We have included the Chronology of the Planning Process in the East End (see table 9.1) to assist the reader in following the twists and turns of the city's efforts.

THE SETTING

At first glance, Cincinnati's East End would seem to be an ideal locale for additional market-rate housing. One of the oldest communities in the city, the East End is a six-mile strip of land between the Cincinnati central business district and the mouth of the Little Miami River (figure 9.1). The plan discussed below actually serves a slightly smaller area. Bounded on the north by steep hillsides and on the south by the Ohio River, the community offers outstanding river vistas and views to Cincinnati's famous downtown skyline.

As we shall see, housing planning in this community has been fraught with controversy. This is a low-income community with decaying housing that has largely been neglected by the city. Distrust among residents towards the city has made planning for middle-income housing difficult.

The East End was originally settled by Germans and Irish. Today the community is heavily urban Appalachian, with a minority of blacks (12%) and a sprinkling of urban pioneers who have rehabilitated single-family homes. In this community of 1,445 (down from 15,000 in 1950), nearly half the population has not completed the eighth grade, the median income is about $12,000, and 30 percent of the population receives welfare or some other form of governmental assistance (Miller and Kavanaugh 1991).

Objective demographic and housing data provide only a partial picture of the community, however. Rhoda Halperin, a University of Cincinnati anthropologist, noted at a 1992 city hall hearing on the East End plan that this is a community where helping out and watching out for one's neighbors is a way of life. People have strong ties to the area even when they move away. At the annual Family Day, 10 to 12 percent of those in attendance are residents of the East End; the remainder come from other communities, including many who had lived in the East End.

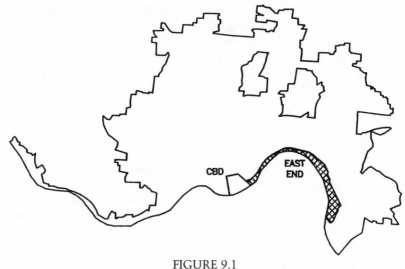

FIGURE 9.1
East End Community Vicinity Map. *Source:* Cincinnati City Planning-
Data Services, October 1991

Riverfront Advisory Council Concept Plan

The East End Riverfront Community Development Plan dates
back to 1986, when, in response to a councilman's motion, a special
team of representatives from the city planning department, the
department of neighborhood housing and conservation (NHC) and
the Riverfront Advisory Council (RAC) was formed by the city manager to promote housing development along the eastern part of the
city's riverfront. The motion reflected the fact that, because Cincinnati is a built-up environment, there are few places where it can add
to its share of market-rate housing. The exceptions are areas along
the river with views. The 1986 motion was based on the belief that
there was a lot more that the city could do with the eastern riverfront
as well as similar areas. The city controls 22 miles of riverfront in
Hamilton County.

About a month later, an ad hoc committee under Gene
Watkins, department of neighborhood housing and conservation,
initiated a ten-month assessment of the area. The ad hoc committee
consisted of representatives of the Riverfront Advisory Council, an
officially designated advisory group to the city manager, city agen-

cies, community councils, and the Development Corporation of Cincinnati. In its final report, the task force emphasized the need for both infrastructure improvements and housing programs: "Removal of rail lines should be high priority; and the development of low-income housing funds through the development of new housing should be used to mitigate displacement and facilitate rehabilitation" (Meyer 1991: 1).

About this time, the Riverfront Advisory Council released a preliminary concept plan (Riverfront Advisory Council and the Cincinnati Department of City Planning 1988). This plan, distinct from the multiagency study just mentioned above, recommended that further studies be conducted in order to respond to the city council motion. The directors of the city planning department and NHC and the chairperson of the RAC recommended that the planning department undertake these analyses. Because of limited staff resources at the planning department, the city decided to have a consultant prepare the plan.

THE LDR ECONOMIC FEASIBILITY PLAN

In the summer of 1988, a team headed by Land Design/ Research Inc. (LDR) was selected for the effort. Work on the land use plan began in January 1989 and was completed by June of that year.

The challenge for LDR was to create conditions whereby more market-rate and middle-income housing could be built in the community without displacing existing low-income residents. A second test was to develop a plan that would pay for itself. Donald Highlands of the Riverfront Advisory Council was the first person to stress the idea of the plan paying for itself. City officials agreed that in order to get improvements for the community funded, it would be good to show that the revenues from the project would compensate the city for infrastructure costs. Wayne Lemmon, an economist on the staff of LDR, recalled: "It wasn't absolutely said that the plan had to pay for itself but it was strongly suggested that our ability to get the infrastructure improvements funded would enhance our ability to sell the plan in city council."[1] LDR needed to answer the following questions: What would the different projects cost and what revenues would be generated? At what point in time would revenues and costs meet? In other words, how would the plan shake out?

The LDR economic feasibility plan (1989) sought to provide a mix of housing types and community improvements that would pay for itself through higher tax revenues, while at the same time minimizing possible displacement. The company made four key recommendations: (1) the retention of virtually all existing residences; (2) the development of 1,370 new residential units with a wide variety of prices and styles; (3) a new shoreline greenway extending the length of the community; and (4) a new village square providing convenience stores and services for both new and existing residents. It was estimated that the plan would pay for itself within eleven years through increased tax revenue from the increased business and increased property ownership. The project would cost $28.8 million to get going. Of this, $17.4 million would come from the city, and $11.4 million would come from the federal government. If built, the project would add $75 million to the city's tax base, adding taxes totaling $4.2 million per year. In addition, the project would generate as much as $250,000 per year in additional income taxes, over and above what was being collected at the time.

The plan did not attempt to address all the housing and housing-related problems in the community. In this respect, it differed philosophically from the Housing Blueprint (a citywide housing strategy, see Housing Blueprint Technical Working Group 1989) discussed in chapter 7, which sought to address all underserved market segments during the 1990 to 2000 time period.

There was little reaction to the plan at first from residents of the East End. The silence was deceptive, however; there were elements of the plan that later were to become highly controversial. The community was not sufficiently organized at that time to provide a coherent reaction to city officials. Suspecting that there might be problems of communication between community residents and the city, two RAC members (Lynne Coward and Estelle Berman, then a city council member) contacted Michael Maloney, an advocate for Cincinnati's Appalachian community and a city planner by training. Maloney confirmed that there was a strong sense of distrust felt towards the city that affected the ability of residents to engage in a dialogue. He also criticized the plan because of the lack of a social component.

Maloney, along with a local consulting firm, Applied Information Resources (AIR Inc.), was hired by the Legal Aid Society to help East End residents better articulate their concerns. The Urban Appalachian Council cosponsored the study with Legal Aid. The resulting study, *The East End Community Report* (Michael Maloney and

Associates and Applied Information Resources 1991) was based on 180 interviews with residents, 22 key informant interviews with a cross section of community leaders, planners, and service providers, and an evaluation of the plan by the consultants. The report criticized the LDR plan because it would lead to displacement and because it lacked specific strategies to address housing and social problems in the community: "Most of the residents had heard of the Eastern Riverfront plan . . . Resoundingly, both homeowners and renters were concerned about displacement" (i).

Critics of the study argued that since interviews were mostly completed during the day, the working population was missed. In fact, this criticism was only partially true. In the first place, not all working people work a 9-to-5 shift. Second, census information indicates that the survey covered the community pretty well with respect to tenure status. Third, this was not a "head-of-household" survey; interviewers were usually able to find at least one adult at home to speak for the household.

Maloney, acting as an advocate planner for the community, did not claim scientific accuracy. However, partly due to the large sample size (about 25% of the households), the results were given considerable credence by city officials. The importance of the study goes beyond the statistical results. Some elements of the East End Area Council's "Recipe for Success," to be discussed below, came from Maloney's study. Patrick Ormand, the president of the East End Area Council at the time, noted that by acknowledging fear of displacement and eminent domain as problems in writing, the report made a new level of dialogue with the city possible.

Ironically, the study was also criticized by some residents because it portrayed the community in too negative a way, for example, by highlighting the high rates of illiteracy and welfare. Rhoda Halperin was brought in to correct for some of these alleged methodological weaknesses—that is, to do nonquantitative ethnological research. She avoided the 9-to-5 framework, which had been used in Maloney's study, and began her research focusing on kinship ties (one of her specialties). Since that time, she and a group of her students (unofficially called the "University of Cincinnati team") have been working in the community, combining advocacy with research.

Michael Maloney, Rhoda Halperin, and AIR Inc. were not the only mediating agents involved in the East End planning process. The city's Community Action Agency (CAA) also played an important role. Staff included Janet Howard, a neighborhood worker in the East End, and Bailey Turner, a highly respected black civic official, an administrator in the central office of CAA.

The CAA has been involved in the East End since the 1960s and has been a primary mechanism for the involvement of black professionals. It played a crucial role in the East End in June 1990. At that time "two black brothers" ("neighborhood types," according to one informant) fought the plan claiming that the plan would cause displacement. By castigating those working in the community (including Jacquelyn McCray, project manager from the planning department) the "brothers" almost single-handedly were able to bring the planning process to a stop. McCray brought in Bailey Turner, of the CAA, to mediate the conflict. Turner backed up Janet Howard and convinced the two men to stop attacking those working on a plan for the community. Thus, the CAA helped the planning process to continue at this critical point.

THE EDAW INC. URBAN DESIGN PLAN

EDAW Inc. was chosen for the next stage of the project, the urban design plan, because of its experience with the mixed-income component of riverfront development. However, because EDAW had a small budget, staff were only able to visit the East End a few times.

In April 1991, in a show of unity, the East End Area Council endorsed a "Recipe for Success"—seven actions members wanted the city to adopt as part of the eastern riverfront plan: (1) scale back the number of proposed housing units and make the majority of new homes single- and two-family units; (2) protect existing residences from acquisition through eminent domain; (3) authorize relocation fees of up to $2,500 for displaced residents; (4) create a housing trust fund for the rehabilitation of residences and new housing construction for senior citizens and low-income renters; (5) grant a fifteen-year tax abatement for existing homes; (6) provide that the redevelopment plan not be required to pay for itself (seemingly an assumption of the LDR plan); and (7) give the community a line item veto over the redevelopment plan. The "Recipe for Success" was prepared with the assistance of Ed Burdell, a planner and a partner in AIR Inc.

The East End Area Council achieved agreement with the city on the second condition in the spring of 1991, when city council unanimously passed a resolution that stated eminent domain would not be used. Whether the city would have ever used eminent domain, other than on tiny pieces of land to make projects possible, is an open question. Nevertheless, many community residents saw the city's action as at least a symbolic victory. Ironically, as we shall see later in this chapter, the city might have wanted to use eminent domain at a later date when some properties were turned into junkyards.

The sixth condition was also acceptable to the city since the concept of the plan paying for itself was a dead issue by then. Most of those involved in the planning effort felt that there was no need for the city to box itself in regarding the ability of the plan to pay for itself. One city staff member noted that it was clear that the plan "would pay for itself but it was hard to say when."

During the spring and summer of 1991, the department of city planning and the department of neighborhood housing and conservation expanded their efforts to involve community residents. A public forum on the plan attended by the Ohio author of this book showed how far the city needed to go in order to win over the community. The point person for the city (Jacquelyn McCray, project planner, planning department) spent much of the meeting listening to accusations that the city was working with developers to remove low-income residents from the East End. It seemed apparent that at this stage in the planning process an "us-versus-them" mentality prevailed (that is, community residents against the city and developers).

Some faltering steps took place in 1991 to add to the community's low-income housing stock. In May the East End Area Council gave tentative approval to Family Housing Developers, a nonprofit organization, to build 24 apartment units. Rents were to range from $275 to $450 a month: the apartments were aimed at people with incomes of $18,000 to $23,000 a year for a family of four. This proposal was later approved for federal tax credits, which were considered necessary in order to make the project financially feasible. The city helped to make the project possible by donating a parcel of city-owned land.

Although an engineer checked the site for problems of hillside slippage, he did not check closely enough. When construction began in the fall of 1991, the hillside began to slip, and, as a result, further work was suspended. The city engineer had been aware of the preexisting slippage problem but had failed to communicate the existence of the problem to the developer. This incident illustrates the lack of coordination between city agencies.

For some time, the Hillside Trust (a nonprofit organization concerned with the thoughtful use of the hillsides) had been anxious about the problem of developing sites in the East End. On October 7, 1991, Robin Carothers, director of Hillside Trust, sent a letter to city officials emphasizing the need to be sensitive to the topography in implementing housing improvements. Carothers recommended that detailed geologic mapping studies be conducted of the relative stability of the hillsides; that this information be included in the final version of the plan; that this information be made available to the city public works department; and that other city agencies consult with the public works department in the case of any public or private proposal for development on the hillsides in the eastern riverfront area. In addition, the Trust recommended that the city refrain from removing healthy trees and other vegetation on the hillside because this could destabilize the hillside and could destroy the views from the hillside to the Ohio River. The plan for the East End that was eventually approved included a geologic and relative stability analysis of the entire study area and identified those areas where development would require hillside stabilization or where development was not recommended.

In May 1990 the city recognized the vulnerability of the community to unrestrained development and placed it under an Interim Development Control (IDC) district. The primary aim of the IDC was to protect the integrity of the planning process. Adding an additional review of demolition and construction permits by the planning commission, it insured that these applications were in conformance with city recommendations that were being prepared as part of the community plan but had not yet been formally approved. The IDC regulation was later extended until November 1991, and then to May 1992. The city council had made clear that it would not extend the IDC beyond May 1992. This put some pressure on city council and the city planning commission to approve a plan for the community.[2]

Under the IDC regulation, owners were required to obtain a permit from the city for demolition or for new construction. Some developers opposed the extension, claiming that they could not make improvements or proceed with development plans because they feared that the city might provide another developer with redevelopment rights on the site ("East End controls likely to remain" 1991).

Code inspection created a thorny set of issues for the city about this time. Many residents of the community believed that, as soon as developers began to show an interest in the community, code inspectors had become more active. In one March week, seventeen families were forced out of their homes because the buildings were condemned (Miller and Kavanaugh 1991a). The Legal Aid Society of Cincinnati chose not to contest the eviction process because of the substandard condition of the buildings, including raw sewage in the basements as well as structural defects. Instead, the Legal Aid lawyer helped the tenants receive the maximum relocation payments at the time ($375), and assisted them in finding a lawyer in order to fight the owner of the building. Some residents felt that in this case, Legal Aid was working in concert with the city and with developers.

Inadequate coordination between city agencies made a code enforcement/eviction situation even worse. The building department did not inform the relocation office in the law department of what it was doing. As a result, evicted families did not have the help that they needed. Fortunately, city staff learned from this incident. After these evictions, meetings were held between the planning department, the building department, and the department of neighborhood housing and conservation to develop a more sensitive approach. Consequently, the next time a code-induced eviction occurred in the East End, relocation staff knew about the problem, and the Red Cross was there to assist.

The preceding examples illustrate the dilemma that cities like Cincinnati face in connection with code enforcement. If the codes are enforced, residents are displaced. If they are not enforced, residents may be injured or killed when there is a fire or when a building collapses.

Another example can be cited to show how uncoordinated city actions can promote distrust. In 1991 the city began making improvements on Columbia Parkway, a major east-west thoroughfare in the community. When highway engineering department employees visited homes to photograph the condition of basements prior to repairs, rumors spread that inspectors were looking for more code violations and that additional displacement could be expected. City staff working on the plan were unaware of the visits until they heard about resident complaints.

THE EAST END RIVERFRONT COMMUNITY DEVELOPMENT PLAN

A working draft of the urban design plan was released in July 1991 (City of Cincinnati Department of City Planning and Department of Neighborhood Housing and Conservation 1991). The consultant sought to create a plan that would blend the old and the new, and would achieve a balance between preserving the existing residential community and managing new development pressures. More specifically, the plan sought to address the following issues:

- Retention and rehabilitation of occupied and vacant residential structures.
- An image for the community that creates a unified focus and is representative of its people, values, and history.
- The existing physical structure of the community and reinforcement of its strong orientation to the river.
- Areas of natural significance and strategies for their preservation and development.
- Buildings and areas of architectural and historic significance and strategies for their conservation and rehabilitation.
- Recommendations on bulk, character, quality, scale, height, and use that form the basis for zoning revisions.
- View corridors to the river from above and within the project area.
- Improvements to existing public spaces and parks, and recommendations for future public spaces and parks.
- Improvements to existing community access points and circulation systems.
- Opportunities for private development, including infill and large development sites.
- Prioritized schedule for private and public improvement recommendations.
- Increased economic activity in the area resulting in increased property tax revenues that support the proposed and recommended public improvements.
- Public improvements that encourage private development and build upon the evolving image of the East End/eastern riverfront community. (8)

The plan's statement of goals does not discuss the subject of market-rate housing. The most relevant goal is to "create broad, community based support for the Plan which reflects the concerns of the community and the goals of the City" (8). It is unclear which city goals are being referred to here. Furthermore, the document does not indicate how the city intends to balance citywide objectives, such as strengthening the tax base, with community objectives like repairing the existing low-income housing stock for existing residents.

The omission of any discussion of these subjects probably reflects a desire to make the plan as agreeable as possible.

When EDAW Inc. was hired by the city to prepare an urban design plan, city staff did not expect EDAW to reanalyze the economic feasibility of the project. Officials felt that the LDR economic feasibility study provided a good base for the design plan. If necessary, city staff could use the LDR model and proformas (calculations of project costs and revenues over time) to see how changes in assumptions regarding the project (for example, number of market-rate housing units, the nature of infrastructure improvements) would result in changes in overall costs and revenues. Moreover, it was understood that it would be the responsibility of the city staff rather than EDAW to write an implementation section for the plan.

The task of preparing such an implementation strategy became one of the main responsibilities of Arnold Bellow, who began as the East End project manager in October 1991. The idea of a project manager originated with the Riverfront Advisory Council, which first proposed a consultant team to work on the project. The city manager at the time approved of the team concept.

When the new manager, Gerald Newfarmer, took office in 1991, he accepted the idea of a project manager, but rejected the notion of an outside consultant, feeling that there was enough talent in-house to fill the post with a city employee. Later in 1991 he hired Bellow as project manager. He had applied for the position of director of the department of economic development. Bellow's hiring added an additional dynamic to the planning process in the East End because he had a vested interest in moving the project from planning to implementation.[3]

The East End Area Council sharply criticized the draft version of the urban design plan because it placed too much emphasis on upscale housing and not enough on addressing the needs of existing residents. More specifically, the president of the council said that the plan placed too much significance on expensive condominiums with prices starting at $170,000. A prominent local developer made the same criticism and recommended instead a mix of rental units and condominiums starting at below $150,000 to target young professionals "who are more willing to take a risk with new development in the East End" (Miller 1991: 5A).[4]

Beginning in July 1991, the city began to work intensively with the East End Area Council to address concerns related to the urban design plan. Staff from the department of city planning (Jacquelyn

McCray and Doug Ruwe) and the department of neighborhood housing and conservation (Ken Bordwell and Gerard Hyland) and the newly appointed project manager (Arnold Bellow) spent hundreds of hours at meetings of the community council and the Riverfront Advisory Council and at public forums concerning the plan. Nevertheless, at these public forums, many of the speakers still viewed the city as the "enemy" working with developers to remove low-income residents from the area.

One of the key problems that the project team faced was identifying what the "community" wanted from the plan. By the latter part of 1991, it was apparent that the East End was composed of at least three distinct interest groups. One group of residents, which included developer-speculators, simply wanted the city to leave the community alone and let private market development proceed unimpeded. The second group of residents believed that a plan for the community was necessary to maintain the community's distinct physical and social character. These people, including the community council president, were in favor of working closely with the city team. The third group of residents was distrustful of both the city and developers. These people felt that, if they were vocal enough in opposition to the city plan, both city agencies and developers would stay away from the community.

This increased community complexity reflected the demographic and housing changes that had occurred between 1990 and 1991. During this period, between sixty and seventy households were forced to move as a result of a combination of evictions, code enforcement activity, and rent increases. Given the rapid population loss in the East End since the 1950s, and the fact that at least some of this migration was involuntary (due to fires, code enforcement, and similar causes), it is hard to say whether the loss of sixty to seventy households represented an increase from what had taken place during the 1980s.

The process of community change was abetted by the activities of speculators, referred to as "junkers" by some community residents. These individuals purchased properties for the purpose of driving down the price of land. In some cases, they did this by storing junk cars on properties, then buying, assembling, and selling these properties to speculators who were interested in long-term price appreciation. Their expectations have some basis in reality. The most recent figures on residential property valuations (Horn 1993) show that the East End has experienced the second highest increase in property values in the city (66%) since the previous valuation. (It is important to point out that the increase was from a very low base.) Sales price data show a more complicated picture. The average sales price per transfer increased from $7,847 in 1987 to $37,475 in 1989 (a 375% increase). This was the time period when the LDR economic feasibility plan was being prepared. People were buying more properties at the time assuming that planning activities would lead to rises in property values.[5] The meteoric price increases did not continue. In 1990 the average sales price dropped to $21,141.

This increased community diversity made it difficult for city staff to use community council meetings to discern residents' feelings on the plan. Different people from the above three groups attended different meetings, and the council went with whoever was at the meeting.

The issue of how to plan with such a split community came to a head in January 1992, when several developers took over a council meeting and convinced those present to reject the city plan. The council had already rejected three earlier versions of the plan.

The rejection had the beneficial effect of uniting community residents as they went about reviewing the community plan. For the next three months (January to March 1992), council members reviewed the plan page by page, identifying areas of agreement and disagreement vis-à-vis the city. This intensive evaluation was used to develop consensus on the community council and in the broader community. City staff were asked not to be present, as the review process was viewed by council members as "family business." The city officials were pleased with this approach because it increased the likelihood that the review process would not be unduly influenced by outsiders.

A major change in community council leadership took place in late 1991. The former president, Pat Ormond, a realtor who lived in a community immediately adjoining the East End and who had served six consecutive terms, stepped down and was replaced by Ruth Coon, waitress/grandmother who lived in the community. Although not as smooth as her predecessor, Coon was quite articulate and quickly developed a reputation for including a wide range of people in the planning process.

Coon's more inclusive approach was demonstrated by her decision in February 1992 to carry out a survey of community residents aimed at developing an alternative proposal to the city's riverfront development plan (Kemme 1992). The survey was carried out, but the results were not presented to the city. The inability of the area council to complete the survey highlights a broader problem, the lack of funding for neighborhood planning efforts in Cincinnati. Other cities such as Dayton, with its priority boards, fund community surveys as a matter of course.

In early March 1992 the city released a "pre-final draft" version of the community plan (Cincinnati Department of City Planning and the Department of Neighborhood Housing and Conservation 1992; page citations below are from the final version rather than the prefinal draft). The document reflected four major changes from the draft urban design plan that was released in July 1991: (1) a name change, (2) an implementation strategy, (3) zoning and land-use regulations, and (4) a capital improvements program.

First, the name of the plan was changed from Eastern Riverfront Urban Design Plan to East End Riverfront Community Development Plan and Guidelines. This was a meaningful change in that it indicated that one purpose of the plan was the redevelopment of the community for existing residents. Furthermore, the deletion of the term *urban design* was significant because that term was required to qualify the area for urban renewal. Dropping it highlighted the fact that the city no longer planned to utilize eminent domain, a key aspect of urban renewal.

Second, in contrast to the urban design plan, the prefinal draft includes strategies to stabilize the residential population once redevelopment begins. By March 1992 the city had agreed in large part to six of the seven recommendations of the East End Area Council in its "Recipe for Success" (see table 9.2).

Third, the completed plan contains a zoning and land-use component that was absent from the earlier urban design plan. The city planning department recognized that the current zoning for the East End contradicted some of the goals and objectives of the plan. The riverfront developed as a river-related business and riverfront industrial area that required intensive and less restrictive business and riverfront zoning districts. Although the character of the area had changed in recent years, the zoning had changed very little from what existed in 1933. Therefore the planning department reduced the allowable density on particular land parcels to conform with what existed in 1992 as well as with proposals that were being developed at that time for the East End plan.

In addition, the plan includes the creation of an Environmental Quality/Community Revitalization district (an overlay zone). This

TABLE 9.2

Status of "Recipe for Success"

a. Eminent domain. The plan explicitly recommended that eminent domain not be used to implement the plan. The urban design plan had recommended that eminent domain not be used for occupied structures but had not mentioned its use in connection with unoccupied properties or the land next to structures.

It is important, however, to note that the city still has the power to use eminent domain under existing state legislation as long as there is a public purpose and the landowner is given fair market compensation. In this plan city officials say that they do not intend to use this power. There is, in fact, nothing to stop a succeeding city council from using it.

b. Tax abatements. The city proposes making tax abatements available on the remodeling and the rehabilitation of existing housing units and for new construction. The plan did not resolve the question of which type of abatement would be used. The first type under Ohio's Community Reinvestment Areas (CRA) legislation is available only in an area identified by the city where disinvestment has occurred. For homes in CRAs, the value of remodeling is not added to the value of the home for up to 10 to 12 years. For new construction in CRAs, tax abatements are given for up to 15 years.

A weakness of this type of abatement, according to the city staff person that we spoke to, is that it is not limited to low-income housing. In some communities, the tax abatement legislation could be abused—that is, used to benefit developers who would have constructed/remodeled the housing units anyway. In order to prevent abatements being used by developers not requiring them, city staff have been trying to qualify the East End under Ohio's Impacted Cities legislation. This would enable staff to target abatements to particular properties rather than to the entire community as under the CRA legislation. For the city to do this, it would normally have to have an urban design plan, including an urban renewal provision permitting the use of eminent domain. Staff from the planning department and the department of neighborhood housing and conservation have been working with the city's law department to get a wording change that would keep the urban renewal title for the sake of tax abatements but would eliminate the eminent domain provision, which is so worrisome for the community. At the time this is being written (May 1993), this issue had not been resolved.

The East End is therefore an example of a community where planners might want abatements limited to low-income housing. As we indicated in chapter 8, there are other communities where economic incentives could make a difference in determining whether market-rate housing is built or not. City staff did not think that the East End is one of the communities where abatements are needed for market-rate housing. These officials felt

(continued)

TABLE 9.2 (continued)

that market-rate householders could be attracted to this area without any form of economic incentive.

It is important to note that the type of tax abatement that we have just discussed is different from what the community had requested in its "Recipe for Success," that is, a ceiling on tax assessments. In the fall of 1991, Cincinnati's Board of Education had lobbied for "circuit breaker legislation" that would limit the tax liability of low-income and elderly homeowners. Board members felt that, if such legislation was passed, low-income homeowners would be more likely to support higher school levies. The school board urged the city of Cincinnati to join in lobbying the state on this enabling legislation. At first (in 1991) the city's law department did not push for the idea because of uncertainty regarding how much it would cost. With the passage of city council's Resolution No. 151–1991 in 1991, the city indicated that it would join the state in such a lobbying effort.

c. Housing Trust Fund. A trust fund—the East End Housing Preservation Fund—has been set up as part of a family of funds operated by the Greater Cincinnati Foundation (a nonprofit organization). Under this mechanism, created by Ed Burdell of AIR Inc., developers on city-owned land pay into the trust fund, which is then used to pay for low-income housing. The target payment for developers is $5,000 per unit, but the amount is negotiable for each property. In one recent case, the developer agreed to pay approximately one-half of this target amount, but acquiesced to contribute to the construction and maintenance of the greenway. This low-income housing linkage program is separate from the bonus program, which is part of the Environmental Quality/Community Revitalization District discussed below.

d. Relocation benefits. The plan urges the city council to designate the East End riverfront as an area to be covered by Chapter 740–9(b) relocation benefits under the city code. Invoking this chapter allows higher relocation benefits to be paid to residents who are displaced through landlord-initiated actions even though such actions are not directly related to the plan.

This recommendation was implemented through a city ordinance (April 8, 1992) which made residents of the East End eligible for special relocation assistance of approximately $2,500 per family. The higher relocation payments were justified based on the premise that residents were being displaced due to city actions.

e. Development of affordable housing units. Through the plan, the city is committing itself towards working with private and nonprofit developers towards constructing replacement affordable housing in the community. Two of the most important programs available to developers are the Housing Implementation Program (HIP) for multifamily units and the

(continued)

TABLE 9.2 (continued)

Renter Rehabilitation Program for buildings with two to four units. The latter program is being terminated nationally but is being reestablished locally under the HOME Investment Partnership program feature of the Cranston-Gonzalez National Affordable Housing Act.

    f. The concept of the plan paying for itself. As indicated above, this idea was "dead" at the time the first draft of the design plan was being prepared.

    g. The line item veto. This is the only element of the "Recipe for Success" that the city disapproved. The city council cannot legally delegate line item veto power to a community council.

---

is the first one of its kind in the city, there already being EQ/Hillside districts, EQ/Public Investment districts, and an EQ/Urban Design district. One purpose of the EQ district in the East End is to limit heights and to protect views. The height restriction is particularly important for the Columbia Parkway Trust, an organization for homeowners and condominium owners up the hillside from the East End. These families are concerned that development in the East End might interfere with their views of the Ohio River. A second purpose of the district is to prevent the demolition of low-income housing. The underlying zoning changes associated with the EQ district should help to address East End residents' concerns about new market-rate developments overwhelming the single-family character of their community.

Under the EQ/CR district legislation, developers are eligible for a 25 percent low-income housing density bonus. That is, they can obtain permission to construct at a higher density if they help to fund below market-rate housing. However, any proposal for increased density or increased height beyond the standards of the EQ/CR district must be reviewed by a hearing examiner. At that point, the community council and community residents have a chance to review the proposal.

Fourth and finally, the East End Riverfront Community Development Plan includes a capital improvement program. A high priority is assigned to acquiring the entire rail corridor in the East End. The first phase involves relocating the rail lines used by four railroads to the lower Mill Creek Valley ($12 million).[6] In the second phase, one rail line in the railroad corridor will be transformed into a bike path. The second line will be left for future public transit use. This second phase will also include removing some of the old rail-bridges over city streets and replacing them with bikeway weight bridges. The cost for this phase will be about $14 million.

Of more immediate importance to the community is the improvement of Eastern Avenue, a major east-west corridor parallel to the river. Improvements in on-street parking and street plantings will be used to give the area more of the appearance of a "Main Street USA" residential community. Currently, the corridor is unsafe because of high-speed traffic.

As community worries moved to the foreground, two citywide goals and issues receded in importance: (1) the need to increase the city's production of market-rate housing and (2) the need to create a continuous greenway path through the entire length of the community.

With regard to the first issue, there is only one place in the plan, a relatively obscure table on page 33, where one learns the total number of units to be added to the East End's housing stock, between 1,100 and 1,300. About three-fourths of the new housing would be in low- to mid-rise housing (four residential floors above two stories of parking) on two relatively large land parcels, 13 and 20 acres respectively. The remainder of the new housing would be distributed among single-family, detached row-houses, and duplexes on infill sites, the riverfront and on the hillsides. No breakdown is provided, however, on how many of these will be market-rate units; nor is any information provided on the extent to which the plan will pay for itself. As Lynne Coward of the RAC observes: "Those involved in the planning process have lost the scorecard."[7] Without any information on the payback period, it will be difficult for city officials to justify city funding for improvements in this community, given the equally pressing needs in other low-income communities. The most current estimate of the plan's total cost is $54 million, of which $24 million would come from the city and the remaining $30 million from state and federal governments.

Although a reanalysis of the economic feasibility of the plan was being conducted just about the same time as the city was acting on the plan, the feasibility information was not used in the planning process. (The plan was approved in May; the report was submitted in July.) Wayne Lemmon, an economic consultant who had worked for LDR Inc. on the 1989 plan, analyzed the economic feasibility of the

1992 one. His report identified several important changes between the 1989 and 1992 versions including a reduction in the number of market-rate housing units and a drop in the amount of commercial development.

These changes resulted in "negative funding" for the project. Lemmon estimated the total direct project revenues to the city would be $8.2 million, while total locally funded capital expenditures would be $34.1 million, leaving a shortfall of $25.9 million. Although the 1989 LDR version of the plan would pay for itself in eleven years, it would take at least twenty years for the 1992 version to pay for itself.

Lemmon (1992) noted an equally serious problem. While significant city revenues were not anticipated until the seventh year of the project, most of the major capital costs would occur before the fifth year. The challenge to the city, according to Lemmon, was to identify sources of funding for these capital improvements external to proposed development projects in the East End. The only practical alternative for the city is to incur debt.[8]

The second area where citywide issues have been given short shrift concerns the proposal for a shoreline greenway. About three-fourths of the greenway would be on land either owned by the city or Cincinnati Gas and Electric Company, the local utility company. On the remaining 25 percent, the project would require taking a fifteen foot strip from some residents' property.

Some East End residents who are directly affected object to the concept of a continuous greenway path whether or not eminent domain is used. They are concerned about security on and near the paths and fear people looking into their yards or homes. Other East Enders who would not be directly affected oppose the pathway because it does not do any good for them.

City staff tried to convince residents about the importance of a continuous greenway, but ultimately the city acceded to residents' requests that the greenway be given a low priority. City staff working with the community did not feel that it was their responsibility to advocate for a higher priority for the greenway, in part because neither the relevant agency directors nor members of city council had taken a strong stand on the greenway. Staff left it to the RAC to advocate for the greenway, but only one RAC member (Lynne Coward) championed the issue. Wayne Lemmon recalled what it was like to attend RAC meetings:

No one was articulating a clear set of objectives. The RAC was reacting to what was presented to it, and collectively it was trying to strike compromises. It was trying to expand the tax base but it was also trying to represent the neighborhood's point of view as well. They [the members of RAC] were not articulating a mission statement.[9]

The reader may wonder: Were there not any citywide documents that the planners could have turned to for guidance as to the city's policies and priorities regarding greenways? In fact, there was none, and there still is no clearly stated city policy. The subject is not discussed in Cincinnati's Coordinated City Plan of 1979. Greenways are addressed in the Cincinnati Parks and Greenways Plan (Cincinnati Park Board 1992), but the latter was approved after the East End plan passed. Thus, the parks plan was of no help to planners working in the East End. Furthermore, the section on greenways in the parks plan was based on the East End plan. Consequently the parks too states that the city will not override residents' views if they object to sections of the greenway crossing private property.[10]

Although giving low priority to the path may have helped to win community approval, this action seriously weakens the plan. The city must develop the riverfront for recreational uses in order to maximize its competitiveness with the suburbs and with other cities that have utilized their waterfront as a mechanism for economic development. For example, Portland, Oregon, removed an interstate highway along the downtown riverfront and replaced it with a greenway and mixed developments consisting of market-rate housing, boutiques, and restaurants. If Cincinnati is to be competitive with cities like Portland, it cannot always meet residents' desires.

There are two key reasons why citywide issues such as the need for market-rate housing and the need for a greenway were not given more attention in the planning process. First, city council members and civic leaders from citywide groups rarely attended public forums that were usually held in the East End. When civic leaders did attend, they preferred to remain quiet rather than bring up controversial issues. (There were not sufficient citywide interests represented in the East End planning process to pursue a public forum elsewhere in the city.) Second, Jacquelyne McCray, the lead person for the city, did not strongly advocate for citywide goals, because she did not think this was one of her main responsibilities. Instead, she expected representatives of the Riverfront Advisory Council to champion citywide issues and goals.

The East End Riverfront Community Development Plan and Guidelines moved closer to acceptance in mid-March 1992, when it was considered at a joint meeting of the city council's community development, housing, and zoning committee and the city planning commission. At this meeting, the most vocal opposition came from residents on the hillside communities above the East End, who were worried about the effects of development on their views (Sturmon 1992). At the same meeting, the president of the East End Area Council praised the changes that had been made in the plan, indicated the need for additional protection against economic displacement, but in general raised no serious objections that could affect the plan's eventual adoption by the city.

The following week, the planning commission approved most of the zoning changes based on the plan. However, a number of property owners contested the zoning changes, arguing that the changes limited their ability to benefit from the land that they owned. To a degree, the owners were expressing a legitimate concern. If the downzoning proceeded too far in trying to maintain the scale of the area, the economic feasibility of the market-rate projects would be threatened. Furthermore, it would be hard for the city to justify infrastructure improvements, given the community's small and declining population. Ruth Coon, president of the East End Area Council, supported a developer seeking a less restrictive land use category—R4 rather than R3.[11] Observing this conciliatory gesture on the part of the community council, Daphne Sloan, a planning commissioner and director of the Walnut Hills Redevelopment Corporation, one of the most respected nonprofit housing agencies in the city, offered the following comment: "Private incentives have to be there. For a community to be developed, there must be incentives for private development and for middle-income people to have a place. What makes a solid community is to have diversity" (Cincinnati Planning Commission meeting March 13, 1992).

The planning commission sided with the developer rather than with departmental staff and approved an R4 zone. In May 1992, both the city planning commission and the city council approved the plan along with the accompanying zoning regulations, including the EQ/CR district. For the East End Area Community Council to have approved the plan and to have indicated a willingness to work with developers would have been unthinkable two years earlier.[12]

The long hours that city staff had spent in the community had paid off.

IMPLEMENTATION

Even though the East End Riverfront Community Development Plan and Guidelines has been passed by city council, there is considerable uncertainty about its long-term prospects for implementation. First, the linchpin for the plan is the relocation of the railroad lines from the East End to the Lower Mill Creek Valley so that the right-of-way can be transformed into a bikeway. As mentioned in the preceding section, it will cost $12 million to buy up the land for the right-of-way and relocate the rail line to the Mill Creek Valley.

Second, the community has tremendous infrastructure needs, including but not limited to its aging sewer system. The city cannot justify all the needed improvements, because of the area's small and declining population. The community is therefore dependent upon private market housing. Whether this housing is actually built will be determined by market considerations, and at present the higher end of the market appears glutted.

Furthermore, as this chapter has shown, the city cannot promote market-rate housing too actively, because the approach is offensive to some residents. The community residents are primarily interested in addressing the redevelopment needs of the East End rather than in adding to the city's stock of middle-income housing. A large-parcel development with mid-rise residential buildings—a key component of the plan—will not begin construction until the year 2000 in order to avoid competition with Adams Landing, a luxury housing project immediately to the west of the East End. Postponing the opening of this project will slow the return of tax revenues to the city.

Third, at present the city's ability to implement the plan is limited because the budget is so tight. Specifically, inadequate funds are available for such things as soil studies, property purchases for public improvements, and title searches. The shoreline greenway and the bikeway right-of-way are particular sources of concern with respect to implementation because they constitute large new facilities and the ongoing maintenance will be expensive. Current park board and recreation commission budgets are inadequate to cover these costs; additional sources of funding will have to be identified.

Furthermore, if the city acts below the flood plain, it cannot by law use Community Development Block Grant funds. Other city funds will have to be expended, and, because of the tight budget, such funds are not readily available.

Finally, despite the concessions made by the city in response to the East End Area Council's "Recipe for Success" (low-income housing programs, tax abatements, a guarantee against the use of eminent domain), the future of the East End as a mixed-income community is uncertain. Even with these protections and programs, some homeowners may sell their properties at a handsome profit and move elsewhere. The situation of renters is even more precarious. There is no way to guarantee that landlords will keep their housing units in low-income occupancy. The construction of new low-income housing by a nonprofit corporation will only partly address this problem.

An Update on the East End Planning Effort

Several meaningful steps in the implementation of the plan occurred between March 1992 and June 1993. First, an Implementation Advisory Team was set up, including residents and others to oversee the implementation of the plan. The team had already held several meetings. One of its priorities is to turn the Pendleton Club building back to the community for community meetings. Originally a train station, the club was later closed and used for storage and for painting city swimming pool diving boards. Although it is crucial for the Implementation Advisory Team to consider the results of Wayne Lemmon's reanalysis of the feasibility of the plan, this is not likely to occur. In general, the team is not dealing with broad issues such as how the plan would be funded.

Second, two nearby properties (Ferry Street Park and Vance Street) were in the process of being sold to adjoining developers for infill housing.

Third, a revised version of the Lewiston project (the project that was suspended when the hillside began to slip) was moving forward and was expected to be completed by March 1994.

Fourth and last, the purchase of the railroad line was moving ahead. This is a very complex and plodding process involving a number of city, state, and federal agencies, as well as the railroad company. The final outcome was still uncertain.

CONCLUSIONS

The tendency for communities to resist unwanted facilities and land uses is no longer restricted to middle-class areas. The strong opposition of East End residents to proposals for middle-income housing shows that NIMBYism is alive and well in lower-income communities as well.

In the East End, the first thing that set off the alarm was the fear of eminent domain—a realistic concern because the city had used this power in the Adams Landing project, just to the west of the East End. Later, homeowners became concerned that the migration of higher income residents would lead to higher property taxes. Tenants worried that higher rents would force them to move. A final group of residents wondered what the city planned to do to deal with the serious housing, schooling, and health problems in the community.

Marxist scholars looking at the community in 1991 probably would not have been too surprised. They would have viewed the community through the perspective of class conflict. Fights over the plan would represent yet another example of a city working with developers to move low-income people out of an area to make way for higher-income residents. However, later steps in the planning process refute the Marxian analysis. City staff worked intensively with the East End Area Council and produced a plan that promoted the interests of the city as a whole, existing residents, and developers. The "city as polity" perspective developed by Norton Long corresponds much more closely to what actually happened in the East End than the framework utilized by Marxists.[13]

One reason the Marxist perspective is of limited value in understanding community development is that it ignores the role of individuals. In fact, personality variables played a key role in the turn-around that occurred in the East End. Ruth Coon, the former president of the East End Area Council, deserves much of the credit for the plan's approval. She helped to bring the community together and stressed a convergence of interests between the city and the community rather than confrontation. In addition, she was patient in working with both developers and "hilltop people," owners of luxury apartments and homes, who were concerned with river views. Despite later problems (footnote 12), her contribution was invaluable.

The city team working in the East End also merit recognition. Not only did they spend hundreds of hours at meetings in the community and at community forums, they were also "good listeners," a trait that helped them to earn the respect and trust of community residents. The appointment of Arnold Bellow as project manager was also valuable because it demonstrated the city's concern with implementation and results. Further, Bellow's ability to develop a good relationship with some of the more antagonistic actors in the community helped to push the plan forward.

The turnaround was also attributable to the technical assistance provided by advocate planners and researchers from outside the community (Ed Burdell, Rhoda Halperin, and Michael Maloney). Some of the most important mechanisms for addressing the concerns of the community (for example, the low-income housing trust fund) came from outside the city government. Had this external help not been available, city officials might still be arguing with community residents.

Members of the Riverfront Advisory Council played a meaningful role in the East End planning process. Lynne Coward's involvement was important because she brought others, such as Michael Maloney, into the process and because she continued to provide a "citywide perspective" on such issues as the greenway. Often she was a minority of one in her viewpoint. Others on the RAC played an important behind-the-scenes role in bringing different city agencies together and in working with other groups such as the Hillside Trust. This is not to say that the planning process in the East End was perfect. A number of mistakes were made, but an examination of these errors offers three important lessons for neighborhood planning efforts in low-income neighborhoods similar to the East End.

First, the case study emphasizes that the city gets a better plan when community residents are involved. However, this type of participation should begin as early in the process as possible.

Second, better coordination between city agencies is vital to reduce community distrust. This goes beyond agencies such as the building department and the highways department dealing with physical improvements. The underlying problems in communities like the East End are fundamentally social in nature. Therefore, in Cincinnati it is crucial to involve such agencies as the city health department and human services office, as well as the board of education, which is distinct administratively from the city.

An example of the importance of including the board of education in local planning efforts is appropriate here. An early draft of the "Recipe for Success" included a recommendation for a new public school. Serious consideration of this recommendation was hampered by the absence of any school board officials on the city planning team.[14]

Third and last, it is important that neighborhood plans like the one for the East End be linked with citywide housing, land use, and social welfare strategies. Work on a citywide housing strategy—the Housing Blueprint—occurred during the same period as the East End planning process, but there was little linkage between the two efforts. Most of the participants in the East End planning process (including city staff) either were unaware of the Housing Blueprint, or did not think that it was important!

A closer linkage would have meant that the Blueprint's philosophy of addressing all low-income housing needs in the city within a ten-year period would have applied to the East End as well. This consistency did not exist in the early stages of the East End planning process. The LDR plan did aim to minimize displacement, but it was still basically a physical land use plan that did not address the serious housing needs in the community. Had the LDR plan expressed the same commitment in relation to low-income housing goals as the Blueprint, much of the initial mistrust among community residents might have been avoided.

One of the lessons of the East End case study is that when such a citywide strategy is adopted, it is essential for the city manager, mayor, and directors of city departments to communicate not only the existence of the plan, but also the importance of using the plan to guide local programs.

Cincinnati needs but does not have a coherent citywide strategy for neighborhood revitalization indicating the combinations of programs that are appropriate in different types of communities. Such a document would indicate the role market-rate housing plays in redeveloping low-income areas like the East End, the way such housing benefits low-income residents indirectly, and the types of programs that the city is prepared to implement to deal with concerns about gentrification-induced displacement. Having such a statement of policies available before the initiation of a neighborhood planning process could go a long way to reducing fears among existing residents.

One possible location for a city's neighborhood revitalization strategy is its comprehensive plan. Unfortunately, Cincinnati's plan, The Coordinated City Plan, adopted in 1979, scarcely touches upon the subject of neighborhood revitalization. As a result, city officials rarely consult it in connection with redevelopment issues. Cincinnati officials could reduce the likelihood of future conflict over revitalization projects in the inner city by beefing up the 1979 plan.

10

METROPOLITAN SCHOOL DESEGREGATION

In the previous three chapters, we have shown that cities have successfully implemented a wide range of middle-income housing programs and that cities can balance programs to retain or attract middle-income families while simultaneously meeting the needs of low-income families. The mobility analysis showed that public school problems deterred central city choices. The problems of central city schools remain a major obstacle to middle-class retention within and attraction to the city. With the number of white middle-class students in central city schools greatly declining in the last few decades, the attention of city schools has naturally turned to its low-income, predominantly disadvantaged, minority clientele. Can cities currently serve middle-income as well as low-income students in the public schools?

We seek to understand the issues that arise when cities adopt schooling programs to retain and attract middle-class families while trying to serve their lower-class clientele. In this book, we focus on two approaches—metropolitan school desegregation and city magnet schools—and analyze them in the context of our two settings. Under Cincinnati's Alternative Schools Program, which we analyze in the next chapter, parents within the city are given a wide choice of specialized (magnet) schools focusing on science, language, business, and so forth. The assumption is that these high quality programs will help to attract and hold middle-class families in central city neighborhoods, thereby increasing the level of racial integration in the schools. The creation of four distinct school districts in New Castle County, Delaware (each encompassing city and suburban neighborhoods), represents a very different approach to integration. The hope behind the second approach is that, if both suburban and city districts are racially integrated, the incentive to migrate away will be reduced, thereby promoting stable integration in both city and suburban schools.

In this chapter, we begin with introductory comments concerning middle-class families and city public schools. The first major part of the chapter then considers the more controversial approach offered to retain and attract the middle class through schools—metropolitan school desegregation. We review the legal basis of this policy and then examine several plans that have been implemented. The second part of the chapter is a case study of the Wilmington, Delaware, metropolitan school desegregation plan. We examine this case in detail, considering its origins, the nature of the plan, and implementation issues. As we focus on the Wilmington metropolitan plan, we ask: Is it possible for metropolitan school plans to address simultaneously the concerns of middle- and low-income parents? Will the metropolitan plan raise the test scores of both types of students? Will it retain middle-income children in the system? Will whites and blacks be satisfied with the plan? Can it be implemented without racial tensions and perhaps promote racial understanding? We conclude that, while the plan has been successful in desegregating schools and offers some hope for city revival, a number of problems, including class and racial conflict, limit its utility in reversing city decline.

CENTRAL CITY PUBLIC SCHOOLS AND MIDDLE-CLASS FAMILIES

The decision of Bill and Hillary Clinton not to send their child, Chelsea, to a public school, focuses our attention on issues surrounding middle-class family location decisions and central city schools. In January 1993, when a spokesperson for President-elect Clinton announced that daughter Chelsea would attend the Sidwell Friends School (unlike his Democratic predecessor's daughter, Amy Carter, who was sent to a public school), many were upset with the decision (Friedman 1993). Highlighted in the analysis of the Clintons' choice was the status of public schools in the nation's capital, "notoriously underfinanced, overcrowded, and far from ideal" (Friedman 1993: A14).

The preceding leads us to reflect on the situation and ask what actions have been taken in the area of schooling to retain and attract families to the city and how successful these efforts have been. We recognize that in recent years city schools have been one of the factors that led to middle-class abandonment of cities. As Jones (1990) has stated, "Families able to do so have moved away from city centers in an effort to find 'good' public schools—ones without difficult children and without social problems" (244). The reasons for the decline, as discussed in chapter 4, go beyond middle-class avoidance of city schools (for example, preferences for suburban living), but there is no doubt, as our mobility analysis confirms, that homebuyer perceptions of the poor quality of city schools play a significant role.

Over time, the movement of middle-class families to the suburbs and minorities to the central cities has led, in Witte and Walsh's words, to "two very separate educational worlds" (1990: 192–93). Focusing on the Milwaukee metropolitan area, they describe the urban and suburban schools as two worlds, the suburban one of educational achievement, educational and financial resources, and student success, and the urban one of inadequate (although not necessarily less) resources and student failure and hopelessness. In the urban world, almost 60 percent of the Milwaukee students are minority, and 44 percent qualify for a free lunch. In the suburban world, only 5 percent of the students are minority, and the same percentage have low incomes. The two-worlds dichotomy recently documented in the Milwaukee area is the rule rather than the exception in the United States. The suburban educational world of superior schools makes it more difficult for cities to keep and attract middle-class whites, who could contribute to the financial and political base of the central city. Middle-class families that remain in the city are likely to send their children to private or parochial school. And city school districts have understandably turned their attention to what steps they can take to serve disadvantaged and minority students. (For a summary of city school programs and programs and policies to help at-risk students, see Raffel et al. 1992).

One approach advocated to overcome the city-suburban dichotomy is metropolitan school desegregation.

THE CASE FOR METROPOLITAN SCHOOL DESEGREGATION

The traditional argument for metropolitan school desegregation is based upon the presumed positive effects of school desegregation on black students. While not all agree (see Bates 1990; Monti 1991), school desegregation is generally viewed as a policy that helps black students achieve more academically (Mahard and Crain 1983) and function more successfully in society (Crain 1972).

There is no consensus among scholars on why school desegregation has a positive impact on minority achievement. Several reasons have been offered, two of which are related to metropolitan plans. Students are greatly affected by their peers, and, when peers are middle-class, they are more likely to set high educational standards for all students (Coleman et al. 1966; Mahard and Crain 1983). In addition, it is argued that educational institutions in our society respond more to the parents of well-off white students than poor minority parents, so desegregation leads to school improvements in formerly black and therefore neglected schools. This theory explaining the positive effects of school desegregation is the so-called hostage theory.

Three reasons for adopting metropolitan school desegregation plans have been offered. First, metropolitan school desegregation maximizes the probability that the students in a desegregation plan will be white as well as middle-class. The higher percentage of white students makes it more likely that there will be enough white students to go around; the higher percentage of middle-class students maximizes the number of students with strong educational values and, thus, the positive impact of school desegregation. In contrast, city-only plans often lack white students and sufficient students with values supportive of education. Therefore, metropolitan school desegregation increases the probability that school desegregation will positively affect black achievement. In fact, Mahard and Crain (1983: 117) report that "the metropolitan desegregation plans analyzed show stronger achievement effects than the plans examined in other studies," where integration was limited to the city.

The second reason given for the attractiveness of metropolitan school desegregation is that it is more demographically stable than city-only school desegregation. That is, it is more likely to minimize white flight. In 1978 Orfield concluded that "where desegregation plans include the suburbs, residential stability is greater" (as quoted in Klaff 1982: 260–61; see also Pettigrew and Green 1976; Armor 1982). Recent studies confirm this (Orfield, Monfort, and Aaron 1989; Orfield and Monfort 1988; Orfield and Monfort 1992). The increased stability results from the difficulty experienced by white families trying to relocate to areas not covered by the plan and the higher percentage of whites in schools in metropolitan as opposed to city-only plans, which may keep schools below the "tipping point" of minority students (Rossell 1990).

The third reason why metropolitan plans are favored is a function of the problems caused by the division between the financial resources of the suburbs and the educational problems and needs of those in the cities. Some argue that this division can be best bridged through metropolitan school districts, although there has been much historical opposition to such reorganizations (Zimmer and Hawley 1968). A metropolitan school desegregation plan tied to a metropolitan school district with a single tax rate and governance structure allows for more equitable educational programs throughout a metropolitan area.

The recent New Jersey court decision on school finance (*Abbott v. Burke*, 575A.2d359 [N.J. 1990]) lays out the dilemmas of urban school districts caught in this resource bind. The court concluded that there is a "constitutional failure of education in poorer urban districts" (100) in New Jersey and that a thorough and efficient education does not exist in these districts. According to the court, "the social and economic pressures on municipalities, school districts, public officials, and citizens of these disaster areas—many poorer urban districts—are so severe that tax increases in any substantial amount are almost unthinkable" (99). These resource disparities are reflected in major deficiencies in educational services provided to urban students and higher city tax rates. The court did not order any metropolitan remedies but did mandate the state to fund poor districts at the level of wealthy districts, and the state legislature, under Governor Jim Florio's leadership, did pass a responsive, but politically painful, funding plan. The Democratic legislature, largely because of their support for this plan, was voted out of office at the next election. Florio's defeat came at the subsequent election.

Given the advantages of metropolitan plans, Orfield (1975) argues that a metropolitan plan "may lower some of the barriers to the return of middle-class families to the central cities and their schools" (55–56). Orfield contends that metropolitan desegregation removes schools as a constraint on migration into cities and that more "reverse migration" (213) into cities of families with children who will attend public schools would result from such a plan.

ADOPTION OF METROPOLITAN PLANS

While metropolitan approaches to school desegregation may help to revive cities, major legal and political obstacles to such efforts exist. Historically, the major impetus for a metropolitan desegregation plan has been the federal courts. But the U.S. Supreme Court's decision on the inappropriateness of a metropolitan remedy to alleviate school segregation in Detroit stands as a major, although not insurmountable, obstacle to metropolitan remedies to city segregation. If metropolitan plans are ordered by the courts in the future, they are likely to be the result of state, not federal, action.

Metropolitan Busing in County Districts

The Supreme Court's *Swann v. Charlotte-Mecklenburg Board of Education* (402 U.S. 1 [1971]) decision opened the door to federally ordered metropolitan busing plans. In North Carolina the Charlotte city and Mecklenburg county school districts had merged in 1960. Black plaintiffs had brought suit against the merged district in 1965, charging that the schools remained segregated. The protracted legal battle was punctuated with violence and hatred. For example, in 1971 the law offices of the attorney for the plaintiffs were burned (Egerton 1976). Despite the protests, U.S. District Court Judge James B. McMillan ordered a comprehensive school desegregation plan, which included the busing of white and black students out of their "neighborhood schools" and across city-county borders, for fall 1970 implementation.

The April 1971 decision of the U.S. Supreme Court, affirming Judge McMillan's order, held that southern school districts must use all feasible means, even if they involved extensive busing, to achieve a desegregated school system. At the time of the order, this meant busing over 30,000 students to over a hundred schools in a district of 84,000 pupils. A decade later, while acknowledging the turmoil that occurred in the first years of the plan—student riots, falling test scores, and white flight—Superintendent Jay Robinson noted the accomplishments of the plan along political, financial, and educational dimensions (Robinson 1982). While the district has certainly had its share of problems, including the "continuing concern" of discipline cases involving black students almost twice as high as the proportion of blacks in the enrollment, the implementation of the plan is generally viewed as a success by outside observers as well (Egerton 1976).

As a result of the *Swann* decision, several southern county school districts implemented school desegregation plans that, by the nature of the county school district, involved metropolitan areas. Almost all of these were located in Florida—Dade County (Miami), Hillsborough County (Tampa), Broward County (Ft. Lauderdale), Duval County (Jacksonville), Pinellas County (Clearwater), and Orange County (Orlando)—where each of the 67 counties had its own independent school system (Cataldo, Giles, and Gatlin 1978). A number of other southern counties were ordered to adopt similar plans. These include Davidson County, Tennessee (Nashville); Guilford County, North Carolina (Greensboro); Greenville County, South Carolina (Greenville); and Mobile County, Alabama (Mobile).[1]

These plans have met with limited success. Three weeks after the *Swann* decision, the federal judge in the Hillsborough County/ Tampa case called for a complete school desegregation plan in the county district to be implemented beginning in September 1971. Desegregation has been relatively stable, but some implementation problems have occurred. School attendance areas had to be adjusted each year to maintain racial balance, the board had no black member in the years following the plan's implementation, and the number of suspensions of black students doubled after, as compared to before, busing (Egerton 1976).

In Nashville-Davidson County, the desegregation plan has not been as successful. The federal district court judge did not want to have students bused for more than one hour and therefore left about one-third of the schools, on the outer edge of the suburbs, free from the pupil assignment plan. His major goal was to desegregate the formerly all-black schools in the city, not to desegregate white schools in the suburbs. Much white flight from the schools involved resulted, especially in city schools (Egerton 1976).

The south, however, is unique in having county school districts. The possibility of a metropolitan plan being ordered by a federal court in an area with the more typical "doughnut" configuration of a central city district surrounded by suburban districts was greatly diminished by the Supreme Court's decision in the Detroit case.

Limiting Interdistrict Plans—The Detroit Case

The U.S. Supreme Court's July 25, 1974, *Milliken v. Bradley* (418 U.A. 717 [1974]) decision has limited the ability of city plaintiffs to argue successfully for a remedy that includes suburban school districts in any desegregation plan. In the *Milliken v. Bradley* decision, the U.S. Supreme Court concluded that forcing the Detroit suburbs to be involved in a remedy to undo the school segregation found in Detroit could only be based upon previous involvement of the suburbs or the state in the creation or the maintenance of the school segregation in Detroit. That is, the court ruled that particular suburbs do not have to be part of the solution if they are not clearly part of the problem. To quote the court (*Milliken v. Bradley* as quoted in Kirp et al. 1987):

> [T]he notion that school district lines may be casually ignored or treated as a mere administrative convenience is contrary to the history of public education in this country. . . . The controlling principle consistently expounded in our holdings is that the scope of the remedy is determined by the nature and extent of the constitutional violation. Before the boundaries of separate and autonomous school districts may be set aside by consolidating the separate units for remedial purposes or by imposing a cross-district remedy, it must first be shown that there has been a constitutional violation within one district that produces a significant segregatory effect in another district. (554)

The court also raised a number of practical questions concerning the difficulty of a metropolitan plan consolidating fifty-four independent school districts involving more than three-quarters of a million students (Tatel, Lanigan, and Sneed 1986). For example, the court asked what would happen to the elected school boards, various tax rates, and differences in curricula under a massive consolidation plan.

When the Detroit case was decided, a number of metropolitan cases were pending that involved the more typical metropolitan area situation—a minority-dominated central city school district surrounded by multiple, predominantly white suburban districts. But the court's decision in the Detroit case slowed down metropolitan remedies to a trickle. The trickle has included cases in the metropolitan areas of Louisville, Kentucky; Indianapolis, Indiana; St. Louis, Missouri; and Milwaukee, Wisconsin.

Post-Milliken Metropolitan Plans

The Jefferson County-Louisville case, decided after *Milliken*, was quite complicated. In this metropolitan area, two school districts served virtually all the area's students—the Louisville city district and the surrounding suburban Jefferson County school district. (A small, third district, initially involved in the litigation, was not included in the final plan.) In 1972 the Kentucky Human Rights Commission recommended merging the two districts to foster desegregation (Orfield 1978). In December 1974 the court of appeals ruled that the desegregation plan to desegregate Louisville could include the suburban district. In considering the relation of this case to the *Milliken* decision, the court found that both legal and practical issues were not obstacles to school district consolidation and metropolitan school desegregation in this case. In 1975, after the U.S. Supreme Court refused to delay the implementation of school desegregation throughout the county, Louisville's school board voted itself out of existence; under Kentucky law, this automatically transferred authority for the schools to the Jefferson County school system (Orfield 1978). Busing between the former city and suburban districts began in September 1975.

The Jefferson County pupil assignment plan was developed in a few weeks time and featured the busing of students based on grade level and the first letter of their last name (McConahay and Hawley 1977). Even though most schools were to be 14–18 percent black and most white students were to attend city schools for only two years, "all hell broke out in the white community . . . [including] protests, demonstrations, sit-ins, fire-bombings, boycotts, and other acts of resistance" (7). While white opposition has calmed down over the years, problems still exist in the district. For example, "bussing assignments are redone yearly to maintain the racial balance goals of the district, and some students can be forced to change schools three times before completing elementary school" (Marriott 1991).

Indianapolis also has a court-ordered metropolitan plan, implemented in 1980, which involves one-way busing of black students from the city to suburban districts. The state legislature had voted to allow most of the governments in Marion County including Indianapolis to merge into "Unigov" (see Rusk 1993: 93). But the legislature, to avoid school districts merging concurrently, changed a state law. The court viewed this state action as harming desegregation efforts, thus opening the door to an interdistrict school desegregation remedy.

While the Detroit decision makes it less likely that metropolitan school desegregation plans will be ordered by the federal courts, the decision has not fully shut the door. In fact, it is not clear how open the door is. Interpreting court cases and projecting future decisions is not a straightforward exercise. For example, in Orfield's 1978 book advocating metropolitan desegregation, he calls the Wilmington, Delaware, case "a most important case" (36) at one point and "not of decisive importance" (400) at another. In an environment of such ambiguity, the threat of a mandatory, comprehensive interdistrict remedy may be sufficient to lead suburban districts to accept a voluntary and limited interdistrict remedy. This is what happened in the St. Louis metropolitan area.

According to Colton and Uchitelle (1992), the 1983 court-approved settlement of the St. Louis school segregation case, which included a voluntary transfer plan for a projected 15,000 black city children to attend suburban schools, resulted in part because suburban districts worried about their legal case. Among their concerns was the pre-Brown busing of suburban black students to city black schools. The Eighth Circuit Court of Appeals felt that *Milliken* standards—that is, the presence of a state- or suburban-based violation—were not insurmountable, and hearings were set on the question of interdistrict liability. The suburban districts agreed to settle the case before the hearings began. The 1983 settlement led to 13,500 minority students attending suburban schools from the city by the 1993–94 school year, with the city receiving half of the state aid for these pupils and the suburban districts receiving their full state allotment. The settlement included magnet schools, largely funded by the state, which have been successful in attracting over eleven hundred private school and suburban students to the city schools in the fall of 1993 (Voluntary Interdistrict Coordinating Council 1993). This number is "far short of the 6,000 interdistrict magnet seats provided for by the settlement as modified by the 8th Circuit" (La Pierre 1988: 40–41). A capital improvement plan for city schools, to be funded equally by the state and city board, was also part of the settlement (Colton and Uchitelle 1992). The cost of the St. Louis metropolitan plan has been substantial. The financial incentives paid to suburban school districts to accept city minority students and transportation costs totaled $700 million from 1980 to 1990 (Smith 1990).

Milwaukee is also involved in a plan that includes voluntary interdistrict transfers. Milwaukee initiated a city-suburban transfer plan in the late 1970s. The city opened 10 percent of its seats in magnet programs to suburban students. Schmidt (1993) reports that 870 white suburban students are attending magnets in Milwaukee and 5,850 city minority students are attending suburban schools.

Thus, under circumstances involving explicit state (or suburban) action and high practical feasibility (for example, limited number of school districts and students), the federal courts may order a metropolitan school desegregation order. Under court pressure, city and suburban officials may even adopt a plan "voluntarily." But the *Milliken* decision has made such plans less likely.

State Courts and Metropolitan Plans—Hartford, Connecticut

While the likelihood of federal courts ordering metropolitan school desegregation seems rather improbable, an important case that may lead to a metropolitan plan based on a state constitution is being tried in a suburb of Hartford, Connecticut. The civil rights lawyers arguing the *Sheff v. O'Neill* case claim that "the racial and economic segregation in Hartford's schools deny children the equal educational opportunity guaranteed by the state's constitution" (Judson 1992: B14). They contend that only a metropolitan remedy can bring relief to the children. Connecticut Governor Lowell Weicker has called for voluntary metropolitan desegregation plans in six regions in the state (Johnson 1993) and building up to eighteen new multi-district schools per year.

Ironically, the 92 percent minority Hartford district is surrounded by suburbs that do participate in one of the nation's few voluntary metropolitan school desegregation plans. Project Concern, however, like similar programs in Boston and Rochester, involves a limited number of minority students bused from the city to the suburbs.[2]

A victory by the Hartford plaintiffs could open up the flood-gates of successful state lawsuits like the state court school finance cases that followed the U.S. Supreme Court's denial in *San Antonio Independent School District v. Rodriquez* (411 U.S. 1 [1973]) (see Bass 1992 for a more restrictive view). A recent ruling in New Jersey raises this as a distinct possibility. A three-judge panel of the appellate division of the New Jersey Superior Court decided in June 1992 that de facto school segregation within or across school district lines violates the state's constitution (Schmidt 1992b). The panel concluded that the state has the power and obligation to eliminate such segregation. The decision allowed the state department of education to study how three school districts could be combined to eliminate segregation.

Retreat from Mandatory Busing

While metropolitan remedies with district reorganization and mandatory busing are possible, although dependent on the particular circumstances of the case, in recent years the courts, as well as many other groups in society, have turned away from mandatory busing independent of the geographical area involved (Gurwitt 1992). Using Cleveland as an example, Gurwitt argues that because there is great cynicism about the wisdom of busing, the courts seem willing to allow different approaches. U.S. District Court Judge Frank J. Battisti told the parties in Cleveland's desegregation suit that he encourages innovative programs and "that the court did not set out to run a busing company" (31). According to Gurwitt, Oklahoma City and Dallas have dropped mandatory busing programs at lower grade levels, and other districts such as Akron and Dayton are considering districtwide choice plans. The Supreme Court's 1991 decision in *Board of Education of Oklahoma City v. Dowell* 498 U.S. 237(1991) "sanctioned school districts' efforts to reduce the use of busing as a tool for desegregation" (Fuerst and Petty 1992: 68). In the 1992–93 school year, Las Vegas (Schmidt 1992c) and Indianapolis were discussing backing off from their busing plans. Indeed, Rossell (1992) has noted that only two mandatory plans have been ordered by the courts since 1981. Thus, the likelihood of the federal courts ordering a metropolitan, interdistrict desegregation plan with mandatory city-suburban busing seems quite low.

A backing away from mandatory busing is also evident in the two landmark cases of metropolitan plans cited above: Charlotte-Mecklenburg and Louisville-Jefferson County. In both cases there is movement away from metropolitan busing. Louisville-Jefferson County is considering changing to a voluntary approach and more segregated schools (that is, from a maximum of 40 percent to 60 percent black students in a school, Marriott 1991). Charlotte-Mecklenburg has voted to turn its mandatory desegregation plan into a magnet-based, voluntary plan (Applebome 1992).

Significance of Wilmington

Despite the *Milliken* decisions and the movement away from mandatory busing, the Wilmington, Delaware, metropolitan area desegregated its schools in 1978. Analyzing this case is important for several reasons. First, it is important to determine what factors led to a metropolitan plan in Wilmington despite the Detroit decision. Might other metropolitan areas follow the Wilmington area to a metropolitan remedy through the federal or even state courts? Second, our mobility analysis indicated that, despite the hopes for the metropolitan school desegregation plan, Wilmington area homebuyers were not more likely to buy homes in the city, other factors being equal, than homebuyers in the Cincinnati area. Census data reported in chapter 3 indicated that no middle-class renaissance of the city took place concurrently with the metropolitan plan. Why did the metropolitan plan not lead to more city homebuying? Third, while city homebuying seemed unaffected, homebuyer attitudes in the Wilmington area towards city schools were relatively positive. What lies behind these attitudes, and can they be duplicated in other metropolitan areas? Finally, in chapter 1 we raised Monti's question about the feasibility of meeting both middle-income and low-income needs within cities. Have officials in the Wilmington metropolitan area been able to achieve such a balance within the metropolitan school system, and, if so, how have they been able to do so?

The answers to these questions are based upon participant observation as well as analysis of census, school enrollment, mailed questionnaire survey, and personal interview data. From 1974 to 1978, the Delaware author was executive director of a diverse 50-person committee named by the governor, the mayor of Wilmington, and the New Castle County executive to ease the transition brought on by the court order (Raffel 1976). His three children attended public schools in Wilmington and the suburbs, and he served as chair of a suburban high school's community advisory council for two years. He has also been involved in policy-level activities from observing teacher negotiations through various state-level school reform efforts. Finally, he has served in a professional role as a consultant and survey research investigator to two of the four districts implementing the court order, to the state's teacher union, and to the state board of education and the department of public instruction.

WILMINGTON METROPOLITAN AREA SCHOOL DESEGREGATION PLAN

Appropriately for this book, the origins of the Wilmington metropolitan school desegregation plan originated in the actions of a middle-class, white, city homeowner. An analysis of the derivation of the school desegregation suit that led to metropolitan desegregation indicated that the "primary initiator" of the suit was concerned about the transfer of low-income blacks into a well-respected city school. She viewed the demographic change in the high school causing a culture clash and middle-class white flight (Schmidt 1979). Housing issues, blockbusting, and declines in property values, for example, were part of this process. She thus sought to expand the catchment area of this and other Wilmington schools and began inquiries that ultimately led to the reopening of the school desegregation suit supposedly decided by the *Brown v. the Board of Education* decisions.

The Suit and the City

When the *Evans v. Buchanan* federal court case was reopened in Delaware in 1971 by five black plaintiffs, the Wilmington metropolitan area had many of the same characteristics of the Milwaukee, Cincinnati, Washington, D.C., and other northeastern and midwestern metropolitan areas, albeit on a smaller scale. The much maligned Wilmington school district served an almost exclusively black student body, while the generally better reputed suburban districts of New Castle County served almost only white students (Raffel 1980). When Wilmington entered the court suit, there were few white students in city schools and the city's white population was rapidly declining (Schmidt 1979).

Wilmington's officials realized the impact that the suit could have on the city beyond the schools. Wilmington's Mayor Harry Haskell (1968-72) understood that metropolitan consolidation would almost certainly result in a single school tax throughout northern New Castle County. Haskell calculated that Wilmington would benefit financially as suburban tax rates increased while Wilmington's decreased. (Indeed, after the federal court order, the suburban tax rate went up by 20% and the city rate declined by 36%.) The Haskell administration successfully urged the Wilmington Board of Education to contribute to the plaintiff's court costs (Wolters 1984). The court order was seen as a boon to the city, helping to stabilize the white population and improve public education. When Wilmington's Mayor Tom Maloney (1972-76) heard about the federal court decision that would inevitably mean a metropolitan school desegregation plan for the area, he was reported to be quite positive, stating, "the benefits to the city in terms of education and property values are clear" (Raffel 1980a: 103).

Wilmington versus Detroit

Whatever the value of a metropolitan school desegregation plan to Wilmington, the *Milliken* decision, announced in the middle of the court suit, seemed to put a halt to any metropolitan remedy. Why then did the Wilmington metropolitan area come under a federal interdistrict metropolitan desegregation order with a mandatory city-suburban busing component? In Delaware, the entire state had de jure segregated schools prior to the *Brown v. Board of Education* (347 U.S. 483 [1954] and 349 U.S. 294 [1955]) decision. State-sanctioned segregation gave the state the affirmative obligation of desegregating the schools statewide. Moreover, the plaintiffs proved to the court's satisfaction that state action had perpetuated the segregation of the Wilmington schools through the Educational Advancement Act of 1968. This act of the Delaware General Assembly gave the state board of education one year to reorganize any school district in the state with the exception of Wilmington, thus walling off the city from the suburbs. The plaintiffs also argued successfully that the state provided funding for bus transportation to private schools, an action that subsidized many white Wilmington pupils to attend suburban nonpublic schools and thus avoid school desegregation in the city. In short, the court found that several city schools were basically all black before school desegregation and remained almost all black (over 90%) after the state acted, despite the state's affirmative obligation to eliminate state-instituted school segregation.

While the suburban school districts in the Wilmington metropolitan area were not implicated in causing or maintaining the segregation of Wilmington schools, they too were creatures of a strong state role in Delaware public education. The district court ordered, and the U.S. Supreme Court upheld, a plan that reached into the suburbs since a city-only plan could not desegregate the city schools.

Thus, in July 1978, the Wilmington School District merged with ten suburban school districts to form the New Castle County School District (Raffel 1980a; Wolters 1984). The court had invited the state legislature to develop an alternative consolidation plan, but, as one state representative put it, the legislature "refused to pull the trigger." In September 1978, the nearly one hundred schools of the new district were desegregated peacefully, without protest, violence, or disruption. To accomplish this, over 20,000 of the district's 65,000 pupils were bused across the old city-suburban school district lines. Under the desegregation plan, city children were bused into suburban schools for nine years, and suburban children were bused into the city for three consecutive grades. Kindergarten was excluded from the plan, as was a small rural district at the far southern end of the county. This pupil assignment plan was the consequence, however, of major conflict in court, and has resulted in some significant dilemmas.

Pupil Assignment Plan

In the remedy proceedings in the Wilmington metropolitan case, a major battle was fought over the pupil assignment plan. The city plaintiffs put forward plans that would maximize the number of years that city pupils would spend in city schools. The suburban defendants did the opposite. Each side had to face two major limits— the area's school capacities and the demographics of school enrollments. For example, a 6–6 plan (kindergarten was excluded in the battle) would require enough seats in the city for half the district's projected pupils. Sufficient space for this number of seats, however, was not available in the Wilmington schools. A plan requiring ten years in the suburbs and two in the city would require great suburban school capacity. It was assumed that new schools would not be built for the purpose of school desegregation. In fact, excess capacity meant that some schools would be closed.

To minimize white flight, school officials sought to achieve racial balance at each school even though the court of appeals had removed a quotalike percentage goal from the U.S. District Court's remedy order. If there had been more students from the city—that is, more black students—the city representatives could have argued for a more favorable plan for city students with respect to minimizing being bused outside the city.

Thus, the Wilmington situation illustrates a dilemma limiting the utility of metropolitan desegregation plans for helping cities attract middle-income families. As noted above, the success of metropolitan plans is a function of the percentage of suburban middle-class students and schools in middle-class areas involved in the plan. A 6–6 plan would share the burden but would imply a student body about equally split in geographical origins and presumably in race. This would put the city on equal footing in years bused, but would imply a more divided and unstable student body.

In addition to the conflict over the number of years busing for city and suburban students, there was also a conflict in court over how many of the suburban districts would be involved. By the end of the battle, the suburban school districts adjacent to the city successfully argued that nonadjacent districts were still within reasonable driving time from the city (that is, one-half hour) and should be included in the desegregation order. Thus the practical dilemma: less busing from the city and shorter busing time to the suburbs generally means fewer white students, and therefore less racial balance and stability, in the plan.

A further dilemma revolved around pupil assignment plans and the definition of a desegregated school to whites and blacks. In general, whites view a school as desegregated if its student body reflects the overall population of the district's student body. In a district 75 percent white and 25 percent black, whites view a desegregated school as one where the 3-to-1 proportion would exist in each school. Blacks, however, are more likely to view a school as desegregated if the percentage of blacks and whites is equal—that is, a 50–50 split.[3]

In Delaware many blacks viewed the pupil assignment plan as unfair because whites were in the majority at each of the schools. In fact, one of the original plaintiffs in the suit exclaimed, "They can't do that!" when she heard the details of the plan (Raffel 1980a: 188). Presumably she would have advocated a plan that would have resulted in schools with equal numbers of blacks and whites. This plan would have bused more suburban students than the plan preferred by whites and would have created white enclaves in distant suburban schools. Thus, a "fair" plan for blacks is seen as an "unfair" plan by whites, even if blacks and whites can agree on desegregated schools as a goal.

While the 9–3 plan in the Wilmington metropolitan area maximized the probability of racial stability, it limited the benefits to city residents. That is, one practical limit on the attractiveness of cities with a metropolitan plan relates to the number of years that children are bused—that is, attend schools out of their neighborhood attendance zones in the city or suburbs. If a family examines similar housing in the city and suburbs and finds that the city location will require children to be bused for nine years while the suburban location requires only three years of busing, the suburban location will be more attractive. The attraction of the suburbs is reinforced when one realizes that many children will already be older than the grades that require busing from the suburbs to the city. Thus, a move to the suburbs will mean avoiding being bused across city-suburban lines altogether.

Consolidation: Political and Administrative Issues

The merger of the ten suburban school districts with the Wilmington School District brought with it many issues of governance. The major problem during the first year of school desegregation was a five-week teachers' strike resulting from a failure to upgrade teacher salaries and benefits across the new district to the levels in the city of Wilmington, the highest in the county before desegregation began (Sills 1982). A problem less frequently discussed but also significant was the political pressure that occurred as parents argued for a leveling-up of school programs and resources (for example, gifted and music programs) throughout the new district. Everyone—parents, teachers, administrators, members of the state legislature, and other members of the educational constituency—seemed to dislike the single, basically countywide school district. Complaints of bureaucratic bumbling and inertia abounded. In testimony before the Subcommittee on Civil and Constitutional Rights of the Committee on the Judiciary, U. S. House of Representatives, in 1981 (see Raffel 1982), Raffel concluded "the problems in the New Castle County School District today result in as large a measure from the school district reorganization difficulties as from mandatory pupil reassignment or busing" (513).

Public opinion against the court order and the single school district affected the financial status of the school district. A 1980 attempt to pass a school revenue referendum was a dismal failure, with 90 percent of an extraordinarily high voter turnout voting against it and all it represented (Raffel 1980b). Voters waited in line up to two hours to indicate how they felt. Not surprisingly, support in the state legislature for the county district was weak.

Following the old adage "better late than never," the Delaware General Assembly reorganized the New Castle County School District into four new school districts in time for the opening of school in September 1981. Three districts (Brandywine, Red Clay Consolidated, Christina) included a substantial part of Wilmington; the fourth (Colonial) included what once had been a district with about half-black enrollment and a minute section of the city. These districts are more analogous to the traditional Delaware school district, each independent, with approximately 10,000–15,000 students, about 25–30 percent minority.

Each of the new districts had a five-member school board elected at-large from five "nominating" subdistricts. That is, all residents vote for board members representing individual subdistricts; candidates must reside within the "nominating" subdistrict. This method was supposed to balance concerns for the district as a whole with the need for area—especially racial—representation. Indeed, the procedure has been relatively successful. Black candidates have been elected from city areas, and white candidates from suburban areas, ensuring racial balance and representation on the school boards, although a few times the reverse has occurred. Superintendents of two of the four districts in early 1993 were black, and there has been a mix of black and white administrators throughout the four districts over time.

IMPLEMENTATION AND SECOND-GENERATION PROBLEMS

Metropolitan school desegregation plans do not escape from the more general problems of implementing school desegregation plans—that is, so-called second-generation problems (see, for example, Orfield 1975) that come after the pupil reassignments are made and, in interdistrict cases, after school district governance changes are settled. These include: (1) problems related to demographic changes that threaten racial balance and raise the specter of white flight; (2) black concerns about racial discrimination—for example, inequitable treatment in disciplinary action and educational program placement; (3) white fears that the quality of education will be harmed, coupled with black expectations for improved black student achievement; and (4) concerns about the level and nature of public support for the public schools. In this section we examine these problems in the Wilmington metropolitan case.

Racial Balance

The racial balance among school officials over time has been mirrored in the racial balance among students. Analysis of enrollments indicates that, while limited white flight to nonpublic schools has occurred, the public schools of the Wilmington metropolitan area have remained desegregated and racially balanced. This is evident from analyzing student enrollment statistics and interracial exposure over the years since desegregation began.

County Enrollment Changes. White enrollment in New Castle County schools has dropped from over 56,000 before the metropolitan desegregation plan was implemented in 1978, to 39,000 in September 1992, a drop of about one-third (figure 10.1). This drop is substantial and appears to be the result of white flight to nonpublic schools and a decline in white births.

We can compare the white school enrollments expected, given the births to New Castle County residents five to eighteen years prior to a particular school year. Given the decline in births from 1957 to 1968, we would expect white enrollments to decline from 1972 until 1990. If public schools were holding their own, the ratio of white enrollment to births should be constant. However, this ratio drops from .874 in 1972 to a low of .591 in 1979, the year after desegregation began. While the ratio has increased from this low point, it has only returned about one-third of the way back (to 0.672). Thus, these data suggest that flight did occur simultaneously with the implementation of the desegregation plan, although some return followed.

We have estimates of the school-age population for the period 1980 to 1990 from the Delaware Population Consortium. The ratio of white enrollments to white school-age population, like the ratio of enrollment to births, also dropped during the beginning of this

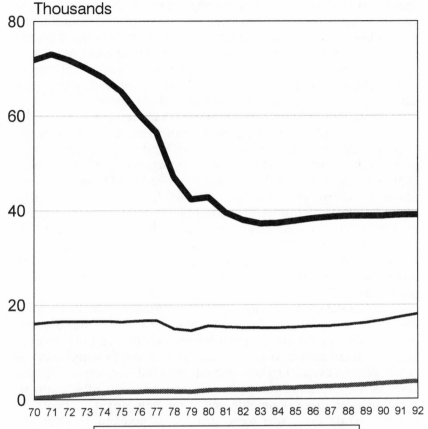

FIGURE 10.1
New Castle County Public School Enrollments by Race, 1970–1992.
Source: Racial and Ethnic Report, Public Enrollment, Delaware
Department of Public Instruction

decade and then returned to the level it was at the start of the 1980s. The pattern of changes in these ratios suggests white flight followed by limited white return.

The flight that occurred could have been the result of two processes: increased enrollment in nonpublic school or residential flight to surrounding counties. The drop in the public school enrollments/births ratio could be due to net migration of children—

that is, families with children moving out of the desegregation area and not being replaced. Indeed, the drop in the enrollment/ population estimate ratio suggests flight from the county to nearby suburban areas just over the border in Pennsylvania and Maryland. However, since New Castle County ended the decade with more white school-age children than the relevant number of births years earlier, it is hard to argue that residential flight occurred.

White flight occurred, but by means of movement to nonpublic schools rather than migration away from the county. Prior to the implementation of school desegregation, white enrollment in non-public school among New Castle County residents was under 14,000. By 1976 nonpublic enrollment topped 15,000 and had risen to over 17,500 in September 1980. In 1988 this number was down to under 15,000 again but has increased in recent years, reflecting the baby boomlet. A second way to measure flight to nonpublic schools is to examine the percentage of New Castle County white pupils in nonpublic schools over time. This grew from 17 percent in 1975 to almost 30 percent by 1980. In 1987 it had dropped somewhat to 28 percent and has remained below 30 percent ever since.

Anecdotal evidence supports the conclusion that the flight in New Castle County was to nonpublic, rather than out-of-state, schools. During the implementation period, the Catholic diocese and several private schools reported great increases in school applications. While several of these schools adopted restrictive policies, such as no admissions based on expressed antibusing sentiment, enrollment at these nonpublic and a few new private schools increased. While there was some increase in housing development across the Delaware/Pennsylvania and Delaware/Maryland boundaries, much of the building was a function of cheaper land and more acreage available for building rather than a desire on the part of builders to respond to increased demand stemming from whites fleeing the county's public schools. The housing market in New Castle County certainly did not suffer because of busing during the 1980s, although 1989–1991 were difficult years for real estate.

Wilmington Enrollment Changes. In the years prior to school desegregation, approximately twelve hundred white pupils attended public school in Wilmington. A majority of these students were located in the Highlands and Browntown parts of the city, where middle-class and working-class families respectively were concentrated. These students attended two elementary schools and one middle and one high school in the city.

In 1980, two years after school desegregation the number of white pupils in the city attending public schools had increased to over fifteen hundred. This number has not been maintained, however. Through most of the 1980s, the number of white pupils living in the city and attending public schools has hovered between thirteen hundred and fourteen hundred, and now stands near the original twelve hundred. This suggests a stabilization but no major change in public school attendance concurrent with the metropolitan plan. Of course, this stabilization has occurred while overall white enrollment in the county has declined.

While the numbers are small and no major increase in white enrollment has occurred, this result is quite significant in relation to trends in other cities. For example, the decline in the percentage of white students from 1980 to 1988 has been from 24 to 16 percent in Los Angeles, 19 to 12 percent in Chicago, and 30 to 19 percent in Dallas (Orfield and Monfort 1992). Similarly, the percentage of white students has declined by 9 percent in Boston and Milwaukee, 4 percent in New York and Philadelphia, from 1980 to 1986 (Orfield and Monfort 1988).

Interracial Exposure in Schools. Despite some white flight, racial balance in New Castle County schools, as measured by the Interracial Exposure Index, has been significantly increased and has become stable as a result of the metropolitan plan. This index is the average percentage of white students in the average black student's school; it measures a key goal of school desegregation. The opposite, white exposure to black students, is not often measured (Rossell 1990).

In New Castle County the interracial exposure in the desegregation area was 27 percent before the order was implemented in 1976. In 1979, one year after the plan was implemented, the interracial exposure index was 70.4 percent. In September 1987 the index was 67.5 percent. Thus, even with the drop in interracial exposure over the eight years after implementation, blacks in the desegregation area had over twice as many white students in their schools as before school desegregation.

Examining only the students in the city schools in 1976, the interracial exposure index has increased from 7.3 to 65.6, almost ten times as much (Rossell 1990: 157). Indeed, Orfield's (1983) comparison of changes in interracial exposure for black students in the largest metropolitan areas of the southern and border states from 1970 to 1980 placed the Wilmington metropolitan area among the three areas with the greatest increase in integration. More important for our purposes, the high degree of racial balance means that white students who live in the city are in majority white schools.

The extent of racial balance in New Castle County can be seen in the degree to which students are now in desegregated schools. In September 1990, a dozen years after the implementation of the metropolitan desegregation plan in New Castle County, less than fifteen hundred of the 58,853 public school pupils, or under 3 percent, were in schools more than 20 percent over the percentage of black students in the county (28%). None were in schools 20 percent under the average. In comparison, Rossell (1990) reports an average of 65 to 83 percent of pupils in schools meeting the +/–20 percent criterion across her categories of school plans in other metropolitan areas. All of the pupils in New Castle County schools with high proportions of black students were in kindergarten, which was not covered by the court order, or in an Intensive Learning Center. All of the regular schools in the desegregation area were still desegregated, and 56 of the 91 schools and centers were within +/–5 percent of the average percentage of black students in the county. In short, racially identifiable schools had been eliminated in New Castle County.

Further evidence of the success of the Wilmington metropolitan plan exists. Despite pessimism about whites sending their children to city schools (Armor 1982; Levine and Eubanks 1986), New Castle County has maintained desegregated schools in the city. In 1992–93, the city schools had a median percentage of white pupils of 60 percent, just a few percentage points less than the suburban schools.

Politics of Maintaining Racial Balance. These statistical conclusions mask some dilemmas revolving around maintaining racial balance at individual schools. Some of the attendance zones have undergone racial change, and as a result it has been necessary to redefine the zones to maintain racial balance. School officials are reluctant to make changes since rapid changes in attendance areas can decrease the satisfaction of parents with the system and lead to school flight. The tradeoff between racial balance and stability of assignments has also been a problem. In this sense, metropolitan plans are quantitatively, if not qualitatively, different from city-only plans; metropolitan plans face the same problem as city-only plans, but balance is usually more easily solved in a metropolitan plan because of the larger size of the desegregation area and greater number of white students available.

In Delaware, the Red Clay Consolidated School District has been the center of pupil assignment battles, and high school assignments the reason for many skirmishes. The federal court ordered that at least one high school in the old Wilmington School District be maintained in the city under the metropolitan desegregation plan. Wilmington High School (WHS), on the border of Wilmington next to posh suburban neighborhoods, was chosen. WHS is now in the Red Clay Consolidated School District.

White parents in the WHS attendance area have charged district officials with keeping the Alexis I. DuPont High School (referred to simply as "AI"), in the high-income part of the district, predominantly white, while not ensuring that WHS is also predominantly white. In 1980 both schools had white majorities; WHS was 70 percent white and 25 percent black, and AI was 75 percent white and 17 percent black. By 1990 WHS was 44 percent white and 43 percent black, the second highest percent black among the area's schools and a cause for concern over racial "tipping" and white student abandonment of the school. AI was becoming less diverse in the opposite direction: 74 percent of the students were white and 12 percent black. The remaining percentage of students for both schools were Asian or Hispanic. Red Clay's school board has been split over this (as well as other issues) and has had many public battles over the boundaries of attendance areas for the high schools.

To balance the need for school desegregation with a resolution of the conflict between the AI and the WHS white parents, the district has tried to move to a magnet school or choice plan. In fact, when the district's first superintendent, Dr. Joseph Johnson, retired, Red Clay hired Dr. Reginald Green from the Cincinnati Public School District. Green was hired to help the district design and implement a magnet or school choice plan to move from mandatory to voluntary high school assignments. His Cincinnati experience in developing curricula for magnet schools was considered a key asset by the board. However, Green's tenure was a stormy one. Controversies over Wilmington High School, magnet plans,[4] and personnel issues led to a 1993 announcement that he was leaving.[5]

The public conflict and intrigues surrounding the Red Clay board, and later its superintendent, have not been reassuring to those parents seeking a quality education for their children. Those in the attendance areas beyond WHS have feared changes in where their children would attend school. Those in the WHS area have been angered by the board's unwillingness to change the race and class composition at WHS. And those with children in the prehigh school stage have been concerned about all the wrangling and posturing.

Educational Quality

The meaning and measurement of quality education are quite elusive. Even standardized achievement test scores, despite their apparent precision, may not be valid indicators of student achievement. Nationally, we are aware of the so-called Lake Woebegone effect, where all states and districts report above-average test scores. In New Castle County congressional testimony indicated great increases in test scores in the first year after school desegregation was implemented, despite a 5-week teachers' strike, but skepticism about these results abounded (U.S. House 1982).

Analysis of 1992 Stanford Achievement test scores for New Castle County reported by the state's department of public instruction indicated that the gap between white and black students in Delaware's schools is substantial at all grade levels tested (2, 4, 6, 8, and 11). The most encouraging result is that the 11th grade gap has narrowed from 1982 to 1992. However, the state has not conducted a formal analysis of racial differences in test scores to determine whether the reduction in the gap may be attributed to the desegregation plan, national trends, or other factors. National Assessment of Educational Progress (NAEP) (1991) results show that the gap between Delaware's white and black students in mathematics is smaller than the racial test score gap in the northeast and the nation as a whole. White student scores are above the national norm on the Stanford test but not on the NAEP test. These reports suggest that blacks are catching up with whites in New Castle County, but the racial gap remains quite substantial.

Perceptions about the quality of education have been mixed; city school ratings have increased and suburban decreased. Survey results right after desegregation was implemented indicated a huge drop in suburban evaluations of the quality of the public schools. The percentage of respondents rating schools in their district as "good" or "excellent" dropped from 80 percent before desegregation to 37 percent in 1979. While ratings have recovered a good deal, they have not reached predesegregation levels (Raffel 1983). Public schools in the suburbs, once rated as well above average, are now at the national level (Raffel 1992). However, the percentage of respondents rating the city schools as equal to suburban schools doubled the year after implementation, and, as indicated in the homebuyer survey reports in chapter 4, the majority see little difference in quality between the city and suburban schools.

Racial Discrimination

All four school districts have faced challenges concerning the over-representation of black students in special education and as targets of disciplinary action. In New Castle County the vocal black group on educational issues and its representative in federal court, the Coalition to Save Our Children, has charged districts with disproportionately disciplining blacks and placing blacks in special education classes. While the numbers certainly support the conclusion that, on the average, blacks are treated differently from whites—blacks are disproportionately disciplined and assigned to special education programs—the reasons for this are not clear.

Examining special education placements points out some of the difficult issues here. The number of black students in special education classes in the county shot upward after the implementation of the school desegregation plan. Raffel and Warren (1987) found that the proportion of blacks assigned to special education in the county increased from 11 to 18 percent after the desegregation order was implemented, while the white proportion held steady at 8 percent. Black leaders claimed that this resulted from racial bias and/or an inability of white teachers to cope with inner-city black children and that they therefore used special education as a dumping ground. School district personnel claimed that, in general, this resulted from the professionally wise placement of children with multiple problems who needed the smaller classes and other services available in special education programs.

Discipline has been a continual problem in New Castle County's desegregated schools. In 1992 New Castle County respondents in a statewide survey conducted for the state school board overwhelmingly cited discipline as the major problem for the public schools (Raffel 1992). A decade before, three years after busing began, the black superintendent of the Red Clay School District, Joe Johnson (1982), testified to Congress that one problem in implementation had been classroom discipline. According to Dr. Johnson, "students from various family structures and communities have different perceptions of what is permissible" (447). The diversity of views, he went on, "increases friction between those with high expectations and those who come from families who have gained very little from the educational system" (447). Charges of differential treatment accompany this friction.[6]

Again, it is difficult to separate ideology from fact. A special project to oversee discipline after school desegregation began called the Delaware author in as a consultant. The black director of the program sought to determine what research would be appropriate to better understand the higher rates of disciplinary action against blacks than whites. The author suggested starting with measuring different student behaviors. The program director opted instead for a detailed study of differential rates of punishment. She assumed that the differential punishment resulted from discriminatory treatment; the author hypothesized that the differential treatment resulted from appropriate teacher and administrator action to cope with disparate student behavior. Analysis of the problem is influenced as much by ideology as by fact. The inability of experts to discuss interrelated problems of race and discipline make the solution to the problem much more difficult.

It is hard to measure discrimination and behavior objectively. But, whatever the objective measurement, the focus of attention of the four school districts has definitely turned to race-related issues, handling discipline problems, and concerns about academically weaker students, at least as represented in the media. For example, in the summer of 1992, the Wilmington *News Journal* published two articles on the same page on the same day about such matters: "Probe sought in school expulsion of blacks" (Ruth 1992) and "Red Clay doesn't cloak the problems—jackets OK in class" (Dennison 1992). The former article focused on the coalition's charge that blacks were being expelled at a much higher rate than whites, and the latter on whether jackets could be worn in class.

To the extent that publicity and school board/administrator attention focuses on second-generation desegregation issues rather than issues of academic quality, middle-class attachment to the public schools is weakened. Many middle-class parents resent the preoccupation of school officials with such issues. The concern of white parents is fueled by the anger of many teachers caught in the dilemma of professional judgment (for example, this child needs special education help) versus administrative directives and hints (for example, we need to lower the number of black children in special education classes). The fact that the districts are being operated under a federal court order makes administrators and school board members especially sensitive, and generally responsive, to the charges of resegregation and differential treatment by black leaders. The desire to avoid court action or negative publicity leads to defensive reactions.

Public Support and Attitudes toward Busing

Given the problems noted above, it is not surprising that busing is not popular in New Castle County. Surveys in Delaware have shown continued opposition to busing since before the desegregation order; an overwhelming percentage of whites still oppose rather than favor it. And blacks, even in the city of Wilmington, are at best split over busing. Given the importance of this opposition, we present data about these views over time below (see Raffel 1985 for a detailed description of the several surveys).

Advocates for metropolitan school districts argue that over time parents' fears and concerns about busing will disappear and they will develop more positive attitudes towards this mechanism. This has not been the case in New Castle County. While some fears and concerns have lessened, New Castle County residents have not become more positive about "busing both black and white children between Wilmington and suburban schools to achieve school desegregation." Three-quarters (74%) of the desegregation-area population opposed busing in 1977. In 1983, almost five years after busing began, slightly more people (80%) were opposed to busing. There was an insignificant drop in support for busing from 19 percent to 18 percent. Basically, the slight increase in opposition comes from a decrease in the percentage of respondents in the "don't know" category. In short, there is no evidence that support for busing in the general population increased after the metropolitan desegregation plan was implemented.

The overall results mask interesting subgroup changes. Parents with children in the public schools were about as much against busing in 1983 (81%) as in 1977 (78%). Opposition to busing increased among respondents with children in nonpublic school and those with no school-aged children, that is, those not involved in implementation—suggesting that opposition was not based on direct experience but rather on other grounds (for example, ideology, racial prejudice, media reports focusing on school problems). The percentage opposing busing increased from 78 to 89 among nonpublic school parents and from 70 to 79 among nonparents. These changes result from quite different black-white and city-suburban reactions to busing.

Suburban opposition to busing essentially held steady between 1977 and 1983. City opposition to busing, however, increased greatly over this period. The percentage of respondents in the city opposed to busing jumped from 34 percent in 1977 to 60 percent in 1983. All city subgroups showed an increase in opposition to busing. Opposition among city public school parents, almost all of whom were black, increased to half in 1983 from 41 percent in 1977. Those without children living in the city were twice as likely in 1983 to be opposed to busing as in 1977 (60% vs. 32%); the few nonpublic school parents in the city showed far greater opposition in 1983 (85%) than in 1977 (20%).

Racial breakdowns indicated that black public school parents and nonparents in the city and suburbs also increased their opposition to busing. Although the number of responses were small, opposition to busing in 1983 was twice as great among black suburban public school parents as in 1977, and the increase was almost as great among black city nonparents. Whites in the city in all parental status groups also were more opposed to busing in 1983. For city and black subgroups, the symbolic victory that metropolitan school desegregation brought was replaced by the reality of their burdens—9 of 12 years of busing for city students and second-generation problems faced by black students, such as perceived racial bias in discipline and resegregation in special education classes.

Results from the Wilmington metropolitan desegregation area thus indicate that the introduction of busing in New Castle County did not lead suburbanites and whites to alter their opposition to busing, while city residents and blacks hardened their opposition significantly. In fact, early in 1993 state officials promised to ask the federal courts to declare the four districts unitary (that is, desegregated) so that the districts would no longer be bound by the court order (Merriweather 1993). In June 1993 the formal request was made. The recently elected governor, Tom Carper, who defeated an opponent who blanketed the state with "Stop Forced Busing" billboards, warned the public that the state would not return to segregated schools when and if the order was lifted.

The federal judge asked the two sides, the Coalition to Save Our Schools/city of Wilmington and the state board of education/state of Delaware/four local school districts to attempt to negotiate a settlement. When the negotiations seemed fatally stalled, U.S. District Court Judge Murray M. Schwartz intervened to reinvigorate the talks and then reclused himself from the case. When the talks bogged down again, James H. Sills, Jr., the newly elected black mayor of Wilmington and an ardent desegregation advocate, and Governor Carper intervened together to help the negotiators reach a settlement. Sills set aside $100,000 of the city's contingency fund to pay for the services of nationally known desegregation lawyer Louis Lucas to represent the city. Sills saw a major interest of the city in these negotiations. He wrote that "people are less likely to locate their homes in cities where schools are seen as socially and economically isolated" (Sills 1993: H1), and that desegregation had helped to reduce some of the isolation. Carper hoped to resolve the long-standing conflict without a costly and acrimonious court battle while achieving a lifting of the court order.

The two sides announced an agreement, in the form of a draft consent decree, after Thanksgiving weekend negotiations in 1993. The agreement called for a declaration of unitary status for the four districts, a phaseout of the pupil assignment provisions of the court order over a four-year period, numerous programs to deal with discipline and multicultural issues, and a change in the school board election procedures from at-large to election district voting. While the state board of education and four local boards voted for the settlement, several members of the general assembly balked. Some judged the agreement a bad deal and argued that the agreement should be race-neutral. They attacked Mayor Sills for spending city money in an area out of his authority.

In early March 1994 Schwartz's replacement in the case, U.S. District Court Judge Sue L. Robinson, a recent Bush appointee to the federal bench, scuttled the negotiated consent decree for two reasons. First, she concluded that the agreement involved the court in the educational process, which is not the court's role. Second, she argued that a declaration of unitary status was incompatible with a consent order calling for new programs to remedy problems with implementation of a desegregation plan. The state expected that a court battle over whether unitary status had been achieved would drag on for at least three more years.

CONCLUSIONS

Despite the two worlds of decaying city school districts and educational achievement in the suburbs and the arguments for metropolitan school desegregation, few metropolitan plans have been implemented. The U.S. Supreme Court's *Milliken* decision established high barriers to those seeking metropolitan remedies in city school desegregation cases. The Wilmington metropolitan remedy was based on several unique factors, including the state's history of segregation and a school district reorganization act of the state legislature that maintained segregation in the city. Nevertheless, although the federal courts seem to be moving away from busing plans and the *Milliken* barriers are high, a new wave of state court metropolitan desegregation orders is possible.

Has the Wilmington metropolitan approach been effective? White student population in the city has stabilized. The perceived gap between the city and suburban schools has narrowed. The schools are desegregated; racial balance exists in all schools throughout the city and suburbs. The four districts involved in the desegregation order have provided students with a quality education, at least as measured on achievement tests.

However, in the minds of the public the metropolitan plan cannot be called a resounding success. There has been some white flight to nonpublic schools. Both black and white parents are dissatisfied with busing, although for different reasons. Racial contact has increased, but at the cost of some increased racial tension. Some of the dissatisfaction is due to characteristics of the system (the greater busing imposed on city students). Some of the difficulties are societal in nature, especially the problems of black families and the resulting impact on school safety and discipline. City and suburban representatives still battle over schools, busing, and race.

Thus, the study of the Wilmington plan suggests that this metropolitan desegregation plan with mandatory assignments has not achieved the long-term goal of promoting the revitalization of Wilmington but has helped to achieve more modest objectives— desegregating schools across a metropolitan area in a stable way, helping to slow down city population loss, and changing attitudes about city schools.

11

Magnet Schools

Magnet schools have been viewed as an important means to retain and attract middle-class students to city schools. Since middle-class families living in cities and dissatisfied with city schools generally can move to the suburbs or send their children to nonpublic schools, cities have tried to provide alternative schools within their own borders to keep their middle-class students or even attract new ones. Magnet schools are now found in city school systems across the nation from Cambridge, Massachusetts, to Houston, Texas, to San Diego, California.

In the first part of this chapter we examine the rationale for magnet schools, their advantages and disadvantages, and focus on the major bone of contention over magnets—student selection procedures. The second part of this chapter is a case study of the Cincinnati Public Schools, where a magnet school plan serves as the centerpiece of a voluntary school desegregation plan. Analyzing Cincinnati, we consider the issues surrounding the ways magnet schools can retain and attract middle-class families while meeting the needs of poorer families. Specifically, we ask questions parallel to those in chapter 10: Has the Cincinnati magnet plan held middle-income and white students in the city school system? What improvements in education have resulted, at least as measured on achievement tests? Are blacks and whites satisfied with the school system? What are the levels of racial tension and understanding? Finally, what role has the business community played in reshaping the city's schools? Has it done so to help business interests or to improve educational equality for middle- and low-income students?

ADVANTAGES AND DISADVANTAGES OF MAGNET PLANS

A magnet school has been defined as a "school, or program within a school, that has four characteristics:

1. a special curricular theme or method of instruction;
2. a role in voluntary desegregation within a district;
3. choice of school by student and parent; and
4. access to students beyond a regular attendance zone." (Fleming et al., as quoted in Blank 1990: 78)

Magnet schools have spread rapidly in central city school districts since the early 1970s, because they offer a voluntary approach to school desegregation, provide a variety of educational and curricular options to students, often focus on outcomes and careers, and indicate a renewed concern about educational quality (Blank 1990).

Interest in magnet schools has recently greatly increased because of their philosophical basis in school choice. As Cibulka (1990) points out:

> [C]hoice has become appealing in recent years for at least two reasons. First, its link to private school aid (objectionable to the political left) and to desegregation (resisted by the political right) has been blurred. Now "choice" frequently refers to reform within the public school sector. . . . This reformulation of choice permitted it to be defended on terms of appealing to a wide (although by no means universal) spectrum of ideologies and a broad range of public opinion. . . . A second reason why choice is more popular than in the past is that this reformulation has been executed within the context of the public school reform movement. (44)

The push for school choice, even if many proponents seek to increase private school enrollments through voucher plans, has thus created support for magnet school plans.

At this point in time, it is hard to argue for magnet schools on their proven educational effects. While the argument that students learn more in magnet schools has been offered, this claim is not based on solid social science research. Blank (1990) located twelve studies of the achievement impacts of magnet programs, but only one included a control group. The better test scores of students in magnet schools could well reflect a "creaming" effect—that is, more motivated and higher achieving students seeking and actually attending magnet schools. Rossell (1990) concludes that, without a comparison group of nonmagnet students and a statistical control for premagnet achievement, one cannot determine if magnets are causing the higher achievement of magnet students. Orfield (1990) has not only been skeptical about the quality of the evidence that purports to show that magnets improve educational achievement, he has also asked whether any positive effects of magnets are the result not of the curriculum or other aspects of magnet schools but of the desegregation of the student body. That is, Orfield is suggesting that the improved achievement scores are a function of the ability of magnet schools to attract better students (generally white, middle-class), who may in turn improve the educational climate at the school. These students, not the magnet programs, may be the cause of the increased achievement.

Retaining and Attracting Middle-Class Students[1]

Higher test scores of students in magnet schools may reflect the pull of magnets for the middle-class rather than the educational effects of magnets. Magnet schools have definitely been used by school officials to keep and attract the middle-class to cities. Perhaps overstating the argument a little, Metz (1990: 144) concludes, "It is no accident that magnet schools are springing up and becoming visible as the upper middle class grow tired of commuting from exurbia and looks to gentrified city neighborhoods for new places of residences." Good magnet schools may well attract students into the public schools who otherwise would have attended nonpublic schools. Magnets may "hold students who would be in private education or whose parents would have made another residential choice to be in another public school system were it not for the availability of at-tractive magnet school programs" (Bennett 1990: 142).

The justifications for magnet schools thus include "more effec-tive desegregation, satisfaction of consumer demand . . . and reten-tion of the middle class in urban areas (useful, among other reasons, for preserving the tax base and, thus, the viability of the school system for poorer students," Clune 1990: 393). The latter justifica-tion is, of course, the focus of our analysis.

Much of the support for the contention that magnet schools hold, or even attract, middle-class students, predominantly white, is anecdotal. For example, Wong (1992: 19) asserts that a Washington, D.C., community in the northwest section of the city, near Ameri-can University, helped keep its elementary schools open by working with the school district to convert them to magnet schools. The boundaries of the attendance areas of the schools were combined to allow parents to select schools within the six-school area. In 1987 almost two-thirds (63%) of the students came from the more affluent (upper middle-class) neighborhoods to the Six School Complex. (For a detailed analysis of this complex, see Gale 1987 and Jones 1988.)

Gale (1987) cites a magnet school plan in Prince George's County, Maryland, outside Washington, D.C., which attracted four thousand applications, including one thousand from private school pupils. Montgomery Blair High School in adjoining Montgomery County, with an enriched math, science, and computer program, was designed to attract whites and Asians into the predominantly black and Hispanic school. The school has not only attracted white and Asian students, three of its students were named as Westinghouse finalists in 1993, the most of any high school in the country. Rossell (1987) cites another example of middle-class attraction. In Buffalo between 1977 and 1986, over twenty-eight hundred pupils, 80 per-cent white, left the nonpublic sector to enroll in magnet schools in the Buffalo public schools. Successes like these prompted the Wash-ington, D.C., school board, in a March 1993 vote, to support ten magnet schools to lure white students into the district's schools "D.C. schools plan new programs . . ." 1993).

The most extensive, systematic, and quantitative study of the effect of magnet schools on student enrollment has been conducted by Christine Rossell (1990). Rossell found that districts with magnet schools as the basis of voluntary desegregation plans were more likely to reduce white flight from schools and improve the interra-cial contact of minority students over time than mandatory plans.

She sees magnet schools as a more effective mechanism for desegregation than mandatory busing plans, even the mandatory metropolitan plans, that have been advocated as plans most likely to retain white students (see chapter 10). Rossell's work, however, is limited to school enrollments and does not measure city demographic changes.[2] The success of city magnet plans in retaining, or even attracting, middle-class families in cities is not well researched. While magnet schools are now common in city school districts, their impact on retention and attraction is not well established. Our own empirical analysis, presented in earlier chapters, provides little evidence of Cincinnati's magnet schools attracting and holding middle-class families with children in the city.

Criticisms of Magnet Schools

Given the questions raised above, it is hardly surprising that participants and observers of the urban educational scene disagree on the value of magnet schools. As Finn (1990) notes, "there are holdouts, most commonly found within the ranks of professional educators and local school administrators" (12). Their opposition is based on two arguments—"that choice is disruptive, costly, and logistically cumbersome; and that choice ill serves poor, disadvantaged, and minority students" (Finn 1990: 13).

Critics of magnet schools, as noted by Finn, are concerned that such schools siphon the better students from a school district, leaving the problem of educationally at-risk students in the nonmagnet, neighborhood schools. They worry that magnet schools are aimed at an already well-served middle-class clientele, thus removing resources from those students most in need and, in the words of Metz (1990: 112), creating "bastions of privilege." Indeed, as we have noted, one of the major arguments for magnet schools is that they make city schools more attractive to middle-class families, and magnets do seem to draw disproportionately from higher social classes (Rossell 1990). Magnets are not generally instituted as a major solution for the problems of at-risk students (Blank 1990). Orfield (1990) skeptically writes that magnets are often cheered because they are instituted in cities where few good schools exist and "the most powerful and vocal citizens" have their children in these "few options for substantial middle-class education" (123).

Selection Procedures and Balancing Class Interests. Attempts to attract or retain middle-class parents in cities with magnet schools must include a reasonable expectation that the children of these families receive a place in a quality magnet school. But providing seats to middle-class students is viewed by many as denying others, especially poor minority students, equal access. An empirical study conducted by Designs for Change (Moore and Davenport 1990) lays out the argument that magnet school selection processes are inequitable. An analysis by Metz (1990) explains why these selection processes are necessary. We summarize the opposing arguments because they are critical for understanding dilemmas associated with balancing class interests when implementing magnet plans.

Moore and Davenport conducted an analysis of high schools that indicates that at least in the cities they studied—Chicago, New York, Boston, and Philadelphia—the recruitment and selection procedures favor middle-class students. Moore and Davenport report that today big-city students have a much more extensive menu of options for high school than they did before 1970. These choices include: selective exam/academic high schools—for example, Bronx High School of Science, Peter Stuyvesant, and Brooklyn Tech in New York City—selective specialized theme schools (that is, magnet schools), selective vocational schools, or nonselective neighborhood schools. The percentage of students in selective high schools in the four cities they studied ranged from 19 percent in New York City to 28 percent in Boston. Included within these percentages were the 5–6 percent in New York City, Chicago, and Philadelphia in selective exam schools. All of Boston's students in selective schools at the high school level, 28 percent, were in such selective exam schools.

Moore and Davenport (1990) argue that "school choice seems to have become a new form of segregation" (189), "a new improved sorting machine" (187). Certain groups—blacks, the poor, low attenders—are more likely to wind up in nonselective neighborhood high schools. The causes of this segregation can be attributed to the recruitment and selection processes, including junior high counselors who work more with students likely to succeed in option programs, selective recruitment of better students, unclear and questionable admission standards, and, in general, "the persistent political pressure that middle-income parents of all races exert to shape the policies, practices, and individual decisions of option schools to benefit their children" (213). Moore and Davenport are concerned because "those families who took the time and had the connections to master its intricacies were at a major advantage" (197).

Moore and Davenport see three reasons for this bias. First,

teachers prefer to work with better students. Second, schools are recognized as good when their pupils score well on achievement tests, so school officials seek high-achieving students for their schools. Third, white middle-class parents have more political influence, which they use to retain rules favorable to their children getting into selective schools. Moore and Davenport's concern for equity leads them to see the magnet schools in these four districts as part of a new system of segregation that must be abolished. They seek to achieve a student body at each school representative of the school system as a whole.

Metz's analysis stands in sharp contrast to the views of Moore and Davenport. Metz (1990) sees the same "facts" as Designs for Change but is much more sympathetic about the appropriateness of selection processes. "Administrators have pragmatic reasons to want to please . . . well-educated, relatively affluent citizens" (132). These reasons include the need to get city leaders to be enthusiastic about voluntary school choice and to spread the word about the program through the mass media and word of mouth. Moreover, administrators know that the well-educated, relatively affluent have choices beyond the public schools, and cities need their financial and political support.

Metz agrees with Moore and Davenport that middle-class parents will expend extraordinary effort to get their children in certain schools:

> First-come, first-serve admissions lead to long lines of parents, who sometimes camp out for several days in line. Single parents and parents with inflexible working hours are obviously disadvantaged by such a system. The student body of such a school is slanted toward students from higher-income, better-educated families. (131–32)

Metz argues that admission by lottery may be fairest, but "it undercuts the sense of parental control over children's fate that is a very significant benefit of choice" (132). Magnet schools are a way of coping with the inequalities in cities—helping some lower-class children, while maintaining schools attractive to the middle class. Metz concludes that critics of magnet schools are looking at only one set of inequities and ignoring the bigger inequity, the major differences between city and suburban schools. To put it another way, if middle-class children are the resource, there are few of them in most cities to go around because of the attraction of suburban schools. Therefore, city school administrators need to be concerned about attracting sufficient numbers of middle-class students to these schools to insure that these schools serve their original purpose for middle-class as well as poorer families.

The Moore and Davenport/Metz difference of opinion raises serious questions about the ability of cities with magnet and selective schools to meet the needs of middle-class families, while serving poorer families. This conflict has been played out in a number of places across the nation—in Richmond, Virginia; Washington, D.C.; and San Diego, California. In each case, the call for equity resulted in the threat or reality of middle-class abandonment of city public schools.

The first case occurred in Richmond, Virginia, over so-called clustering of white pupils in a magnet school. "After busing was instituted to comply with a 1970 court order to desegregate the schools, many middle-class families, white and black, left the city" (De Witt 1992: B15); many schools lost all their white pupils. However, in the Bellevue Model Elementary School in the fall of 1992, whites constituted 12 percent of the student body, up from 3 percent. The area, predominantly black and low-income, had been undergoing some gentrification from middle-class blacks and whites moving to the area. The magnet school's black principal had been "clustering" the white pupils—that is, grouping them in a white majority (but presumably racially mixed) class. A black clergyman and his wife, Hylan Q. and Valerie Carter, complained to the school board, which led the school superintendent "to reassign them to achieve better integration" (De Witt 1992: B15). Among other things, the Carters had been upset that their child received a low priority to be accepted into the magnet school, while all whites had been accepted. Soon after, a second school in Richmond was also accused of clustering, and the district moved to investigate and eliminate this practice.

The second case of an attempt to be equitable in conflict with the goal of middle-class attraction led to a lost opportunity in Washington, D.C. (Gale 1987). Attempting to meet the needs and desires of middle- and upper-income whites, Washington, D.C. school district officials tried to establish an integrated, high-quality, academic, selective high school in the city in 1980. While "residents of the predominantly white Capitol Hill neighborhood wanted to locate the school in the building then housing the Hine Junior High School in their neighborhood . . . some black board members objected" (102). They were afraid that "whites would take over the school . . . [turning it into] . . . an elitist institution" (102). The school, Banneker High School, was then located near Howard University, in a black neighborhood. Despite attempts to draw white students, none were in the school's first graduating class. Gale cites fears of safety, based at least in part on actual incidents occurring near the school grounds, which kept white students away; "it is doubtful that white parents in Washington will succumb to the appeal of Banneker's admirable curriculum as long as the school continues in its existing location" (103).

As a final example, Rossell (1992) describes a classic case of equity before common sense. In San Diego, "the plaintiffs were able to convince the court that (magnet) programs-within-schools (PWS) were elitist" (14), so the plan was changed. Under the revised plan, white parents had to volunteer their children for schools that were 80–100 percent minority. The result was predictable. All the whites left these schools, and many left the school district. The equitable solution was only equitable (and wise) on paper.

The controversy over the selection procedure for magnets suggests two conclusions. First, to some degree, there is a tradeoff between equity in magnet selection procedures and attracting/retaining middle-class students. Moore and Davenport's goal of representative schools would probably lead to white loss in majority black districts. The proportion of white students in New York, Boston, and Philadelphia is less than one-quarter.[3] In Chicago, the proportion is approaching one-tenth. It is likely that, faced with "representative" schools, white parents will seek alternatives to city public schools. This would be self-defeating for the city. Such flight does not hurt those who leave but does harm those left behind who must shoulder more of the tax burden and lose the advantages of having more educationally motivated children in their schools.

Second, the inequality more fundamental than selection inequity lies outside the influence of city officials. Jonathan Kozol (1991), in his indignant book, *Savage Inequalities*, argues that cities face this difficult choice because of the structure of the situation foisted upon them—not enough middle-class, well-off families to support city schools. Kozol (1991: 185) reports an interview with a Washington, D.C., urban planner who explains that "poor people in the District . . . want very much to keep the middle-class children, white and black, from fleeing the city's schools." To keep them, parents accept a dual system of magnets for the wealthy and traditional neighborhood schools for the poor, even if both schools are housed in the same physical building. But Kozol points out: "this compromise would not be needed if the city were not isolated from the suburbs in the first place. . . . If the urban schools were not so poor, if there were no ghetto system, people wouldn't be obliged to make this bleak accommodation" (186). Poor people will support a two-tiered system in order to keep the few well-off students and families. This inequitable compromise results from the disparities between the city and suburbs.

Financial Requirements. The second major criticism and limitation of implementing magnet plans is financial, but "determining the cost of magnet schools above and beyond the normal operating cost of a school system is fraught with difficulty" (Rossell 1990: 137). Magnets usually involve construction or renovation costs, one-time teacher training costs, transportation costs beyond those normally associated with a neighborhood-based desegregation plan, equipment costs, and, depending on the plan, added personnel costs—for example, funds for specialists. It is difficult, however, to separate expenditures needed for magnets from those for traditional programs.

Rossell (1990) reports the cost of the Savannah-Chatham County magnet plan as over $3 million for one-time start-up costs and over $2.6 million for operating costs. The program includes eleven magnets for 3,450 students. The Yonkers school district implemented twelve magnets for a start-up cost of $843,000 and operating costs of $633,000. These estimates exclude new school construction and transportation costs. The magnet and theme schools established in Kansas City, Missouri, the heart of "perhaps the most ambitious school desegregation plan ever attempted," involved an income tax hike of almost $1 billion (MacNeil/Lehrer News Hour, February 7, 1993).

Despite the concerns about equity and financial requirements, many cities have established extensive magnet programs. Among the most far-reaching and longstanding is Cincinnati's Alternative Schools Program. Below we analyze the Cincinnati public schools with respect to factors helping and hurting the attraction and retention of middle-class families. We discuss the issues in Cincinnati that limit the impact of magnets on middle-class attraction and the prospects for balancing middle-class (primarily white) attraction with meeting working/lower class (primarily black) needs.

CINCINNATI PUBLIC SCHOOL DISTRICT

Cincinnati has faced the problems confronted by many other central city school districts. The district suffered from a controversial desegregation plan, white flight, teacher unrest, conflict on the school board, which included a "well-publicized fistfight between board members," and ten years of rejected school tax increases (Hill, Wise, and Shapiro 1989: 13).

Alternative Schools Program

Cincinnati has had a history of commitment to choice and alternative schools since the mid-1970s (Griffin 1977). In a 1977 analysis of "Alternative Programs in Cincinnati," former Superintendent Donald Waldrip highlighted a new program in Inland Waterways Occupations as well as several other options for students at all levels. The superintendent at that time, James N. Jacobs, noted, however, that major problems were linked to the plan, most significantly a strong attachment of parents and students to neighborhood schools despite the attractiveness of alternatives (Felix and Jacobs 1977).

In 1984 the city school district signed the Bronson Settlement Agreement with the National Association for the Advancement of Colored People and the Ohio State Board of Education, ending a ten-year lawsuit. The district agreed to utilize alternative schools and school pairing to attempt to reach the standards, measured by the Index of Dissimilarity or Taeuber Index, set in the agreement. The Taeuber Index measures the degree to which blacks and whites are distributed across individual schools in comparison to how they are distributed across the school district.[4]

According to Hill et. al. (1989), "the fortunes of the city district changed in 1986 when John Pepper, the new president of Proctor and Gamble, the city's largest business, returned from a National Alliance of Business conference on public education determined to marshall the talents and resources of Cincinnati's business community on behalf of poor minority students" (13). Soon after, Lee Etta Powell, a black female, was appointed as superintendent. With the help of J. Kenneth Blackwell, a black city councilman, a Youth Collaborative was formed to develop a comprehensive strategic plan for education in the city (Hill et al. 1989). The plan met with some success during the late 1980s. In Hill, Wise, and Shapiro's judgment, "since 1986, the school system has made modest improvements in curriculum and staff development, improved staffing in the most disadvantaged schools, implemented teacher career reforms, and simplified the district administrative structure" (14).

By 1990 the city had developed an ambitious alternative schools program with roots two decades old. There were twenty-six different academic programs at forty-nine sites. About 35 percent of Cincinnati's students, more than 18,000 of 52,000, attended magnet schools (Clark 1990a). Programs included a High School of the Communications Professions, where students learned journalism, advertising, public relations, and photography. Other magnets included two math and science academies, two academies of physical development, an International Studies Academy, a Fundamental Academy, and a School for the Creative and Performing Arts (Clark 1990). Despite the extensiveness and success of the system, questions about the magnet schools draining neighborhood schools, an issue that surfaced when magnet plans were first proposed, remained (Clark 1990a).

In the 1992–93 school year, two schools served most of the white middle-class high school students who stayed in the city. The School for the Creative and Performing Arts, with an enrollment of 48 percent black and 52 percent white, is part of the alternative schools or magnet program. Students interested in this school, which spans grades 4 to 12, audition for admission. An attempt is made by the school and district to keep the racial enrollments approximately even.

The second high school that attracts large numbers of middle-class students is Walnut Hills High School, Cincinnati's "Boston Latin," a selective college prep school. Technically, this school is not in the alternative schools program, but it serves as a magnet. All 6th-grade Cincinnati students take an examination to determine eligibility for this school. In 1992–93, the school served 68 percent white students; the remainder were black or Asian. School officials have tried hard to encourage black students to apply and remain in Walnut Hills because of the pressures of the court agreement. Since success in desegregation is measured on the Taeuber Index, the large percentage of whites in this school places it far from the average percentage of whites in the district overall and hurts the school board in its effort to show progress towards desegregation. Thus, attracting and retaining black students at Walnut Hills is a priority. Ironically, this is probably the best integrated school in the system in terms of stability. The Walnut Hills situation demonstrates the problems associated with a strict adherence to the Taeuber Index.

At the junior high school level, there are no schools with a high percentage of whites beyond "double neighborhood schools"—that is, those paired for desegregation (for example, the Dater and Porter schools). But as noted above, both Walnut Hills and the performing arts school serve junior high students.

Some attractive public school choices for middle-class families exist at the elementary level. For white middle-class parents, the three Montessori alternative schools are the most popular. The North Avondale, Sands, and Carson schools, which have this program, all have a slight majority of white students enrolled. Although no data are available, it is likely that many parents are unwilling to locate in the city despite these choices, because they are unwilling to have children travel so far from their home neighborhood. Furthermore, those considering moving into areas near popular schools cannot be assured that their children will go to the magnet schools. For example, those wanting to locate in the North Avondale neighborhood in Cincinnati (one of the few stable racially integrated neighborhoods in the city) have no assurance that their child will be able to attend the North Avondale School, because selection is based on race. Thus, this type of selection procedure works against efforts to maintain the area's racial stability.

Selection Procedures. Not surprisingly, since many of the alternative schools are extremely popular and oversubscribed each year, Cincinnati has faced questions about its alternative schools selection procedures. The district established three eligibility levels to set priorities among students and parents. Within each level of eligibility, seats are assigned on a first-come, first-served basis, although racial balance is also taken into account. Those students with siblings in a school are given the first chance to select the same program and location. This cuts down on the number of contacts a parent or parents need to have with their children's schools. Those students at racially isolated schools, where at least 90 percent of the students enrolled at the school are of one race, receive the second highest priority for admission. This list includes about six thousand students, almost all of whom are black, since in 1992–93 only one school was 90 percent white. Finally, after those with siblings and those at racially isolated schools apply, all others may do so.

Students from outside the Cincinnati school district may apply for seats in alternative schools that are not filled, although they must pay tuition to attend a Cincinnati school. Approximately one hundred suburban students were enrolled in 1992–93, most in the School for the Creative and Performing Arts.

While the school district has been trying to increase the number of alternative school places available, the demand for seats in the magnet programs exceeds supply. Less than half of the applicants receive one of their three choices. A higher percentage of whites than blacks receive a seat in a school of their choice because so many more blacks apply for the limited number of seats. Competition for seats in the most desired schools has led to parents waiting in long lines and even camping out overnight. The district has tried to cope with this, to the point of not announcing until the last minute where registration would take place. One observer said that the race to get to the appropriate registration spot was like the Western land rush. The school board has discussed using a lottery procedure, but it recognizes the value in parents being directly involved in the application procedure and in the serving of middle-class families. Fortunately, these selection procedure dilemmas have not escalated into major class or racial conflict or controversy.

The district has responded to demands for various programs and has even cut less popular alternative programs. For example, the district reduced the number of elementary schools using an accelerated curriculum, given the limited parental demand. Because of cost considerations, the number of magnets can only be expanded as funds become available. Ironically, the district is not under a court order but rather a consent decree, and thus has received low priority for federal magnet school funds over the years. The federal Emergency School Aid Act has been the major source of such funds, but the act was repealed in 1981 and the Magnet School Assistance Program, which ultimately replaced it, in 1993 was funded at a level of only $108 million for the nation (Clinchy 1993).

In October 1993 the 19-year desegregation suit against the Cincinnati public schools ended when the school board approved an out-of-court settlement. The settlement calls for monitoring and sets specific goals in areas of staff and student segregation, student discipline, and academic performance for at least two years. The settlement parallels desegregation cases throughout the country where a concern over racial balance has been replaced by concern with how much black students are learning. The most difficult part of the settlement is the discipline provision. The teachers union felt that teachers were assigned too much of the responsibility for enforcing discipline and that this responsibility should be shared with administrators and parents as well. (For a discussion of this issue, see Shanker 1994.)

At the time of the settlement there was considerable disagreement as to what benefits the Alternative Schools approach had achieved. Some such as Robert Manley, a Cincinnati lawyer involved in desegregation cases, noted that the approach Cincinnati used (alternative schools and open enrollment for voluntary movement to integrate schools) had achieved greater integration and less loss of white students than would have occurred if a mandatory busing scheme had been used.

Others such as Judge Nathaniel Jones, former general counsel for the NAACP, questioned the impact of Alternative Schools on the performance of black students. He argued that the reliance on magnet schools was a predictable loss of funds for neighborhood schools, most of which contain black students. "It's left a district in which some students move along very well and others get left behind," concluded Jones (Ramsey 1993: 1)

Homebuyer Attitudes about City School Strengths. If magnet schools have been successfully marketed to the middle class, we would expect homebuyers to view Cincinnati's alternative schools program as a major strength of the city school district. In addition, we would expect that middle-class homebuyers would be the most likely to view the alternative schools program positively. In our Hamilton County survey, we asked: Which of the following is the *main* strength of the Cincinnati Public Schools?

1. Quality of the facilities
2. Alternative schools/diversity of programs available to students
3. Quality of the teachers
4. Discipline in the schools
5. Safety in the schools
6. Mixing of students of different races
7. Mixing of students of different social backgrounds
8. No major strengths exist.

As we expected, Cincinnati's alternative schools were viewed by Hamilton County homebuyers as the major strength of the city schools. When given a choice of the seven potential strengths, 39 percent of homebuyers picked "alternative schools/diversity of programs available to students," more than the total of all other chosen strengths. The next most chosen strength was the "quality of teachers"; 8 percent selected this alternative. As expected, social class was highly related to this selection. Respondents with more education, occupational status, and income were far more likely to note alternative schools as the major strength of the city schools. These correlations held among city and suburban homebuyers. In addition, white homebuyers were more likely than nonwhites to see alternative schools as a strength of city schools. Thus, as suggested by our earlier review of the literature on magnet schools, Cincinnati's alternative schools have succeeded in appealing to middle-class homebuyers. But this strength has been constrained by problems in the district.

Administrative and Educational Problems

In recent years, despite the optimism of Hill et al. and its ambitious magnet program, the Cincinnati district has had to cope with a number of administrative and financial challenges as well as concerns over student discipline and student achievement.

Financial Stress and Administrative Restructuring. The 1990 school year was a difficult one for the Cincinnati public schools. Discipline problems and financial needs loomed large. To heighten public confidence and help the district deal with financial problems, the district asked for the help of the business community. Superintendent Lee Etta Powell requested that Clement L. Buenger, chairman of the board of Fifth Third Bancorp, create and chair a business task force to examine the district's administrative structure and management (Olson 1991). Before the newly formed commission could issue a report, the district wound up in state receivership, a form of bankruptcy for public agencies. A November 1990 school tax levy was soundly defeated.

Reporting in September 1991, the Buenger Commission found the school system to be "plagued with problems [including] political discord, inefficient management, antiquated systems, and an administrative structure that had a tendency to maintain the status quo" (Olson 1991: 20). The commission recommended severely cutting the district's central office staff and placing more authority in the hands of those at the local school level (Shanker 1992). The commission also advocated providing incentive pay for teachers, principals, and administrators, and transforming the superintendent's position into two jobs—a president to handle educational policy issues and a vice president, with a business, rather than education, background, to deal with the district's day-to-day affairs (Olson 1991).

Superintendent Powell was forced to resign in the summer of 1991. The hiring of a highly visible black female had not provided a simple cure to the district's problems, as had been hoped. She joined many other fired/nonrenewed superintendents of big city school districts such as New York and Chicago. In the fall of 1991, her white replacement, J. Michael Brandt, promised to follow the Buenger Commission's recommendations if the November 1991 referendum passed (Celis 1992). Indeed, the passing of the referendum in November did lead to reforms and the lifting of state receivership (Celis 1992).

In May 1992 Superintendent Brandt and the Cincinnati Public School District acted to streamline its central administration. The number of central office administrators was reduced from 127 to 62, and, "as a result of these and other cuts in administrative personnel, the Cincinnati district [was to] save $16 million dollars over the next two years, and this money [was to] be put back into the schools" (Shanker 1992: 7). Specifically, the district eliminated "several layers of bureaucracy including the district's area assistant superintendents and the entire departments of administration, curriculum, and instruction" (Gursky 1992: 13). The position of vice president of the district was also created to oversee human resources, management information systems, administrative services, and public and legal affairs (Gursky 1992). As recommended by the Buenger Commission, the district has been working on an incentive-pay plan (Celis 1992) and has taken a number of other steps to improve the district's administrative efficiency (Bradley 1993). Reflecting the Buenger Commission's emphasis on restructuring and cost cutting, the 1993/1994 budget of the Cincinnati school district was $292 million, down from $306 million the previous year. It was the first balanced budget since 1986 and only the fourth in two decades. The budget called for eliminating 404 jobs (Weintraub 1993).

While generally receiving rave reviews, the Buenger Commission has received some criticism. For example, a group of black professionals criticized the commission because it was all white and therefore (according to the group) did not adequately represent black interests. Obviously, the reform effort in Cincinnati has not escaped the burden of racial conflict.

Discipline Concerns. Cincinnati, despite its well-received magnet program, has spent the years since 1990 trying to cope with the issue of discipline in the schools. The district has faced much negative publicity over discipline problems. Headlines such as "Fear Factor Grows in City Classrooms" (Clark 1990c) have been all too common. While the extent of the concern for discipline in the Cincinnati schools is well documented (Clark 1990b, 1990c), it is not clear how discipline problems are distributed across magnet and nonmagnet schools. We do not know of any studies of this subject.[5] Our homebuyer survey, however, does highlight the significance of the discipline and related safety issue.

Homebuyer Attitudes about City School Weaknesses. We expected that homebuyers in general and middle-class homebuyers in particular would be concerned about discipline and safety problems in the schools. The Hamilton County homebuyer survey asked respondents: Which of the following is the *main* weakness of the Cincinnati Public Schools? The same list of options as provided for the district's strengths was given.

1. Quality of the facilities
2. Alternative schools/diversity of programs available to students
3. Quality of the teachers
4. Discipline in the schools
5. Safety in the schools
6. Mixing of students of different races
7. Mixing of students of different social backgrounds
8. No major strengths exist.

As expected, 43 percent of respondents in our Cincinnati homebuyers survey viewed discipline as the major weakness of the Cincinnati schools, more than all the other weaknesses selected combined. Another 9 percent viewed safety as the major weakness. The only other response at this level was "quality of teachers;" twelve percent viewed this as a weakness. In order to determine which factors affected safety/discipline as compared to other factors, we combined these two in the crosstabular analysis. Social class, as expected, was related to perceiving discipline or safety as the major weakness; those with greater occupational status and education were more likely to be critical of the city schools on these dimensions. Thus, the major target group of school efforts at middle-class attraction and retention were the most concerned about disciplinary and safety problems in the city school district. The Cincinnati survey results suggest that, unless cities are able to address the discipline and related safety issues, they will be unable to take full advantage of the demonstrated attractiveness of magnet schools (see also Gale 1987 on this point).

Some people would argue that the discipline issue partially reflects cultural differences. A recent (Clark 1992) incident provides an example. A white Cincinnati school board member attending a high school graduation recorded the fact that many more black than white members of the audience continued to applaud for individual students even after the principal asked them not to do so. The school board member was strongly criticized for publicizing such information, and for concluding that this was an indicator of black-white differences in school behavior. Although he did not resign when asked to, he decided not to run for reelection to the school board the next time around.

There are a number of possible explanations for the incident. More black than white parents may have been exhibiting their lack of respect for the principal. Alternatively, the blacks in attendance, parents, relatives and friends of the graduates, may have been especially proud of the black graduates, leading them to be more expressive. Finally the behavior may have reflected a lower-class black cultural lifestyle, one that stresses this type of expressive behavior. The school board member considered this type of disruptive behavior to be a violation of middle-class decorum and respectfulness at a graduation ceremony. Middle-class parents regardless of race would be reluctant to send their children to schools where disruptive behavior, whatever the rationale, is tolerated.[6]

The district has taken some action to address discipline concerns. For example, in response to the large number of suspensions, in-school programs have been developed to prevent the students from creating trouble in their home communities. Local school discipline committees, composed of teachers, administrators, parents, and students, and mobile area impact teams, to assist with identifying students with chronic behavior, attention, and achievement behavior, have been instituted by the district (Clark 1990b, 1990c). The stricter discipline policy has been criticized by some blacks (and by some liberals, including a former dean of the College of Education at the University of Cincinnati) because a larger number of students (mostly blacks) have been suspended.

As statistical reports became available during the 1993 to 1994 school year, it became apparent that efforts to improve discipline were not succeeding. The most recent evidence, available in March 1994, is disquieting. Second-quarter suspensions rose almost 3 percent and expulsion rates rose by nearly 18 percent over the first quarter. A total of 3,627 suspensions and expulsions were imposed in the second quarter of the year. District enrollment is fifty-one thousand students. Blacks make up 80 percent of all expulsions and 78 percent of all suspensions.

Lionel Brown who oversees discipline for the district blamed the sharp rise in expulsions on more violent behavior by students. Physical assault was the leading cause of high school and middle school expulsions, followed by possession of a dangerous weapon (Ramsey 1994).

The Cincinnati School District had tried to react to the high rate of suspensions and the problem of children roaming the streets during the day by introducing in-school suspensions. However, the use of this approach did not mollify critics such as Reverend Michael Cash, chairman of the education committee of the Baptist Ministers Conference of Cincinnati and Vicinity: "A suspension's a suspension, in my estimation . . . They've got a few good ones [in-school programs] but most of the in-school suspension classes are just warehousing kids" (Weintraub 1993: B1).

The school system remains caught in a difficult predicament. (See Bradley 1994 for an excellent discussion of "The Discipline Dilemma.") On the one hand, it needs to improve discipline in order to make the system attractive to families remaining in the city and to make voters confident enough in the system that they will approve tax levies. On the other hand, the system is pressured by the out-of-court settlement to reduce racial disparities in suspensions and expulsions.

Thus, despite the existence of magnet schools, Cincinnati has a discipline problem. Many children come from low-income families (often with only one parent) where educational values are not stressed and restricted finances translate into limited educational supports. Consequently, students do not come to school ready to learn. Cultural conflicts and disciplinary problems are not eliminated by magnet schools.[7]

Academic Achievement. The district reported increasing test scores in the mathematics, reading, and language areas of the

California Achievement Test in 1992 (Gastright 1992). However, only a minority of students in the city's public schools (48% in mathematics, 42% in reading, and 47% in language) received scores above national norms. Furthermore, the variation across schools in tested achievement is great; four elementary schools (including North Avondale and Sands) had over 70 percent of their pupils above national norms in reading, while eight elementary schools had less that one-quarter of their students scoring at this level. Not surprisingly, at the secondary level only the School for the Creative and Performing Arts (over 70%) and Walnut Hills (89% to 95%) had a majority of students scoring at least at the national norm in reading, mathematics, or language. The poor academic achievement of many city students is reflected in the district's dropout rate. Forty percent of the students do not graduate from high school (Celis 1992).

Enrollment Changes in Cincinnati and Hamilton County Schools

Over the last twenty years, public school enrollment in the city of Cincinnati has dropped by 40 percent (figure 11.1). Moreover, the city has gone from a majority white school district to one where over 60 percent of the students are black. The number of white pupils dropped from over 47,500 to under 18,000 from 1970 to 1992. The total enrollment, however, did stabilize in 1981, after magnet schools were emphasized in the desegregation plan. Since magnet schools have been in place, white enrollment has declined, but only by about forty-five hundred students.

It should be noted that white pupil losses and black pupil gains have occurred in Cincinnati's suburbs, although at different rates. Hamilton County has twenty-one school districts, excluding Cincinnati, ranging in enrollments from under one thousand to over ten thousand students. In the suburban districts, 12 percent of the pupils were black in 1991–92, up from 5 percent in 1970–71 (MARCC 1993).

The suburban districts are quite diverse in test performance. Some have average test scores exceeding the city schools. However, some of the working-class school districts have scores not much different from those in the city, and Walnut Hills High School in the city has had average scores above many of the most prestigious suburban schools.

The suburban public schools lost almost 30 percent of their enrollments (in comparison to the city's 40%), dropping from near

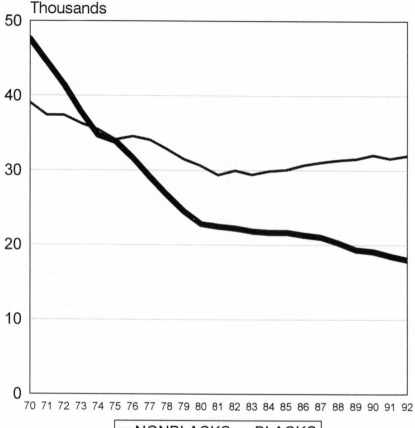

FIGURE 11.1
Cincinnati Public School, Enrollments by Race, 1970–1992. *Source:*
Metropolitan Area Religious Coalition of Cincinnati (MARCC)

100,000 to 72,000 during the same 1970–90 period (MARCC 1993),
suggesting basic demographic rather than school-related reasons for
some of the city's enrollment drop. However, while the number of
nonblack students in the suburbs dropped by one-third during this
period, the city's nonblack enrollment dropped by 59 percent over
this period. This indicates that some flight from city schools certainly took place, although it is not clear how much was residential
flight versus flight to private and parochial schools.

As noted above, the 1984 Bronson settlement agreement was

based on measuring progress away from racial isolation and towards desegregation in Cincinnati on the Taeuber Index. According to the school district (Lewis and Elsey 1989), the district had made much progress on the Taeuber Index through the late 1980s. In the 1969–70 school year, the index of dissimilarity was 67, meaning two-thirds of the students of one race would have to change schools to create a district in which all schools were reflective of the racial composition of the district. Since the percentage of other students—that is, non-black and nonwhite, is so low (1.1 %), the district has calculated the index by comparing black to nonblack students. By 1979–80, the index had dropped to 57, and in the 1989–90 school year, the index was down to 36.6. The settlement established goals, using the Taeuber Index for elementary, junior/middle, and high schools. The district reached 97 percent of the elementary goal, 144 percent of the junior high/middle school goal, but only 61 percent of the high school goal.

It has proved difficult for the school district to maintain the positive trends in racial integration that it had attained through the later 1980s. A 1993 study (see Weintraub 1993b) indicated that the level of segregation in Cincinnati public schools increased for the second year in a row. From October 1992 to October 1993 the Taeuber Index for elementary schools rose from 38.6 to 40.3. The index for high schools rose from 34.3 to 35.9. The figures for middle schools and junior high schools improved during this period. The use of the index of dissimilarity, however, makes desegregation appear more successful in the city than the reality.[8] As we noted above, the number of white students in the city fell at a more rapid pace in the 1970s than did the number of black students. While the index of dissimilarity dropped greatly over time, Rossell and Clarke (1987) found that the interracial exposure of black students to white students in Cincinnati public schools, that is, the percentage of white students in the average black student's school—hovered in the 20 to 30 percent range. The exposure index went from 27 percent three years before the 1970 implementation of a desegregation plan in Cincinnati to a low of 21 three years after implementation. By a year after the Bronson settlement, however, the percentage of whites in the average black's school had increased to 29 percent. Thus, while the index of dissimilarity dropped almost 50 percent over time, the racial exposure index increased 10 percent from before the first plan to the latest measurement. The good news provided by monitoring the Taeuber Index exaggerates the increase in desegregation as mea-

TABLE 11.1
Comparison of White Enrollment and Racial Exposure in Four Ohio Cities

	Percent White Enrollment			*Whites in School of Typical Black Student*		*Blacks in 90–100% Minority School*
	1967	*1980*	*1988*	*1968*	*1988*	*1988*
Cincinnati	58%	42%	38%	26%	29%	20%
Cleveland	43%	28%	23%	7%	22%	0%
Columbus	67%	59%	51%	30%	48%	0%
Dayton	64%	43%	37%	12%	34%	4%

Sources: Orfield and Monfort (1992: 21); Orfield and Monfort (1988: 25).

sured by the racial exposure index. The Cincinnati schools are doing a better and better job of having schools reflect the racial composition of the district, but the changing racial composition of the district—the dropping percentage of whites—means the average black student is exposed to only marginally more whites.

It is instructive to compare enrollment and interracial exposure in Cincinnati to three Ohio cities where a mandatory, court-ordered desegregation plan has been in effect. The decline in white enrollment in Cincinnati has been equal to the average in Cleveland, Columbus, and Dayton from 1967 to 1988 (table 11.1). The loss in Cincinnati has been less since 1980, just before magnet schools were emphasized in the district's school desegregation plan. However, the exposure of black students to whites in Cincinnati has been very modest over this time period in comparison to the three other cities. While the evidence is anecdotal, observers of Ohio schools believe that Cincinnati has done the best job of holding upper middle-class whites, those who have many other choices, because of its alternative schools.[9]

Thus, magnet schools appear to have helped to slow the loss of white student enrollment in Cincinnati. While white pupil loss was quite high during the 1970s, it was reduced greatly during the 1980s. The same slowdown in white loss occurred in comparable cities, although not to the same degree. The proportion of whites in the average black's school stabilized after the magnet school plan was implemented. However, other Ohio cities with mandatory plans did much better on the exposure index.

Homebuyer Attitudes about Changes in City Schools. Given the expectations concerning the magnet school system, we thought that respondents would have perceived marked improvement over the last four years. In the survey we asked the following question: To what degree do you think that the quality of the Cincinnati Public Schools has changed during the last five years?

1. Improved greatly
2. Improved somewhat
3. No change
4. Declined somewhat
5. Declined greatly.

In fact, respondents were far less optimistic than we had expected. Slightly more than one-third viewed the schools as "greatly" or "somewhat" improved (4% and 34%), slightly under one-third saw "no change" (29%), and exactly one-third judged the schools to have declined "somewhat" or "greatly" (26% and 7%). Homebuyers with incomes of $30,000 or more, felt somewhat more positive about changes than those with lower incomes. One-third in this low-income category were positive, versus 45 percent among those with higher incomes.

CINCINNATI'S CATHOLIC SCHOOLS

Up to this point, this chapter has focused on Cincinnati's Alternative (magnet) Schools and the extent to which this approach has succeeded in attracting and retaining middle-class families. It is important to keep in mind that the Catholic school system also plays an important role in attracting and holding families in the city.

Overall, the Catholic school system of greater Cincinnati[10] served 38,616 students in 1993/1994, of whom 6.9 percent were minorities. Student enrollment was up from 36,687 for the 1990/1991 academic year when 7.3 percent of the students were from minority groups (Archdiocese of Cincinnati 1990/1991, 1993/1994).

Most of the evidence on the role of the Catholic schools in attracting families to the city is anecdotal. Archdiocese staff that we interviewed indicated that they routinely receive calls from people working for companies like Proctor and Gamble and Cincinnati Gas and Electric (as well as smaller firms) asking about the availability of

Catholic schools in particular areas of the city and for test results for these schools.[11] Surveys conducted by the department of educational services of the archdiocese indicate that householders choose the Catholic schools for three reasons: (1) educational programs, (2) religious content, and (3) discipline.

The Catholic schools are important for the city because they serve as "neighborhood anchors." Unlike the Alternative Schools (which serve the city as a whole), the Catholic grade schools serve particular parishes. In doing so the schools serve to promote a high quality of life, particularly for parents who are neighborhood-oriented. St. Catharine School (Westwood) and Nativity School (Pleasant Ridge) are examples of quality parish schools that are helping to maintain racially integrated neighborhoods.[12]

The Catholic school system has sought to avoid becoming an outlet for families seeking to avoid integrated public schools. The policy of the archdiocese is that if a parent states that he or she is enrolling a child to avoid contact with children of other races, the school will refuse to enroll the child. If an incident occurs in the public schools that might precipitate flight to nearby Catholic schools, the archdiocese asks principals to interview parents with respect to their rationale for choosing a Catholic school. "Fleeing" the public school is considered an unacceptable reason for enrolling in one of the Catholic schools. In some situations in the past, the archdiocese has told principals that they should not accept students unless they were from families who were long-time members of the parish.

The preceding, and our empirical findings in chapter 4 concerning the city/suburban residential choice, indicates that the Catholic schools could be emphasized as part of a marketing strategy for the city. Cincinnati's Housing Blueprint (chapter 7) made this recommendation, but it has not yet been implemented.

Conclusions

Over the last two decades, the Cincinnati public school system has been a viable, active, and progressive city school district. The district's extensive alternative schools program, selective secondary schools, and genuine reform efforts led by the business community place it in good standing among city school systems. Moreover, Cincinnati has been able to achieve these successes without major racial and class conflict. Magnet schools, for example, are viewed as beneficial to both middle- and lower-class children.

Nevertheless, despite the successes of the city school district, academic achievement is below average across the district and quite low at many neighborhood schools. Discipline problems plague many schools. Financial support for the district has been difficult to muster.

The Cincinnati case indicates that magnet schools alone cannot turn a city around and make it attractive to middle-class families. The city schools continue to lose white students, although the rate of loss has been reduced over the last decade. Magnet schools do not meet the needs of those with young children, who do not want their children bused out of the neighborhood. Furthermore, many families want houses with a yard so they can watch their children, not new condos and townhouses. Concern about cultural differences and discipline issues serves to limit the willingness of middle-class whites to send their children to neighborhood public schools serving a majority of black, lower-income students. Thus, Catholic schools are particularly important for families who are neighborhood-oriented and who seek schools near their homes.

Cincinnati illustrates the complexities of achieving and monitoring school desegregation. Statistics such as the number of white students, the racial exposure index, and the Taeuber Index may move in different directions simultaneously and represent different and competing objectives. The dangers of blindly following a formula are exemplified by the efforts at Walnut Hills High School to improve the district's Taeuber Index by encouraging more black students to attend and stay in the high school. This effort could be self-defeating if the school becomes two-thirds black, like the district as a whole, or if academic standards are sacrificed.

The Cincinnati case also shows that the business community can play a positive role in school change. Despite the criticisms and financial pressures, it is unlikely that the system would have reorganized itself without the outside push provided by the business community in the Buenger Commission report. One of the key lessons from this Cincinnati case study is that the business community can play a key role in educational reform efforts just as it can in housing efforts. For instance, business leaders were active in the Riverfront Advisory Commission, which was involved in the preparation of the East End Riverfront Development Plan and Guidelines. Marxists would argue that, when business leaders get involved in urban affairs, they tend to hurt the poor, thinking only of maximizing profits for their corporations. The "city as polity" perspective, as we noted in chapter 1, says that it is possible for city officials, school board members, business people, and residents to work together to serve the "public interest." The latest business effort in Cincinnati appears to be evidence for the latter view.

Finally, this analysis suggests that magnet schools, as opposed to metropolitan school desegregation approaches, can be a feasible approach to improving the attractiveness of city schools. The most difficult issue relating to magnets is the question of equity, especially in selecting which pupils will be assigned to magnet schools, but this is not a zero-sum question. The additional cost of magnet schools is also a hindrance, especially in difficult economic times. Still, middle-class parents recognize the educational value of magnet schools and may well be attracted to areas served by magnets. Certainly, the Cincinnati case study indicates that, despite equity issues, a city can implement an attractive magnet school system. However, magnet schools will not be enough to produce homebuyer return to the city. In the long run, they must be part of a broader strategy to revitalize areas of a city.

PART 4

CONCLUSIONS

12

FUTURE CITY
REVITALIZATION EFFORTS

Successful boutiques close to restored city homes in cosmopolitan neighborhoods reflecting the wealth and artistry of earlier times, towering condominiums with inviting stores on the first floor serving middle-class apartment owners, and roomy, charming, but inexpensive homes with small neighborhood parks nearby housing middle-income families. Can cities take actions to make these images more of a reality?

As noted in chapter 1, this book has sought to examine prospects for central city revitalization through: (1) an analysis of the underlying factors affecting locational choice decisions and (2) an examination of the political and administrative issues surrounding the implementation of housing and schooling programs aimed at attracting and holding middle-income families (for example, subsidized housing programs for middle-income families, metropolitan school districts, and magnet schools).

Selling Cities is by no means the first book to deal with the subject of central city revitalization. Consequently, chapter 2 sought

265

to place this book in the context of three different literatures: urban political economy, urban sociology, and metropolitan planning. Our review of these literatures led us to three conclusions. First, although there are numerous social, economic, and political obstacles to revitalization, cities can do a better job than they are currently doing in slowing decline. Second, a needed component of central city revitalization is attracting more middle-class families. Third, critical gaps exist in our knowledge of factors influencing city/suburban choices. The existing literature suggests numerous hypotheses concerning programs that could help cities to attract and hold middle-income families. *Selling Cities* tests many of these hypotheses. Let us review what we learned.

A REVIEW OF THE EVIDENCE

We began our analysis of homebuyers in chapter 3 by showing that the homebuyer market does contain a small but meaningful number of households in the prechild stages of the life cycle, as well as a minority with city-oriented residential values. Cincinnati contains a small cosmopolitan cluster of homebuyers, but Wilmington does not, because many "urban type" facilities such as restaurants are more likely to be found in the suburbs. Thus, our findings suggest some hope but also some disappointment for city revitalization.

In chapter 4 we analyzed why some households purchased a home in the city and others in the suburbs. Results from this analysis of determinants of city-suburban choice are also somewhat mixed concerning the prospects for city revitalization efforts. High-status households without children, particularly those with a strong cosmopolitan orientation, exhibit a decided propensity to choose central city locations. In addition, the Cincinnati (but not the Wilmington) results show lower middle-class neighborhood-oriented households and young householders originally from the suburbs drawn to the city. On the other hand, families with children, particularly those with a strong familistic orientation (for example, seeking a new house with a great deal of space, emphasizing quality public schools), have a high propensity to choose suburban locations.

Some Wilmington leaders thought that implementation of metropolitan school districts would make the city more attractive to families with children, since children would attend desegregated schools whether they lived in the city or the suburbs. However, the analysis of city-suburban choice provided no evidence that Wilmington's metropolitan school districts have been able to influence metropolitan shifts toward the city. All other factors held constant, New Castle County homebuyers were less rather than more likely to choose central city locations than those in Hamilton County. Our survey of homebuyers indicated that those buying homes in New Castle County in 1988 did not differentiate between city and suburban schools very much, but this did not translate into white families buying homes in the city of Wilmington.

Chapter 4 results, therefore, provide a glimmer of hope concerning efforts to revitalize central cities. That is, cities can build upon their record of being able to attract upwardly mobile singles and couples without children. In addition, some cities may be able to draw more neighborhood-oriented families, including those committed to Catholic school education. Obviously, city leaders would like such householders to remain in the city through later child-oriented stages of the life cycle. Chapter 5 undercuts such hopes somewhat. As expected, buyers in the central city had more rapid moving plans than buyers in the suburbs. However, in contrast to what we had expected, city buyers with a strong taste for urbanism had more rapid moving plans than those without an urban orientation. Furthermore, there was no evidence that Wilmington's metropolitan schools were helping to hold families in the city. In contrast to what we had predicted, Wilmington city buyers had more rapid moving plans than those in Cincinnati (where there are no metropolitan school districts).

Turning to the positive, the spatial clustering of homebuyers (analyzed in chapter 6) provides some basis for optimism about revitalization efforts. In Cincinnati, and to a lesser extent Wilmington, two clusters of neighborhoods exist in the city that do not exist in the suburbs.

The first cluster is composed of cosmopolitan communities. A wide swath of neighborhoods surrounds Cincinnati's CBD and extends to the Ohio River. Socio-economic status levels and housing prices approach those in the "suburban ideal" cluster, the latter containing prototypical top-of-the-line suburban single family homes. Couples without children are attracted to the cosmopolitan area because of older, distinctive homes and amenities, one of the most important being river views. Wilmington's cosmopolitan neighborhoods ring its parks and the Brandywine River.

The second cluster is composed of baseline neighborhoods.

These are close to downtown with modestly priced older homes in relative good condition. These areas are especially suitable to those starting their housing and occupational careers and, hence, emphasizing economic criteria in the housing search.

Chapters 7, 8, and 9 emphasize the political feasibility of middle-income housing programs. Chapter 7 highlights the practicality of addressing both market-rate and below market-rate housing problems in local housing plans. Although most local plans over the last two decades have focused exclusively on low-income needs, four that we discussed addressed both types of needs: a task force report (Cincinnati); a plan prepared "in house" by the housing department (Montreal); the housing component of the city's comprehensive plan (Hartford); and a study prepared by outside consultants (New York City). Cincinnati's Housing Blueprint highlights the fact that low-income advocates will support middle-income programs: (1) once they become aware of such problems as a weakened tax base and population decline and, (2) as soon as they become convinced that city officials are serious about addressing low-income housing problems.

Cities as diverse as Cleveland, Montreal, and St. Paul have implemented middle-income housing incentives like tax abatements, low-interest mortgages, and tax credits, without much controversy (chapter 8). Often, minority politicians have become strong advocates of these programs as a result of their recognition of the need to preserve the city's tax base and to preserve neighborhood revitalization. Further, these cities have been able to deflect criticism of these middle-income programs because they have good track records with respect to their low-income programs.

Middle-income housing projects in established low-income communities are often resisted by residents who fear being displaced as a result of rising rents and real estate taxes or by more active code enforcement. Chapter 9, the East End, Cincinnati, case study, shows that these fears can be resolved through a community planning process that addresses both low- as well as middle-income housing issues.

In chapters 10 and 11 we examined administrative and political issues concerning schooling alternatives that have been advocated to make cities more attractive to middle-income families. In chapter 10 we showed that metropolitan school desegregation is not a very feasible or practical response to central city decline. There is now little support for this approach from the federal courts or the public; the only path for this major change may lie in state courts. The metropolitan schooling strategy offers little tangible benefit for middle-income families who can access suburban schools by moving to suburbia to avoid seeing their children bused out of the city. In Wilmington parents realize that desegregated schools mean having one's children bused for nine of twelve years to the suburbs. Few see this alternative as attractive. While evaluations of city and suburban schools have drawn closer, support for busing in the Wilmington metropolitan area has not increased over time. Parents still object to young children leaving neighborhoods to attend school miles away. They worry about the shift in focus of the public schools from academics to discipline and race relations. Our analysis therefore provides little hope that metropolitan school desegregation plans alone will lead to city revitalization.

Magnet schools and neighborhood schools offer better prospects for attracting and holding the middle-class. The Cincinnati public school system has maintained a viable, active, and progressive system with alternative schools (and one selective school) as the foundation. Middle-income students are attracted to a number of excellent schools. However, three issues limit the feasibility of this approach in Cincinnati and elsewhere—equity, discipline, and bureaucratization.

Academic experts and community activists question the fairness of providing resources to middle-income children as opposed to poor children. Magnet schools are viewed as primarily serving the middle class and utilizing resources that should be divided among all children in a city. Cincinnati has successfully coped with these tensions, but equity issues affect school selection procedures.

Concerns about safety and discipline undermine central city schools in general and undercut the attractiveness of magnet schools. Many parents are unwilling to have their children use public transportation to get to these schools. They also worry about how they will get from the bus stop to the school. Even a stalwart advocate of the public schools, Mayor Kurt Schmoke of Baltimore, took his daughter out of one of the "best" public schools in Baltimore after a security guard was shot. In Cincinnati, discipline concerns have grabbed the headlines from the success of alternative schools.

Over and beyond safety and discipline concerns, there is a broader class issue that affects middle-income attraction. Middle-class parents seek to have children from middle-class homes pre-dominate in the schools their children attend. Furthermore, white parents are unwilling to have their children attend schools where their child will be part of a racial minority. Efforts to provide parents with some type of guarantee about the racial or class mixture of the student body (as in Richmond) have been so controversial that edu-cational officials are unlikely to consider using these strategies in other cities.

Many big city school systems have been in a state of turmoil as they try to confront racial tensions, promote cultural diversity, in-crease awareness of AIDS, and deal with other societal problems. The superintendents of a number of these school districts (including New York City) have been forced to step down because of their inability to handle these seemingly intractable issues. This state of strife in the schools makes middle-class parents pessimistic about the value of magnet and neighborhood schooling programs. In Cin-cinnati the business community spearheaded the latest reform ef-fort, but parents have no assurances that business will be able to maintain the momentum for reform.

Thus, while magnet schools offer the prospect of quality educa-tion to attract and retain middle-income students, and metropolitan schools the prospect of stable, desegregated schools, these positive factors have not been enough to overcome the appeals of suburbia and the limits of city living.

City policymakers need to recognize the importance of includ-ing parochial and private schools as cities develop marketing efforts. Highlighting the Catholic schools is particularly important for neighborhood-oriented families who do not want to have their chil-dren participate in citywide alternative schools as well as for parents who want to stress religious values as part of their child's education. While providing information about private and parochial schools without undercutting public schools may be difficult, such market-ing efforts are critical to attracting families to cities.

SHORT-TERM STRATEGIES FOR CENTRAL CITY REVITALIZATION

In the short run, cities need to build on their strengths. Policy-makers need to target members of those subgroups who have demonstrated interest in city living. Our results, as well as previous research, show college-educated singles and couples interested in living near downtown as key target groups. Another key target group in cities like Cincinnati (which have many viable middle-income communities) is neighborhood oriented families, many of whom are committed to Catholic school education.

Efforts to attract upwardly mobile households should take advantage of the city's competitive advantages, especially the cosmopolitan neighborhoods that exist in the city but not in the suburbs. These are areas with concentrations of upwardly mobile households, attractive neighborhood business districts, proximity to downtown, and, in the case of Cincinnati, river views.

There are a number of things that cities can do to reinforce their competitive advantage in attracting upwardly mobile singles and couples. First, cities need to make their downtowns lively and interesting.[1] The development of "entertainment districts" is a step in the right direction. Such districts are a planned attempt to concentrate facilities that appeal to the middle-class such as theaters, ice skating rinks, and restaurants. Cincinnati and Minneapolis are two cities pursuing this strategy.

Second, cities ought to consider developing and implementing "demand-side" programs such as the ones discussed in chapter 8. These should be coordinated with supply-side initiatives such as those in Cleveland and Montreal; they should be implemented through semipublic nonprofit corporations such as the ones in Wilmington; and they should be targeted to declining but still salvageable neighborhoods.

Third, most cities could do a better job of marketing the types of attractive neighborhoods that are available to homebuyers.[2] This should involve a partnership among city government, the chamber of commerce, the school district, the archdiocese, and others. With limited city funding, such "city-living committees" could publicize the existence of attractively priced homes, and fine magnet schools, in newspaper articles and at citywide cultural and recreational events. Cleveland and Pittsburgh are among the cities with active city-living committees; Cincinnati has used its "A Day in Eden" to increase awareness of different city neighborhoods to the thousands of metropolitan residents who come to the park event each year.

Fourth, cities need to expand their efforts to construct new housing (and to rehabilitate existing units) for middle-income families near downtown. Many cities lack a supply of "upscale housing" so that middle-income families wanting to be close to the central business district cannot do so. These city efforts could be on vacant land (as is occurring in a development south of The Loop in Chicago, see Kent 1993) or in established low-income areas like the East End of Cincinnati. Chapter 8 described a number of relatively successful models from cities as different as Cleveland and St. Paul. Cleveland is taking advantage of vacant land made available as a result of widespread abandonment, whereas St. Paul is encouraging middle-income families to upgrade and enlarge its large stock of old but basically sound homes. Factors critical to increasing the market-rate housing stock include: (1) streamlining the development process in city hall so that the "playing field is leveled" between the city and its suburbs, (2) achieving a balance between demand-side, supply-side, and neighborhood marketing efforts, (3) obtaining support from the mayor and other elected officials, and (4) attracting and holding capable staff.

Up to now, we have emphasized things cities can do to attract middle-income families. We agree with Anthony Downs (1990) that it should be the responsibility of states and localities to fund housing programs for the nonpoor while the federal government shoulders housing programs for the poor. Nevertheless, there are five things the federal government can do to facilitate local and state efforts.

First, the U.S. Department of Housing and Urban Development (HUD) should take on the responsibility of publicizing these more successful efforts. A recent report prepared for the Canada Mortgage and Housing Corporation (Hulchanski et al. 1990) may serve as a model. Second, HUD should also consider allowing a broader range of middle-income housing programs to be eligible for Community Development Block Grant funds. Congress has provided HUD with a mandate to target CDBG funds to low- and moderate-income people and areas. However, there is not necessarily a contradiction between funding middle-income housing programs and targeting lower-income areas. Programs to foster greater socio-economic diversity could be part of efforts to improve living conditions for existing residents. Attracting middle-income people could, for example, help to make viable neighborhood shopping districts feasible.

Unfortunately, HUD has not developed a logical and consistent basis for choosing which middle-income programs can be funded in these areas. Chapter 8 highlighted this issue. HUD allowed Cleveland to use some of its CDBG funds to offer subsidized below market-rate mortgages because these loans were part of an effort to revitalize a blighted inner-city area. However, HUD rejected St.

Louis's use of CDBG funds to implement a marketing program to attract families to inner-city areas. HUD's decision seems arbitrary; marketing is critical to efforts to attract younger families to the central city.

HUD officials face a serious problem. They do not want to be criticized for allowing CDBG funds to be used to build tennis courts or swimming pools in middle-class areas (or similar projects). Still, if these administrators only seek to avoid scandals, their fear will lead to inaction. Well-thought out middle-income housing programs that might promote neighborhood upgrading efforts will continue to be rejected.

In writing this book, we were impressed by the level of competence and commitment of staff in housing departments and non-profit agencies around the country. HUD might well defer to the wisdom and experience of these officials with respect to middle-income housing programs that are part of broader revitalization efforts. After all, the Community Development Program of 1974 was based on the premise that local officials are better prepared to develop programs in their communities than are administrators in Washington.

Third, the federal government can help to put middle-income housing programs on a firmer financial footing. The 1980 reforms (the so-called Ullman legislation) in the tax system hurt local efforts by restricting their issuing of tax-exempt mortgage bonds. These tax regulation changes have had a significant impact on St. Paul's efforts to reduce middle-income migration. St. Paul's Middle-Income Housing Fund, which has made available $20 million in subsidized mortgages, was created by refinancing bonds from authority available before 1980. When these funds are exhausted, the city will no longer be able to offer these types of loans. Recognizing this problem, the city of St. Paul has developed a proposal to amend current tax law to authorize a qualified Middle Income Housing Opportunities (MIHO) initiative. This proposal, whose fate is highly uncertain, deserves serious consideration by the Clinton administration.

Fourth, serious thought ought to be given to a recommendation made by Tom Bier and Ivan Maric (1993) of Cleveland State University, which would help to reduce overrapid middle-class suburbanization. As was pointed out in chapter 8, the Internal Revenue Code concerning capital gains permits homesellers to defer payment of any tax liability resulting from the increased value of the house. This capital gain provision spurs sellers to buy more expensive homes, which are typically found in the suburbs. Bier recommends that the capital gain provision be modified so as not to hurt sellers who move down in price. The change in the provision might spur some sellers to invest in less costly homes in older neighborhoods.[3]

Fifth, HUD should encourage individual cities to expand the scope of their Comprehensive Housing Affordability Strategy (CHAS) documents to deal with middle-income as well as low-income housing problems. As part of the broadened effort, HUD should encourage cities to coordinate community land use plans with citywide housing strategies. Cities should consider, for example, how the construction of middle-income housing, in particular low-income neighborhoods, promotes revitalization efforts while at the same time helping to expand the city's tax base. Had this type of coordination existed in Cincinnati between the East End Riverfront Community Development Plan and Guidelines and the city's housing strategy (the "Housing Blueprint"), much of the conflict between the city and the East End might have been avoided. If HUD is serious about making the CHAS documents truly comprehensive, it should: (1) provide needed technical guidance to local communities and (2) reward cities with better plans with additional nonearmarked funds.[4]

We are aware that our proposals at the national level (more flexible CDBG guidelines, changes in tax law) are controversial. One reviewer of an earlier draft of this book stated that it would be "foolish" for HUD to be more flexible with its limited funds, that such a proposal would lead to diversions of subsidies from the poor to the middle class. Furthermore, the same reviewer indicated that such proposals would be controversial in part because cities might abuse funds made available by the federal government. Finally, he questioned our argument that subsidies to the middle class would help revitalize the city. How do we react to these criticisms?

In the first place we doubt whether our proposals, either at the national or local level, would be very controversial. As we saw in chapters 7 through 9, middle-income programs have usually not proved to be contentious when implemented. Virtually all of the criticism based on the equity issue has come from academic housing experts rather than practitioners. Furthermore, our proposals are not much different than those put forward by Oliver Byrum (1992), Planning Director, City of Minneapolis. Byrum, hardly a radical, recommends varying the amount of mortgage interest deductibility and the interest rate of mortgage loans based on whether the family buys in the central city or the suburbs. Common to his and our tax proposals is a desire to "level the playing field," to provide economic incentives to live in the city currently offered to prospective suburbanites. Finally even if our proposals prove controversial, this would not be damning criticism. Controversial strategies may be needed today to deal with the serious challenges facing cities.

In response to the second criticism—that the national proposals are costly and regressive—we should first point out that we see local governments assuming the main responsibility for funding programs for the nonpoor. The federal government should continue to focus on programs for the poor. The changes that we propose would not change this balance of responsibilities very much. The tax changes would not involve expenditures for the middle class; instead they would result in taxes not collected. However, revenue losses would be relatively small. Our proposals for changes in CDBG guidelines would not result in massive shifts of expenditures from the poor to middle-class families. (In fact, it is somewhat deceptive to refer to programs like the marketing effort in St. Louis as "middle-class" oriented, since marketing would indirectly benefit low-income families as well through more viable neighborhoods.)

There is of course some basis for concern about tax and CDBG guideline changes being abused. Readers may recall news stories of a few years ago documenting CDBG funds being used by some suburban localities for tennis courts. However, controls have been built into our recommendations to insure targeting and to prevent abuse. For example, below market-rate mortgages financed by proposed tax law changes would have to be used in declining, older areas of central cities. Nevertheless, we recommend that all our recommendations be monitored to insure that stated objectives are attained, that costs (or revenue losses) be in line with expectations, and that misuses be identified and dealt with quickly.

The final criticism gets to the core purposes of this book—that is, that there is little empirical evidence that middle-income programs benefit the poor. In order to respond, it is worth restating some of the main findings of our review of the urban regeneration and neighborhood revitalization literatures (chapter 2):

- Cities like Pittsburgh with strong leadership have been successful in achieving regeneration, measured by changes in the job base from manufacturing to service industries, and by downtown revitalization.

- Although there have been few empirical analyses of the spillover benefits of downtown revitalization in terms of jobs for the poor, there is fairly widespread consensus that cities such as Pittsburgh are better off today having provided subsidies to jump-start downtown revitalization as compared to giving up on their downtowns.
- Frieden and Kaplan (1990) argue that downtown revitalization (which includes middle-income housing projects) offers a more realistic and effective strategy for the creation of low-skill jobs than inner-city economic development, which has been notoriously ineffective.
- There is considerable consensus about the value of community development corporations (CDCs) in implementing inner-city revitalization efforts. The more successful efforts (such as in the Bronx) involve income and tenure mixing. Empirical evidence on the spillover benefits of mixing for individual households is minimal, however.

Thus, relatively strong qualitative evidence exists to support the implementation of middle-income housing programs both to promote the overall economic viability of the city and to promote socio-economic mobility among the poor. Nevertheless, the weakness of existing empirical research is obvious. As part of its mission to help cities, HUD should encourage research on the spillover effects of middle-income housing programs and should take responsibility for disseminating the results.

While there are no panaceas for improving urban public schools to retain or even attract middle-class families, two short-term steps should be taken. First, concerns about discipline and safety in schools must be aggressively addressed. Students and their parents need to have confidence that they will not suffer physical harm when they attend school. Nor will confidence be restored in urban education until disruptions in the classroom are unique rather than routine events. Specific means to improve discipline in the schools include time-out rooms and alternative schools for discipline problems, as well as clear and well-publicized codes of student behavior.

Second, middle-class students must have certain access to quality, desegregated schools. In magnet plans this requires a procedure that provides families with clear information about what school their child will attend and stability in this choice over time. School districts that leave pupil assignments to right before the start of the school year and make assignments only a matter of chance, risk losing middle-class students to the suburbs. In the same vein, cities that spread the few middle-class children around the district to desegregate all schools are doomed to lose them.

The alternatives most likely to have an impact on retaining or attracting middle-class families involve longer-term efforts.

LONG-TERM STRATEGIES FOR CENTRAL CITY REVITALIZATION

In the long run, cities need to develop strategies that reach beyond their current strengths, attracting families during the pre-child and to a lesser extent, postchild stages of the family life-cycle. Policymakers need to establish the goal of attracting and holding increased numbers of middle-class families with children. Achieving this goal will require addressing perceived problems with the public schools. Our results indicate that this will be difficult, but progress can be achieved through improving school quality and coordinating schooling with housing programs and policies.

Improving School Quality

First and foremost, school quality must be improved in order to retain and attract middle-class families to the city. We agree with Teaford (1990) that "certainly, if central cities are ever to rival the suburbs in appeal to families, the gap between the quality of city and suburban schools will have to be closed" (11–12). As he suggests, central city schooling needs to be at the top of the 1990s city agenda, replacing downtown development, for the revitalization of cities to occur.

School quality will be more likely to improve where outside forces take an active role. Efforts to increase the confidence of middle-income parents in the administrative competence of school bureaucracies are needed. In Cincinnati, as we have described in chapter 11, the corporate business community has played a key role in pushing the school district to streamline its central administration and spend some of the savings on educational programs.

The analysis of magnet schools in Cincinnati suggests that magnet schools have the potential to attract and retain middle-class families in the city. We believe, however, that the full potential for magnet schools has yet to be realized. We are struck by a recent article, "Why Paris Works" (Greenhouse 1992), which describes the

Lycée Janson-de-Sailly, "a magnet school sitting in the heart of Paris' equivalent of New York's Park Avenue" (29). According to Greenhouse, "this school simply does not exist in an American city. Janson has 3,200 students, a lengthy waiting list and a substantial number of students from Paris's rich western suburbs, who are attracted by the school's reputation" (29). Greenhouse notes that the school has not only attracted top students but also a number of accomplished novelists and historians as teachers.[5] The lesson from Paris and Cincinnati is significant: magnet schools can attract and hold middle-class students.

The lesson from Wilmington is also clear: metropolitan mandatory busing can at best play only a modest role in slowing middle-class suburbanization. However, the results from the Wilmington metropolitan area indicate that perceived city-suburban differences in school quality can be reduced through metropolitan school efforts as schools lose their racial identification throughout the city and suburbs.

We suggest taking the best of both worlds from the Wilmington and Cincinnati approaches. The major advantage of the Wilmington plan is its metropolitan coverage; the major strength of the Cincinnati system lies in its alternative and selective schools. The federal and state governments should encourage metropolitan areas to adopt metropolitan approaches to education that are based on magnet schools and provide incentives to school desegregation. There are state models for such legislation (Massachusetts, Minnesota), and, as noted in chapter 10, Connecticut's governor is calling on the state to consider metropolitan education in regions throughout the state. Federal legislation focused on metropolitan desegregation rather than on metropolitan education has been introduced before (Orfield 1978).

Cities should build on the popularity of choice proposals to establish magnet schools that serve the metropolitan area. State legislation may well be necessary for such schools, but, given the interest in parental choice, now may be the time to seek such approval. The schools should be based on the strength of the city's institutions. In Wilmington, these would be the chemical industry (for example, high school of science), banking and financial services industry, and the arts (utilizing the Grand Opera House, Playhouse, Delaware Art Museum, and so forth).[6] Cincinnati already has such magnet schools, although they are open to suburban students only on a tuition basis. The extent to which transportation is provided to such schools and the financial incentives offered to sending and receiving school districts will affect the success of such plans. Racial balance should be maintained at each school.

The purpose of these schools is to draw some suburban students into the city to help desegregate the student body and raise the quality of the city school. The number of students attracted from the suburbs to such schools is likely to be limited to the hundreds, depending on curriculum, financial, and transportation arrangements. But such schools serve a secondary purpose. They show that superior education can take place in the city, and they introduce, or reintroduce, families to the city. They also improve school quality for low-income as well as middle-income students, for gifted as well as low-achieving students.

Policymakers should look carefully at St. Louis (see chapter 10), where city magnet schools and a city-to-suburban transfer program are being implemented. The early reviews of these efforts were mixed (see Monti 1986 for the negative, and Levine and Eubanks 1986 for the positive). Recent assessments indicate some success at attracting suburban students to city schools, the successful transfer of many city minority students to the suburbs, and some general improvement in city schools (Smith 1990; La Pierre 1988; Voluntary Interdistrict Coordinating Council 1993). One assessment also indicated, however, that St. Louis schools still suffer from the problems plaguing other inner-city schools—"lagging academic achievement, discipline problems, poor attendance, substance abuse, teen pregnancy, dropouts, and staff turnover (Smith 1990: 25)." Since the St. Louis approach exemplifies the metropolitan/magnet approach to increasing educational quality for all city students, it should be analyzed carefully in the decade ahead.

We recognize that it will be insufficient to improve only the academic quality of public schools serving city students. Discipline and safety issues must also be addressed, even if this involves political risks. In Cincinnati, the overwhelming majority of parents and voters, black and white, favor stricter discipline. Programs have been resisted by some liberals and by some blacks employed in civil rights organizations who find the higher rate of suspensions of black students to be a useful organizing issue. But middle-class parents will not long tolerate schools where they feel their children are not safe or not learning to the level of their potential.

Coordinating School and Housing Planning

Coordinating housing and school planning could also help to make cities more attractive to middle-class families. While such cooperation is not a new approach, it is not often used. For example, in the 1960s planners suggested that educational parks be established to serve students from distant areas. More recently, the Stewart B. McKinney Homeless Assistance Amendments Act of 1990 includes a "demonstration program to fund local education agencies to provide literacy and job training, child care, and substance abuse education services to public housing residents." This program is aimed at low-income individuals, but it demonstrates the possibility of joint housing-education programs.

There are at least three approaches to coordinate housing and school planning to retain or attract middle-class families. First, school officials can place new schools at locations that better serve middle-class parents and students. This may involve neighborhood schools for elementary grades or educational parks for secondary schools. The former will minimize safety concerns of parents in cities, and the latter will increase the options open to older city students. Given the growth in the number of women in the workforce, locating elementary schools at work sites may also be a positive step. The objective is to help schools meet middle-class goals. This will, of course, require close attention to local desegregation mandates and equity considerations.

Fuerst and Petty (1992) cite an example of "intelligent planning and flexibility" in Charlotte for the stability of its long-term desegregation plan, pointing out that "when a new housing development was built outside the city of Charlotte, the school district built a new school midway between the new development and the city itself, so that black and white children from both areas would be bused an equal distance, 20 minutes" (67). Another example of housing-schooling coordination is underway in Seattle. Seattle is trying to avoid becoming a city closed to middle-income residents and families. Mayor Norman Rice has called for a number of "urban villages" in the city—communities of small parks, schools, townhouses, and apartments (Egan 1992, 1993). These urban villages, to be situated where there are now old warehouses and empty lots, are planned to attract people, including families, to a mix of modest to upper-income homes. In contrast, Chicago is home to a $3-billion development of houses, stores, hotels, businesses, and exhibition halls, but the project is not likely to attract families because of "the lack of reputable schools in the area" (Kent 1993: 30).

As a general principle, the racial desegregation of schools should not be allowed to harm the integration of neighborhoods. As noted in the previous chapter, this has been an issue in the North Avondale neighborhood in Cincinnati, where a residentially integrated neighborhood is served by a popular magnet school without residents having guaranteed access to the school. Some school systems have developed creative ways to deal with this problem. For example, Jefferson County, Kentucky (Louisville) excludes integrated neighborhoods from its busing plan. A related option to develop magnet schools in middle-class areas involves setting aside a certain number of seats for residents of the neighborhood.[7]

To provide incentives to homebuyers, builders, and others concerned with construction, school officials can build schools in residentially desegregated communities to promote quality, desegregated, neighborhood schools. A model of such effort is found in Palm Beach, Florida, where school and county officials have made major efforts to attract black families to white areas (Schmidt 1992a). Desegregation/pupil assignment plans that treat desegregated neighborhoods as one encourage residential stability.

Within the context of school-housing coordination, the specific concerns of middle-class parents about school composition must be addressed. Middle-class parents demand that middle-class children be in the majority in their schools. This is likely to be a politically controversial issue. Many lower-income parents may seek to have their children admitted to these schools. Without some "quota" of middle-class children, the utility of the school as a mechanism for attracting middle-income parents will be undermined. Almost twenty years ago, Orfield (1978) discussed the concept of treating whites as a "minority" in cities where few remain. Such a policy would encourage whites to be half of the enrollment rather than limit their proportion in the school to an unstable small fraction.

A second approach to school-housing coordination, beyond school placement and composition, is for school and city officials to increase the availability of suburbanlike services to city middle-class parents. We found that families with children are more likely to have suburban values (emphasizing, for example, homes with yards and good public schools) and are less likely to buy in the city. But at least some of the needs of child-oriented families could be well met in a city if appropriate efforts are made to provide services such as day care and after-school enrichment programs.

Consider the Wilmington school desegregation metropolitan plan. A family thinking of living in the city may accept their children being bused to suburban schools, but will they find family supports in the city, such as good, inexpensive day care, swimming pools and parks, fast food restaurants (important for children of all ages), and supermarkets? In other words, can cities provide a family-oriented package of public and private services? The answer may be that this can only be done in a limited number of neighborhoods. In addition, to what extent are family-type homes available in the city? Because many families seek large yards, several bedrooms, and other housing amenities, cities should seek to locate specific tracts where coordinated efforts to attract families can be focused.

Thus, we are arguing that cities need to be made family-friendly. Today's middle-income family needs day care for preschool children and afterschool care, convenience stores, and fast-food restaurants for hurried lifestyles. While cities have decried the loss of department stores (see Lyall 1992 for a discussion of the latest such loss in Syracuse) and movie theaters, family-oriented institutions may be even more critical to the viability of cities.

A third approach to the coordination of housing and educational policies and programs may require a change in governance structure for some cities. Over twenty-five years ago, Robert Salisbury (1967) called for changing the isolation of school governance from urban governance by having cities include education as a city department. He asked, "What would it be like if schools were a more integral part of the urban political system: if, for example, they were made a regular line department of the city with a director appointed by the mayor to serve at his pleasure?" (156).

While Salisbury's concern at the time was not the middle-class but the poor, his arguments may be relevant to solving today's problems. He asked, as do we, "whether greater mayoral control would lead to changes in school policy (e.g., better coordination and cooperation with urban renewal, recreation, and poverty programs) which would make the educational program more effective in solving the large complex of community problems" (159). Certainly this step would lead to better coordination of education and housing. But given the difficulty of getting the needed state legislation and the resistance of city school districts, other means of coordination need to be explored.

POLITICAL LEADERSHIP

The ambitious agenda we have described above will necessitate strong political leadership. As we noted in chapter 2, leadership has proven to be critical in determining the degree of success that cities have had in dealing with the economic and social challenges that they have faced (see Judd and Parkinson 1990, for example). As the role of external forces, such as the restructuring of the global economy and the cutback in federal funds, have buffeted cities (Savitch and Thomas 1991), it has become more difficult for cities to adopt coherent strategies supported by cohesive coalitions.

An analysis by Swanstrom (1988) of the types of mayoral leadership in recent years helps to identify the nature of leadership necessitated by our recommendations. Liberal mayors, such as New York's John Lindsay and Cleveland's Carl Stokes, dominant in the 1960s and 70s, sought to encourage both economic growth and redistribution of resources and implemented redistributive policies based on the ready availability of federal funds. Swanstrom argues that as federal funds dried up, liberal mayors were replaced by neoconservatives, such as New York's Ed Koch, who concentrated on economic growth, even if inequality increased. Recently a third style of mayoral leadership has developed, which Swanstrom calls "urban populist." Populist mayors "displace ethnic and racial divisions with economic division; the haves versus the have nots" (123). They also seek to change the focus of policies from growth to redistribution. Swanstrom sees Raymond Flynn of Boston and Dennis Kucinich of Cleveland as exemplifying populist mayors.

Our recommendations require a fourth type of mayor, one we call a "pragmatist," who emphasizes downtown development as well as neighborhood concerns, and who is comfortable addressing market-rate as well as below market-rate housing issues. Fortunately an increasing number of mayors are being elected who deserve this label, including Michael White, Cleveland, and Norman Rice, Seattle. Both are black mayors who reject the racial politics of the 1960s and 70s, who practice fiscal conservatism, who are involved in public school issues, and who have supported middle-income housing projects (see Gurwitt 1992; Sleeper 1993). We believe that this new breed of mayor will demonstrate the leadership qualities needed to develop and implement the programs outlined in this book.

THE PROBLEMATIC FUTURE OF CITIES

The chances of success for the above strategies are uncertain. Urban problems such as crime, drugs, and high taxes continue to push middle-income families away from cities, including many who would otherwise prefer to live in cities. The problems faced by cities are complex and difficult to solve—interwoven in a fabric of family breakdown, poverty, and economic restructuring. The dispersion of economic activity may well continue to pull households from the urban center. Governmental policies which provide for highway subsidies, for example, spur suburban construction and continue to pull households further to the periphery. And the fact that suburbanites are in the majority of the metropolitan population means that a growing percentage of the population do not know what city life is like, other than what they read in the papers or see on television.

Nevertheless, it would be a mistake to write off as impossible the types of programs discussed above. First, procity forces are at work at the federal level based on the Clean Air Act and the Intermodal Surface Transportation Efficiency Act (ISTEA). Second, the Los Angeles riots have helped to bring increased attention to urban problems and have led to "Empowerment Zones," the biggest new federal program for the inner cities for more than a decade (Lemann 1994). Third, there has been growing recognition of the need for better metropolitan cooperation and planning to deal with inner-city poverty, "dead" downtowns, and suburban sprawl (Byrum 1992, Judson 1993, Peirce 1993, Smothers 1993). Finally, Cleveland's success in revitalizing its downtown and in changing its image (earning it the nickname "Comeback City") show that it may be possible to slow down if not reverse patterns of economic and social decline.

The continued attractiveness of European cities such as Paris shows that urban living can remain an option into the twenty-first century as long as governments are willing to provide the resources required. Furthermore, within the United States there are major differences among cities in terms of viability. The types of programs we have discussed above are most likely to succeed in cities where decline has not proceeded to severe levels.

Our results imply that there will be considerable variation among American cities in their ability to attract additional middle-income families. The prospects for success in smaller cities like Wilmington may be limited because there is no significant cosmopolitan grouping of buyers in the metropolitan area and because so many of the urban amenities are located in the suburbs. The potential for success is greater in medium-sized cities like Cincinnati with more viable downtowns and with larger cosmopolitan populations. Ironically, the nation's largest cities, such as New York and Chicago, have such clusters, but they are hindered in their revitalization efforts by extreme concentrations of social problems such as crime and welfare dependency.

Cities initiating the short- and long-term programs recommended above may have to be satisfied with small victories rather than a complete turnaround. Marketing an up-and-coming cosmopolitan neighborhood, where the city has helped a few boutiques get started through targeted loans, providing subsidized mortages and tax abatements for couples purchasing townhouses on what had been a vacant inner-city lot, and turning a languishing elementary school into an exciting magnet school with seats reserved for neighborhood children may be difficult work for a city. Achieving limited successes is a way to gain momentum and a sense of optimism about living and working in the central city. Given the prevailing pessimism about our cities, these small victories would be no mean achievement.

DEMOGRAPHIC CHARACTERISTICS

Age 20 to 29. Whether household head was between 20 and 29 years old: 0. No, 1. Yes.

Age 50 years and over. Whether household head was 50 years or older: 0. No, 1. Yes.

Married. Whether the respondent was married: 0. No, 1. Yes.

Children. Whether had any children 18 or younger: 0. No, 1. Yes.

Preschool child. Whether had any children under 5: 0. No, 1. Yes.

School-age children. Whether had any children 5 to 18: 0. No, 1. Yes.

Parochial school child. Whether had one or more children in parochial school: 0. No, 1. Yes.

Income. Total household income: twelve income categories range from under $15,000 to $80,000 and above.

Education: Educational level of principal breadwinner: five categories range from less than high school diploma to college beyond bachelor's degree.

High-status white-collar job. Whether principal breadwinner had professional or managerial/administrative position: 0. No, 1. Yes.

Blue-collar job. Whether the principal breadwinner had a blue collar job: 0. No, 1. Yes. Low-status white-collar job was the reference category.

Two or more workers. Whether the household had two or more adult workers: 0. No, 1. Yes.

White. Whether the respondent was white or "Oriental": 0. No, 1. Yes. In the New Castle County sample the "no" category included Hispanics.

Out of labor force. Whether no adult in the household was employed: 0. No, 1. Yes.

Migration and Housing History

Previously owned. Whether the household owned prior to moving: 0. No, 1. Yes.

Newly formed household. Whether the household was newly formed: 0. No, 1. Yes. Previous renter was the reference category.

Moved from suburbs. Whether the household previously resided in a suburban area: 0. No, 1. Yes.

Moved from outside the metropolitan area. Whether the household moved from a location outside the Cincinnati/Wilmington SMSA: 0. No, 1. Yes. Moved from the city was the reference category.

Central city white. Whether white and lived in the city: 0. No, 1. Yes.

Suburban black. Whether black and lived in the suburbs: 0. No, 1. Yes.

Suburban white. Whether white and lived in the suburbs: 0. No, 1. Yes. Central city blacks was the reference category.

Metropolitan location. Whether lived in Hamilton County/ Cincinnati metropolitan area: 0. No, 1. Yes.

Housing Characteristics

Home price. House price in dollars.

Home size. House size in square feet.

Age of home. Age of home in years.

Single family home. Whether live in a single family home: 0. No, 1. Yes.

Two family home. Whether live in a two family home: 0. No, 1. Yes.

Residential Assessments

Suburban schools better. Index formed by multiplying two items, whether the Cincinnati/Wilmington public schools were better, equal to, or worse than the Hamilton County/New Castle County (suburban) schools; and the importance of the quality of local public schools in the locational choice (five categories from "unimportant" to "very important," "don't know" was the middle category). Scores for the index ranged from 1 to 15. The highest scores identified householders who considered the suburban public schools superior.

City housing prices better. Index formed by multiplying two items, whether the city of Cincinnati/city of Wilmington had housing prices that were worse than, equal to, or better than the suburbs of Hamilton County/New Castle County; and the importance of housing prices in the locational choice (five categories from "unimportant" to "very important," "don't know" was the middle category). Scores for the index ranged from 1 to 15. The highest scores identified householders who stressed good housing prices and who felt the city had better housing values.

Suburban environment better. Index formed by multiplying two other indices: 1. the extent to which the suburbs were perceived superior with respect to the style of homes, the size of the lots, and overall area appearance, and 2. the extent to which the respondent emphasized each of these environmental qualities. Scores for the first index ranged from 3 to 9; scores for the second ranged from 5 to 15. Multiplying these two indices resulted in a new index with scores ranging from 15 to 135. The highest scores identified householders who stressed suburban environmental attributes and who felt that the suburbs offered superior suburban type qualities.

Urbanism. Factor score, degree of emphasis on urban attributes. We summed two items, prefer an "urban" area, and a mix of people, and subtracted a third item, prefer a "suburban" area. The scores ranged from -3 through 9.

Accessibility. Factor score, degree of emphasis on accessibility. We summed three items, prefer being near: work, public transportation, and stores. Scores ranged from 3 to 15.

Neighborhood orientation. Factor score, attempt to preserve neighborhood social relations. We summed five items: prefer homogeneous neighborhoods, near friends/relatives, near churches/

synagogues, safety, and "lived nearby and liked it." Scores ranged from 5 to 25.

Efficient government. Factor score, emphasize efficient government services. We summed: low taxes, the quality of government services, and good housing values. Scores ranged from 3 to 15.

Housing progress. Perceived progress in achieving "ideal" home. Five categories ranged from "no progress" to "achieved goal."

Mobility Characteristics

Choose suburban location. Whether chose a suburban location: 0. No, 1. Yes.

Moving plans. Whether planned to move within five years: 0. No, 1. Yes.

Economic Incentives

Tax abatements. Index formed by summing two separate items measuring interest, the first, a tax reduction of $500 a year for the first five years, and a second, a tax reduction of $1,000 a year for the same time period. The scale scores ranged from 0 (low interest) to 8 (high interest).

Below market-rate mortgages. Index formed by summing two separate items measuring interest, the first, home financing at 1 percent below market-rate (worth about $500 a year), and the second, home financing at 2 percent below market-rates (worth about $1,000 a year). The scale scores ranged from 0 (low interest) to 8 (high interest).

Definitions of Community Variables Included in Factor Analysis

Individual Variable	Community Variable
House size	Average size of homes in square feet
Income	Average income
College	Percentage who attended college (Hamilton County); percentage who completed college (New Castle County)
White collar	Percentage with high-status white-collar jobs (i.e., professionals, managers)
Rooms	Average number of rooms
Home price	Average housing price
Blue collar	Percentage of homebuyers with a blue-collar job
Dwelling unit age	Average age of dwelling units
City	Percentage of homebuyers who previously lived in the city
Married	Percentage who are married
Newly formed household	Percentage who previously lived with other family members
Out-of-town	Percentage who moved from outside the Cincinnati/ Wilmington metropolitan area

(continued)

Individual Variable	Community Variable
Family size	Average number of individuals per family
Children	Percentage with either preschool or school-age children
Single parent	Percentage who are single parents
Owned	Percentage who previously owned
Age	Average age
Black	Percent of homebuyers who are black
Two or more workers	Percentage of households with two or more workers
Parochial school children	Percentage of households with one or more children in parochial school
New home	Percentage living in homes built since 1960
Move	Percentage planning to move within five years
(Specific to Hamilton County sample)	
Suburbanism	Average score suburbanism (appearance + lot size + house style + emphasize "suburbs" + property value appreciation)
Childrearing	Average score childrearing (near schools + public school quality + child care)
Economics	Average score, economic criteria (taxes + government services + safety)
Neighborhoods	Average score, neighborhood orientation (homogeneity + near friends + lived there before and liked it)
Accessibility	Average score, accessibility orientation (public transportation + stores + churches/synagogues)
Urban	Average score, urban orientation (heterogeneity + prefer "urban" area)

(*continued*)

Individual Variable	Community Variable
Nonexperiential	Average score, nonexperiential attributes (accessibility to work + good housing prices)
	(Specific to New Castle County sample)
Childrearing	Average score, childrearing attributes (near schools + churches/synagogues + child care + public school quality)
Suburbanism	Average score, suburbanism (house style + lot size + area appearance + property value appreciation)
Economics	Average score, economic criteria (housing prices + taxes + government services)
Neighborhoods	Average score, neighborhood orientation (near friends + homogeneity + lived nearby/liked it + safety)
Urban	Average score urbanism (public transportation + prefer "urban" setting - prefer suburban setting + heterogeneity)
Accessibility	Average score, accessibility orientation (close to work + near stores)

NOTES

CHAPTER 1

1. A computer-assisted literature search turned up only a handful of recent studies dealing with residential choice and most of these were from the Netherlands. Deurloo et al. (1990) establish the importance of the residential environment (that is, the type of housing made available by the public and private sectors) in addition to income and family compositional characteristics in affecting these choices. Timmermans et al. (1992) highlight the joint decision-making process of dual worker households.

Among the few recent American studies, two stand out. Percy and Hawkins (1992) provide empirical support for Tiebout's assertion that families locate in areas based on combinations of services and taxes that best meet their needs. Waddel (1991) criticizes previous research that has asserted that workplace location is an independent variable affecting residential choice. Using Dallas-Ft. Worth data, he argues that residential choice, work location, and tenure choice are determined together.

CHAPTER 2

1. We recognize that some of the authors we have cited within each of these bodies of literature may have a disciplinary background different from our specification. Many of these scholars see themselves as interdisciplinary. Nevertheless, we believe that we have captured the essence of their thinking by placing them in one of the three groups.

2. Judd and Parkinson exaggerate when they try to link Pittsburgh's leadership with its 1985 designation as the most livable city in the USA by *Places Rated Almanac*. In 1993 Cincinnati was designated as the most livable city by the Almanac (see Carnutte 1993) at about the same time that

the local media were complaining about a lack of leadership ("City's missing 'big picture' leaders say" 1993). Thus, the assertion that there is some type of causal relationship between leadership and quality of life is suspect.

3. The proposal would equalize benefit levels between states and within metropolitan areas, and would contribute to some degree of deconcentration among the poor. However, Peterson's assertion that this recommendation would lead to increased family stability is oversimplistic.

4. Most whites shy away from saying such a thing to avoid being accused of "blaming the victim," which is what happened to Daniel Patrick Moynihan in 1965, following the release of his report on the disintegration of the black family. Elsewhere in the book, Downs's call for greater discipline and improved organization within the black community is watered down considerably, demonstrating just how politically sensitive this issue is. Here is what the cover blurb says: "Anthony Downs . . . sees little hope for racial integration as the central social strategy for solving urban problems, but does see hope in the internal resources of America's minority communities."

5. Kasarda's assertions on the attraction of the city to particular demographic subgroups is based on research on gentrifying communities which comprise only a small part of central cities. These studies may not be generalizable to central cities as a whole.

6. The magnitude of this type of revitalization is not large, affecting less than .5 percent of the housing stock.

7. For a more up-to-date discussion of this demonstration, see Rosenbaum 1991.

8. Elijah Anderson's essay in *The New Urban Reality* highlights the fact that, while racial tensions are not as serious in gentrifying as in "normal" changing communities, in those changing from white to black, the tensions and fears are, nevertheless, profound.

9. Proposals three and five are rather unique for a book published during the 1980s. These themes are emphasized and elaborated upon in more recent writings on metropolitan planning to be discussed below.

10. Whereas we see the glass as half-full, Small, and later Downs in the concluding chapter, see it as half-empty. Looking at these same findings, Small concludes: "This reinforces my previous conclusion about irreversibility of decline" (204).

11. Thus, during the late 1960s and early 70s, a period of urban turmoil, spending levels increased. Typically a large bloc of black citizens involved in political activities led political leaders to campaign on spending. Later in the 1970s, citizens, in the form of a taxpayers' revolt, played a major role in fiscal retrenchment.

12. The more recent writings on metropolitan planning emphasize this theme.

13. This argument is developed more fully in Wilson's 1987 book *The Truly Disadvantaged.*

14. Richard Nathan suggests using workfare as a basis for an incremental strategy to deal with the underclass issue. He suggests improving the way workfare is implemented and using this experience to strengthen other social services. Wilson criticizes such an incremental approach, but does not indicate what fundamental changes are needed.

15. Inner-city community development corporations (for example, the Bedford Stuyvesant Restoration Corporation) are already actively involved in efforts to attract middle-income blacks. The role of CDCs is discussed in greater detail later in this chapter.

16. For a more extended discussion of the role of CDCs in neighborhood revitalization, see Rasey et al. (1991) and Mayer (1984).

17. This approach to revitalization, emphasizing social viability, is more likely to succeed than one emphasizing economic indicators alone (income, property values). For a more detailed discussion of neighborhood social viability, see Schoenberg and Rosenbaum's 1980 research on St. Louis.

18. The preceding raises a question: If programs like Empowerment Zones are inherently flawed, are there any other strategies to provide jobs for low-income residents of these areas? Frieden and Kaplan (1990) suggest making the best use of downtown development. Cities could open up more downtown jobs to low-income residents by requiring the developers of projects using city funds to hire a certain proportion of city residents, or graduates from city public schools. This approach—negotiation/mediation between city government and business—is described in more detail in Frieden and Sagalyn's 1990 book *Downtown Inc.*

19. It is beyond the intended scope of this section to review the now extensive social science literature on housing adjustments, which includes the determinants of housing repairs and improvements as well as the determinants of residential mobility. Readers interested in such a review should consult Quercia and Rohe (1993).

20. It is important to point out that Galster's mobility analysis is part of a larger analysis of housing adjustment whereby housing repair/improvement decisions are viewed as a function of: (1) demographic characteristics, (2) objective housing characteristics, (3) housing and neighborhood-related attitudes, and (4) mobility plans. The results dealing with the determinants of repairs/improvements are more positive than those dealing with moving plans. That is, owner-occupants are shown more likely to maintain

property than absentee landlords. Furthermore, loans and grants stimulated upkeep behavior and also led neighbors to invest in their properties. Thus, the empirical results support a strategy combining subsidized loans/grants for repairs plus programs to expand homeownership.—Two other conclusions from Galster's empirical analysis should be noted. First, public investments to improve neighborhood infrastructure or physical conditions would only have a minimal impact on upkeep behavior. Second, promoting social cohesion could lead to increases in housing investment. However, the policy implications of this finding are uncertain, because little is known about how government could increase social cohesion. Furthermore, according to Galster, even if such knowledge existed, it might not be desirable to implement such programs since such efforts could lead to increased parochialism.

21. As this is being written, January 1994, there is a significant flurry of interest in metropolitan cooperation and metropolitan planning around the United States. Cincinnati's new mayor, in her "state of the city" address, called for area cooperation, including the creation of a two-state (Ohio and Kentucky) port authority (Crowley 1994a, 1994b; Green 1994a).

22. Peirce points out that Baltimore's tax rate is double that of any other Maryland county; this creates a huge burden on businesses and the remaining middle class.

23. Many scholars dismiss the benefits of downtown development for the poor, and it is, in fact, difficult using aggregated data to identify spillover benefits of these projects for the poor. It is important, however, to ask: Are there any other alternatives for promoting economic development? Frieden and Kaplan (1990) note that with the failures of programs like Model Cities it is hard to imagine large-scale initiatives like this in the 1990s. What can be done according to Frieden and Kaplan is to make the most of downtown development. As mentioned earlier, cities could open up more downtown jobs to low-income residents by requiring developers of projects using city funds to hire a certain proportion of city residents or graduates from the city public school system.—The possible benefits of downtown development can be seen most easily at the project level. Take for example, Philadelphia's private-sector Center City District (Levy 1993). CCD has hired disadvantaged hard-to-reach individuals to sweep sidewalks and to do landscape maintenance. It is planning a demonstration involving formerly homeless employees on teams which would conduct daytime outreach to individuals who are living or panhandling on the streets of Center City.

24. In the past, business elites and strong central city mayors might have provided this leadership, but neither can provide it today. Business elites have been decimated as a result of corporate mergers and downsizing, and there are fewer strong central city mayors (like William Donald Schaefer of Baltimore) than there were in the 1980s.

25. Peirce cites two examples: (1) in Baltimore the number of civil servants has remained virtually the same despite large decreases in the city's population, and (2) in St. Paul there is concern that high union wages for civil servants could lead to higher property taxes, producing a situation that could trigger middle-class migration.

26. Part of the marketing and public relations effort is to identify and build upon a "niche" where the city has a competitive advantage over others. Peirce recommends that St. Paul market itself as a "cultural capital" and create a "cultural corridor" of museums and theaters. Such a marketing strategy could help to attract arts-oriented householders to St. Paul.

27. This is the most common approach to metropolitan governments and is the one used in Indianapolis-Marion County. Rusk cites two other approaches: empowering counties as a form of metro government—for example, Montgomery County, Maryland; or combining counties into regional governments.

28. *Citistates* shows how hard it is to improve metropolitan cooperation, let alone achieve metropolitan governments. For the book, Peirce visited six metropolitan areas (Phoenix, Seattle, Baltimore, Dallas, St. Paul, and Owensboro, Kentucky) and prepared a set of recommendations for each one; these were included in a special supplement of each local newspaper. As reported in the book, reception to his recommendations was mixed. The report had the most impact in Phoenix, where metropolitan planning was in its infancy; it had very limited impact in the other four. Had he proposed metropolitan governments, his recommendations would have been dismissed without being considered seriously.

29. Rusk is overpessimistic about the prospects for older inelastic cities. First, his list of twelve cities includes some that are office headquarters and major tourist/convention destinations where future prospects are relatively good (Chicago, Philadelphia, and Baltimore) as well as others (Gary, Newark, Detroit) that are in much worse condition. Second, Rusk understates the importance of leadership in dealing with central city decline; this is illustrated by another city, Cleveland, included on the list. Journalists considered Cleveland "dead" when the Cuyahoga River caught fire a few years ago and the city almost went bankrupt. Journalists and scholars should be careful about declaring Cleveland "dead." Cleveland's downtown is the envy of other cities in Ohio (DiLonardo 1993a, 1993b); in January 1994 Cincinnati's new Mayor Roxanne Qualls headed to Cleveland to talk to city officials and developers about that city's downtown recovery (Green 1994b). This trip was somewhat ironic since Cincinnati was rated as the most livable city in the United States in 1993. In addition, in 1993 Cleveland received a national innovations award for constructing one thousand housing units for middle-income families in previously vacant areas of the city

("Bright ideas" 1993). This omission with respect to the role of leadership is surprising since elsewhere in the book Rusk argues that leadership matters in accounting for the ability of some cities to annex their suburbs and others not.

30. Peirce does not address the criticisms of ghetto enrichment programs offered by Rusk and more recently by Lemann (1994): (1) that the programs of the last thirty years have been ineffective, especially in the area of job creation, and (2) that when they are effective, people move away, resulting in little improvement in the area. The difficulties of ghetto enrichment are illustrated by the upheavals within "Rebuild L.A" (set up after the 1992 Watts riots), including the resignation of its director, Peter Ueberroth, and its chief operating officer, Bernard W. Kinsey (Sims 1994).

31. It is important to contrast Byrum's views on inner-city housing programs with Sviridoff's and Lemann's. Byrum is against funding them since they will, according to him, anchor the poor in the city and prevent them from taking advantage of suburban employment opportunities. Furthermore, funds for housing could be used to address more fundamental problems in the inner city such as education and health. On the other hand, both Sviridoff and Lemann recommend funding because CDCs are adept in affordable housing production.

32. Conservative critics, such as Charles Murray (1984), argue that federal government programs like public welfare do more to worsen than to solve social problems.

33. *Old Problems in New Times* well illustrates the lack of consensus among experts. For example, when Byrum turned to the experts for solutions to the problems of increased levels of single-parent households and welfare dependency, he discovered answers as diverse as parental responsibility programs to prevent early childbearing (Isabel Sawhill), improved employment opportunities (William Julius Wilson), and welfare reform (Charles Murray). These differences in approach are not easily reconciled.

CHAPTER 3

1. The number of single-family units produced in recent years is even more limited than the census data suggests. Information provided to us by the Cincinnati Buildings and Inspection Department on building permits does distinguish single-family units and does highlight the paucity of production of this type of unit. During the late 1980s and early 90s, about 90 new single-family housing units were produced inside of Cincinnati each year. The detailed figures are as follows: 1986–84, 1987–83, 1988–99, 1989–111, 1990–93, 1991–70, 1992–100.

2. The seven metropolitan areas were: Akron, Cincinnati, Cleveland, Columbus, Dayton, Toledo, and Youngstown. The research is being carried out by the Ohio Research Network, a team of researchers from state universities in each of the seven metropolitan areas. Dr. Thomas Bier of the Urban Center, Cleveland State University, is coordinating the research.

3. Although a number of considerations were taken into account in determining how many rings to use, the primary one was to include most of the sellers. For example, in Cincinnati and surrounding Hamilton County the 14 rings included 12,788 sellers, or 84 percent of the total.

4. In this case we are defining the city as the nearest eight rings.

5. The U.S. Bureaus of the Census has published 1985–1990 moving data by area, which identifies the current residence, city or suburb, of movers. The corresponding available national statistics do not include data on whether movers came from the same or a different metropolitan area. Thus, while the data permit the calculation of metropolitan totals, they do not permit calculation of sums for the nation as a whole.

6. The reader should note that more detailed quantitative results were not included in this and following chapters due to space reasons, but that they are available from the Delaware author. We have noted this omission of detail in footnotes to the text.

7. The cluster analysis feature of SPSS-X is very time and space intensive; consequently we utilized a 25 percent sample for the cluster analysis for both Hamilton and New Castle counties. This accounts for the differences in sample size between table 3.1 on the one hand and tables 3.4 and 3.5 on the other.

8. The factor results that were used to define these factors, such as social rank, are available from the Delaware author.

CHAPTER 4

1. Stanback, in *The New Suburbanization: Challenge to the Central City* (1991), analyzes the most recent movement of economic activity and employment to the suburbs.

2. Weiher (1991) provides a detailed theoretical analysis of how individual preferences for racially compatible housing in conjunction with America's political fragmentation leads to a successful sorting process of school districts and municipalities in the St. Louis metropolitan area.

3. Waddel's 1991 article is one of the few urban economic studies to examine residential choices at the individual household level. In contrast to

previous economic research, Waddel argues that work location is not an exogenous factor influencing residential choice. Instead, residential choice, work location, and tenure location are determined together. Data from the Dallas-Ft. Worth metropolitan area suggest that households choose their locations and workplaces to balance distaste for commuting with a preference for large homes and lower densities. According to the research, higher incomes and family status increase the preference for larger homes at the expense of longer commutes. Although Waddel's research represents an improvement over earlier economic work based on aggregate data, his study is of limited value for understanding the movement of some middle-class families into cities. Residential attitudes and preferences help to account for this movement, but Waddel's study relied exclusively on objective characteristics.

4. Although our model emphasizes the role of personal objective and subjective characteristics we also want to stress the role of residential (supply) characteristics. In many cities families seeking upscale housing near downtown will not be able to find it because of the absence of supply. Conversely the tendency of private developers to focus on providing upscale units along the suburban fringe (along with the tendency for government to use zoning and other means to encourage this trend), promotes suburban preferences and choices. This point—the importance of residential characteristics—is highlighted in Deurloo and Dielman's sophisticated 1990 study of residential choices in the Randstad, the major urbanized region in the Netherlands. They found evidence to support the well-documented tendency for households to remain in the same type of housing and residential environment (e.g., for those living in suburban detached homes to remain there). However, there were some interesting exceptions. In large cities, many households choose multifamily rental units when they move, even households who previously owned or were in single-family rental units. This is not necessarily a reflection of preferences for multifamily housing, but rather of the large supply of this type of housing (346).—This chapter does not look at the impact of the residential environment on city-suburban choices. However, in chapter 3 we did take a look at the characteristics of housing supply in the Cincinnati and Wilmington metropolitan areas. The latter results should be kept in mind as we focus on the determinants of city-suburban choice.

5. The analysis in this chapter tests for the validity of this hypothesis based on our complete sample of homebuyers, whether they had school-aged children or not. A priori we expected that the impact of metropolitan school districts on city-suburban choices would be greater among families with than without school-age children. (It could also be argued that these school policies would be salient to families with preschool age children and those intending to have children in the near future, but we anticipated early in the

project that school policies would be most salient to families with school-age children.) Consequently we prepared an additional set of regression runs, in addition to those presented in this chapter, looking at the determinants of city-suburban choices among families with school-age children. The results (not presented here) were essentially the same as those shown in this chapter. That is, a Wilmington area location did not contribute to city choices when other factors were controlled. Therefore, even among a sample limited to families with children, Wilmington's metropolitan busing did not help to attract families to the city.

6. The detailed regression and logit results are available from the Delaware author.

7. From the perspective of a prototypical middle-class homebuyer with children, school quality comparisons across city-suburban lines in New Castle County are difficult. The most readily available measure, mean standardized test scores, do vary by school. But under the county's school desegregation plan (see chapter 10), each of the four northern New Castle County school districts has particular grades concentrated in the city or in the suburbs. Thus comparing schools requires comparing grades. In point of fact, while there is a tendency for those public schools in the city to report lower mean test scores than suburban schools in comparison to the national mean, the differences are inconsistent and quite minimal (Delaware Department of Public Instruction 1991).

8. We considered but then rejected another possible explanation of this finding, that families were attracted to Cincinnati by the existence of a system of alternative schools. First, the alternative schools system has as its primary objective the promotion of racial integration rather than attracting middle-income families. The fact that those who move into the city have no guarantee that their child(ren) will be accepted into the preferred alternative school, would make them uneasy about making this type of choice. Second, our own survey results highlight the low evaluations of Cincinnati's public schools vis-à-vis those in the suburbs and parents' concerns about safety and discipline in the city schools. It is unlikely that the existence of alternative schools could outweigh these concerns among homebuyers with children. Nevertheless, we did use both crosstabular and regression analysis to empirically test for the possibility that families with children were being attracted to the city because of the existence of magnet schools. The results (not presented here) provided no support for this proposition. In the crosstabular run limited to families with children, those perceiving the alternative schools to be the main strength of the system were no more likely than others to locate in the city. Furthermore, the belief that the alternative schools were the system's main strength did not contribute to an increased likelihood of choosing the city when other demographic and mobility characteristics were controlled.

9. We had assumed that single parent households would constitute another market niche because of the greater availability of day care facilities in the city and because city locations are more centrally located with respect to both child care and employment opportunities. Separate crosstabular and regression analyses using the single parent variable and the Hamilton County homebuyer data set failed to support this assumption. The crosstabular results show that single parents are no more likely to choose the city than others (31% in both cases). Furthermore, in the regression analysis (not presented here but available from the authors) single parents were no more likely to purchase in the city than others when the impact of other background characteristics were controlled.—We were not able to test for the validity of this hypothesis (that single parents would be attracted to central city locations) as part of the main set of analyses for this chapter because the index identifying single parent households is intercorrelated with two other predictors (marital status and presence of children).

CHAPTER 5

1. See Galster (1987) for a more detailed review of the literature on determinants of moving plans/behavior, as well as an empirical assessment of the impact of different background characteristics through moving plans to housing repair/improvement decisions.

2. For examples of empirical studies using this framework, see Newman and Duncan (1979), and Varady (1983).

3. In general, the mobility literature emphasizes that recent homebuyers would be in equilibrium with their homes and locations, and therefore would be inclined to stay. Nevertheless, there is considerable debate among scholars about the long-term attachments of the baby boom generation for cities. That is, will members of this cohort who were attracted to near downtown areas in the 1980s remain in the city beyond their early adult years, or will members of this subgroup follow the pattern of earlier generations in relocating to the suburbs as they attain the more mature age categories and as their income levels rise? See Frey (1993).

4. The analysis in this chapter tests for the validity of this hypothesis based on our complete sample of homebuyers, whether they had school-aged children or not. A priori we expected that the impact of metropolitan school districts on mobility plans would be greater among families with than without school-age children. (It could also be argued that these school policies would also be salient to families with preschool age children and those intending to have children in the near future, but early on in the research project we predicted that school policy would be most relevant to those with school-age children.) Consequently (as in chapter 4) we prepared an addi-

tional set of regression runs, in addition to those presented in this chapter, looking at the determinants of moving plans among families with school-age children. The results (not presented here) were essentially the same as those shown in this chapter. That is, a Wilmington area location did not contribute to plans to stay when other factors were controlled.

5. Results are available from the Delaware author.

Chapter 6

1. For a more detailed review of this literature, see Herbert (1973) and Knox (1982).

2. A secondary purpose of the discriminant analysis was to determine the importance of the community characteristics taken together in predicting cluster membership. The results show that this grouping of variables correctly classified nearly all (97 to 98%) of the grouped cases. The discriminant analysis and factor analysis results cited in the text are available from the Delaware author.

Chapter 7

1. For a more complete discussion of the Hartford, Montreal, and New York City efforts, see Varady and Birdsall (1991).

Chapter 8

1. The task of stimulating new housing production is, of course, much more difficult in older, landlocked cities in the northeast and upper midwest than it is in newer cities in the south and west that are able to annex their suburbs by expanding their boundaries.

2. For a detailed discussion of the preparation of the Housing Blueprint, along with an assessment of the literature on local housing plans, see Varady and Birdsall (1991). Analysis for the Housing Blueprint indicated that homebuyers would be better off under a tax abatement program. Such a program, however, suffers from three disadvantages. First, in states with laws similar to Ohio's, tax abatements are relatively inflexible. They are available to all housing units in all designated "reinvestment areas" in a city, regardless of the price of the housing. The lack of targeting can be a source of criticism. Second, while virtually any local government can abate taxes, few can develop and administer a below market-rate mortgage program. Implementing the latter therefore provides a central city with an important mar-

ket advantage over its suburbs. Third, a tax abatement program is probably more controversial because it results in the loss of tax revenue for the school system. Although the Technical Working Group proposed both subsidized mortgages and tax abatements in the early stages of its deliberations, the latter was excluded from the Blueprint itself.

3. In the past, states and localities have funded housing programs for the nonpoor, but these have usually been programs to assist young couples to become homebuyers. These programs for young couples need to be distinguished from the middle-income housing programs discussed in this chapter, whose goal is to promote the economic regeneration of the central city.—In general, it has been the responsibility of the federal government to fund housing programs for the poor and to leave to the states the responsibility of developing and implementing programs for middle-income families. In a broader sense, however, federal housing assistance is not focused on the poor when the tax benefits of homeownership (the ability to deduct interest on mortgage payments) are taken into account. These tax regulations largely benefit middle- to upper-income households. As pointed out by Downs (1990: 75), "the potential tax revenues sacrificed by the Treasury each year because of such benefits are much larger than the direct expenditure costs of *all* housing subsidies to low-income households combined." This type of middle-income tax benefit has stimulated suburbanization beyond what would have occurred otherwise. The rate of suburbanization might be reduced if this tax benefit were eliminated. However, it is beyond the scope of this chapter to discuss the legal, political, or economic ramifications of such a change in any detail.

4. For example, on May 14, 1994, a symposium was held in Cleveland on the Cleveland State University campus to commemorate the 25th anniversary of the arrival of Krumholz in Cleveland. The symposium was set up to coincide with the release of a new book co-authored by Krumholz and Pierre Clavel, *Regenerating Cities: Equity Planners Tell their Stories* (1994).

5. The reader might wonder why we did not follow a different research strategy, comparing cities that have decided to develop middle-income housing strategies with those that have decided against the approach either because it would be too controversial or because of the perception that continuing suburbanization is inevitable and that there is little that cities can do about it. This alternative approach would not have been practical for two reasons. First, few cities consciously consider and then reject implementing middle-income housing programs. Most of the funds available for housing programs come from the federal level and are targeted to low- and moderate-income families. Cities that "follow" existing funding sources are therefore led towards a focus on low- and moderate-income housing needs. Second, there is no sharp break between "having" and "not having" a middle-income

housing strategy. Many cities support market-rate housing through such activities as making land available to developers. If asked, leaders in such cities might say that they do have a middle-income strategy. In this chapter we are concerned with a smaller subset of cities that offer financial incentives to middle-income families and seek to determine whether these incentives have been politically controversial.

6. The reader will note that all the cities to be discussed are from the "rust belt" of the northeast and upper midwest, which is understandable because this type of city has been hurt most by suburbanization. We are aware of at least one middle-income demand program from the sunbelt, San Diego's Housing Trust Fund (Grimes 1991); unfortunately, we learned about it too late to include it in our study. HTF is primarily focused on providing affordable housing for very low-income families, but a maximum of 10 percent can be used for first-time homebuyers. The inclusion of a middle-income component was crucial in getting the program approved. Two specific selling points, related to the middle-income component, were: (1) the need to address employers' inability to attract skilled white-collar workers to relocate to San Diego because of escalating housing costs and (2) the need to rehabilitate housing in the city's older, declining neighborhoods.— Although this chapter focuses primarily on cities providing financial inducements to middle-income families, two innovative supply-side efforts from the northwest should be noted. Seattle's plan for "urban villages" near to downtown (Egan 1992, 1993) addresses the perception that Seattle is becoming a city that is closed to families with children. Mayor Rice has called for the development of a number of communities of small parks, schools, and apartments where there are now old or empty warehouses. The city's role in this project, costing $400 million, would be to acquire the land and to build a park and its amenities. Project costs would be paid for by short-term bonds and from tax money from an anticipated rise in adjacent property values. Private developers would build the housing once the area is rezoned.—In 1974 Vancouver City Council adopted household mix objectives for the False Creek basin (just to the south of the business center of the city), which would reflect the population, income, and household mix of the Vancouver metropolitan area. The six market-rate developments that were built during the 1970s and 80s were successful in attracting middle- as well as low-income families, as well as families with children (City of Vancouver Planning Department 1989).

7. Telephone interview, February 18, 1993.

8. Telephone interview, February 22, 1993.

9. Ibid.

10. Telephone interview, Charles Kindleberger, director of research, St. Louis Community Development Agency, March 1, 1993.

11. Originally the comptroller for the city threatened to sue over the use of Community Development Block Grant funds for this purpose, saying it was not in compliance with HUD regulations. The comptroller's actions led HUD to investigate the use of CDBG funds for the City Living Program and to rule the activity ineligible because of the lack of low/moderate benefit. As a result of the eligibility ruling, a compromise was reached. The city was allowed to produce neighborhood plan summaries for city neighborhoods rather than the City Living brochures. The plan summaries focus on factual information about the neighborhoods and provide a summary of city planning efforts. Marketing information is not included. The city can state, for example, that there are two parks, but it cannot discuss housing price trends. (Interview with Peter G. Sortino, director of intergovernmental affairs, office of the mayor, city of St. Louis, November 12, 1993.)

12. Mayor White is fairly unique among blacks elected as mayors of large American cities in recent years. Whereas most black mayors, such as David Dinkins in New York City, have stressed social programs and have developed mostly minority constituencies, White has focused on economic development and maintaining a middle-class presence in the city (Sleeper 1993). He emphasized the latter point in a visit to Detroit (Marrison 1993): "We can't ultimately end up with a city of all old people and all poor people, because when that happens, they'll call us Detroit and turn the lights out."

13. Interview, April 29, 1992.

14. Cleveland has earned the nickname the "Comeback City" based on nearly $4 billion of construction downtown.

15. Interview, February 4, 1993. The Internal Revenue Code concerning capital gains permits homesellers to defer payment of any tax liability resulting from the increased value of the house. This capital gain provision spurs sellers to buy more expensive homes, which are typically found in the suburbs. Bier recommends that the capital gain provision be modified so as not to hurt sellers who move down in price.

16. Telephone interview with Anda Cook, February 19, 1993.

17. An indication of its activity level is a special advertising supplement, "Buying into Cleveland," that was included in the April 19, 1993, issue of the *Cleveland Plain Dealer.*

18. Robert Sprague, director of planning and economic development, quoted in a news release concerning the program, February 14, 1992.

19. The notion of creating a new middle-class is an appealing one and provided the basis for New York City's most recent master plan (New York City Department of City Planning 1969). There are two problems with this

idea, however. First, social scientists disagree among themselves as to what should be done to create a new middle class. Second, even if it were possible to create a new middle class, it would take a long time to attain this goal. In the meantime, something must be done to maintain the social and economic viability of central cities.

20. A year later, the proposed initiative at the federal level was in limbo. Little progress had been made despite having a Washington lobbyist working for the city. The Association of Local Housing Finance Agencies decided not to support the initiative with its stress on allowing tax-exempt bonds to be used for subsidized loans for middle-income families. Instead the Association proposed expanding the size of the target areas eligible for these loans. Currently in St. Paul only a small number of census tracts, mostly in industrial areas, are eligible for these loans.—Demand for the subsidized loans, which was high when they were introduced, decreased in 1993 when the interest rates for regular loans dropped. As interest rates rose in 1994, demand for the city's program increased. By June 1994, the Middle-Income Housing Fund had resulted in $11.5 million in closed loans. It was anticipated that the Middle-Income Housing Fund would close down by the end of 1994 replaced by a second phase to be created by refinancing bonds from pre-1980 federal legislation. (Interview with Katy Sears Lindblad, city of St. Paul, Department of Planning and Economic Development, June 16, 1994.)

21. This section draws heavily from Léveilée and Whelan 1990.

22. Montreal has also suffered economically in relation to its main rival, Toronto. This decline began in the post–World War II period and accelerated when the Parti Québecois passed legislation to protect the French language; see Levine 1990.

23. It would be a mistake to overstate the problems of central Montreal. Compared to similar U.S. cities, Montreal has far more people living downtown and is far safer.

24. Interview with Martin Wexler, Housing and Urban Development Services, City of Montreal, June 15, 1992.

25. See Wessel and Reich (1992) for a discussion of the controversy surrounding the construction of HarborView, a luxury condominium development on the south shore of Baltimore's Inner Harbor.—Coldspring New Town in Baltimore represents another type of supply-side program for middle-income housing, a planned community away from downtown. In the 1970s, the new town was conceptualized as a $200 million project to produce 4,000 units for middle- and upper-income housing units. The city played the dominant role in the public/private partnership: "The city would acquire the land, pay for the detailed plans, build the necessary infrastructure and act as a mortgagee in financing the final sale of the completed units. In addition,

the city would provide a short-term construction loan at favorable rates to the developer" (Lyall 1980: 47–48). The project was plagued by: (1) an innovative design by the noted architect Moshe Safdie that was difficult to construct, (2) defects in construction that led to a class action suit, and (3) limited market demand resulting from an isolated location in close proximity to a low-income area. As a result, by 1990, only 200 market-rate units had been constructed, and additional construction in the near future seemed unlikely. Coldspring New Town's middle-income orientation also proved controversial. Residents of a nearby black community objected to its construction and argued that housing funds should be directed toward their community's needs.

26. There is some scholarly support for this position regarding the psychological benefits of downtown revitalization. Robin Boyle (1990: 129), observing a comparable uneven pattern of revitalization in Glasgow, concluded that downtown improvement makes all residents, poor and affluent, feel proud of their city.

27. Interview with Reggie Stanfield, Project Coordinator, Vacant House Loan Progam, City of Baltimore, February 9, 1993.

28. Certainly this could not be said of all of Baltimore's redevelopment programs. Hula (1990), for example, reports that aspects of Baltimore's downtown development handled through private sector ventures "generated a great deal of controversy" (199) and that, as we point out in footnote 25 "from its inception the Coldspring project has been plagued by controversy" (204). Wong's (1990) analysis of Baltimore (and Milwaukee) may explain why some programs have been more controversial than others. He reports that, although Baltimore's housing agency was politicized, Mayor Schaefer had sufficient resources to make deals with opponents to temper any public criticism. While Peterson (1981) argues that developmental programs are generally less controversial, more recently neighborhood-based housing rather than downtown-based commercial programs seem to garner the most public support.

29. Interview with Reggie Stanfield, February 9, 1993.

30. Telephone interview, Alan Matas, former project director, March 12, 1993.

31. Ibid.

32. A CDC is a nonprofit community-based organization governed by a board consisting of neighborhood residents and business leadership dedicated to the revitalization of a given area. Sviridoff (1994) sees CDCs as one of the main rays of hope in the midst of inner-city decline.—Thus far, few scholars or policymakers have recognized the importance of including middle-income housing in inner-city revitalization. Although William

Julius Wilson has written and spoken extensively on the subject of the social isolation of the underclass, he has not (to our knowledge) discussed the benefits of attracting more middle-class families to these areas, nor has the idea caught on with public officials. After the Los Angeles riots, a small black development firm approached but was rebuffed by a number of government agencies who were not interested in financing middle-income buyers. Eventually, the firm was able to persuade Wells Fargo Bank to back their plan (Kerr 1992).

33. Koven and Koven (1993) found tht Des Moines's tax abatement program for newly constructed residential housing was successful in attracting homebuyers who would have located in the suburbs without the program.

CHAPTER 9

1. Interview with Wayne Lemmon, March 30, 1993.

2. The zoning that was operative at the time of the IDC was relatively unrestrictive. Had the IDC regulation been lifted without putting replacement zoning and land-use regulations in place, the applicable zoning would have provided the opportunity for virtually unrestricted development in the East End.

3. The idea of a project manager originated with the Riverfront Advisory Council, which first proposed a consultant team to work on the project. The city manager, at the time, approved of the team concept. When the new manager, Gerald Newfarmer, took office in 1991, he accepted the idea of a project manager but rejected the notion of an outside consultant, feeling that there was enough talent in-house to fill the post with a city employee. Later in 1991, he engaged Bellow as project manager. This discussion exemplifies the fact that turnover of high-level city staff can destroy the continuity of city policy. Interestingly, Newfarmer was dismissed by Cincinnati's city council in spring 1993. What impact this type of rapid turnover will have on the East End is not known.

4. In fact, the estimated average market value of new units in the LDR plan was $146,000. However, more than half of the units were condominiums in mid high-rise units expected to cost $175,000. A fourth of the units were expected to cost under $100,000. The majority of these lower priced units were to be built on in-fill sites.

5. Interview with Doug Ruwe, Cincinnati Department of City Planning, June 1, 1993. The analysis of price changes was carried out by the department of city planning using real estate transaction data gathered by Ameristate Inc. Several large industrial property sales were excluded from

the analysis including one—the Sawyer property at the western edge of the community—that sold for nearly $1.9 million.

6. The city is burdening the East End plan with all the costs of rerouting the rail lines from the East End to the Mill Creek Valley north of downtown, even though the benefits of relocation will also go to the areas to the west of the East End including but not limited to Sawyer Point, a project of the city's department of economic development. Officials of the latter agency refuse to prorate costs between the East End and other communities. Offcials feel that if Sawyer Point assumes some of the costs, deals that had been arrived at with developers will be spoiled. (Interview with Wayne Lemmon, March 30, 1993.)

7. Interview, February 25, 1992.

8. As this is being written (September 1994) Lemmon's reanalysis of the economic feasibility of the East End plan has not been publicized. In July 1992 he sent the report to Jacquelyne McCray, project planner from the planning department. She in turn transmitted it to Arnold Bellow, who, starting spring 1993 was the city's deputy director for economic development, as well as project manager in the East End. He did little to advertise the study before he left Cincinnati to take another job. As a result, it continues to gather dust. The Ohio author of this book is one of a handful of people in the city to have read Lemmon's work. One city official said that since the plan had already been approved by the time the report was received, the report was "moot" and therefore there was no need to publicize it. Furthermore, the city had gotten into trouble whenever it released specific numbers (as when it indicated the number of low-income housing units that should be retained in the downtown area). Releasing the report, according to this informant, might make the project controversial at a time when it was moving from the planning to the implementation phase. In hindsight, it might be argued that Lemmon's economic analysis should have been built into the planning approval process that took place in 1992. Had city council members known of the shortfall in the 1992 plan, they might not have been willing to approve it or they might have been willing to support it only if modifications were made in the plan to shore up its financial feasibility. However, not having the report available worked to the advantage of council members, at least in the short run. It allowed them to approve a "plan without a price tag," as another informant put it.—We think that the report should have been publicized even though the plan had already been approved and even though this might have made the implementation phase somewhat more controversial. Those involved in the implementation process need to know how much the plan will cost to implement as well as the limited means the city has to pay for it. These issues cannot be ignored much longer.

9. Interview with Wayne Lemmon, March 30, 1993.

10. Interview with Steve Schuckman, park planner, Cincinnati Park Board, May 17, 1993.

11. The lower the number of the zoning category, the lesser the density of development allowed. A lower density would probably mean less profit for the developer.

12. The East End Area Council experienced a setback in the fall of 1992, when Ruth Coon was charged with misappropriating about $800 in community council funds. The Area Council and the city are pursuing prosecution unless she reimburses the community council. A housing official who worked closely with Coon doubts whether the episode has any broader meaning. He feels that this was simply a case of an individual who confused community council funds with her own. Other low-income community councils have been able to adhere to sound accounting practices.

13. The East End plan did not get destroyed in a political maelstrom. The original political purpose of the land-use plan started off simply as a development to increase the tax base. This limited focus was expanded when the concerns of the community—displacement, poor housing conditions— were exposed. The ability to broaden the focus was attributable to the good working relationship between city staff, advocate planners, and developers. We speculate that the at-large election of city council members increased the ability of the bureaucracy to work out a compromise with the community. Had there been a district-elected councilperson, he or she might well have tried to exploit this situation by killing the planning process entirely.

14. There are other obstacles to the building of a new school: the financial pressures on the school district and the fact that the plan envisioned new housing for singles and couples rather than for families with children.

CHAPTER 10

1. The only metropolitan plan in the west is in Clark County, Nevada, the home county of Las Vegas.

2. Two states have adopted voluntary metropolitan school desegregation plans. Wisconsin provides double funding (that is, funding for the sending and receiving districts) for students from the Milwaukee schools who attend suburban schools. Massachusetts law supports such transfers in several metropolitan areas (Nathan 1990). These plans allow blacks from the city to transfer to suburban districts with available places. These plans are unlikely to help to retain or attract middle-class whites to the city. By reducing the number of black students in city schools, the plans might decrease the likelihood that whites would constitute small minorities in

particular schools, thereby making them more willing to remain within the system. Of course, the volunteers for such transfer programs tend to be those minority children from families most positive about education and successful in school, and their leaving the city could hurt the prospects for positive interaction between black and white students. This conclusion is based on the premise that integration is most apt to succeed in reducing stereotypes if whites and blacks are of the same social class.

3. Exactly the same dilemma occurs in efforts to achieve stable, racially integrated neighborhoods (see Farley et al. 1978).

4. Black leaders have questioned the chances of success of such plans without strong mandatory assignment plans as back-ups.

5. Dr. Green left Red Clay without a new position in hand and with the board paying for his condominium mortgage.

6. The problem of a lack of safety and discipline in schools serving central city minority students is certainly not limited to the Wilmington area. The higher suspension rates of black students from the inner city is not simply a function of insensitive white teachers. Even when teachers are black, discipline is an issue. Each semester Frank Mickens, principal of Boys and Girls High School in Brooklyn, "expels scores of students who fight or cut classes" (Lee 1993).

CHAPTER 11

1. In this section we limit ourselves to American studies, but Menahem et al.'s 1993 Tel Aviv study should be mentioned. The research team hypothesized that the city's system of specialized nonneighborhood schools (SPNN) enabled families to remain in socio-economically mixed areas, whereas if their children had been forced to attend neighborhood schools, they would have left these locations. Only a small minority of the parents said that if their child had not gotten into a SPNN school, they would have relocated to another area. Thus, the impact of these magnet schools on residential choices was apparently quite limited.

2. Rossell's research has also been criticized by Monti (1991), who claims that the marginal increase in desegregation is not worth the various costs of magnet schools.

3. After a ten-year hiatus, in 1993 Philadelphia was under pressure to expand its desegregation efforts, despite its shrinking white student base. Even desegregation advocate Robert Crain had stated that desegregating Philadelphia schools with a mandatory plan "is not going to work" (Crain 1982: 413). According to Crain, mandatory desegregation will lead to white

flight, thus canceling out any hoped for desegregation. In April 1993 a judge did rule that mandatory desegregation was not sensible. For a discussion of the Philadelphia case, see Hinds (1993).

4. The Taeuber Index, or index of dissimilarity, measures the segregation of two groups. According to Klaff (1984: 43), "the index measures differences in the distribution of two groups and is computed as half of the sum of the absolute value of the difference between the two percentage distributions." One calculates the percentage distribution of blacks and nonblacks or whites in each school. The absolute differences for each school are then summed and halved. "The substantive interpretation of the values of the index is given in terms of the percent of one population which would have to move to different [schools] in order to have the same percent distribution over the [schools] as another population" (Klaff 1984: 44). Thus, if we were examining census tracts, "a value of zero corresponds to a completely even distribution of black households, i.e., the black fraction of every block or census tract is equal to the proportion for the entire city or metropolitan area, while a value of 100 indicates complete segregation, i.e., every block or census tract is either one-hundred or zero percent black" (Kain 1988: 14). The analogous numbers apply to schools—100 is a totally segregated school and 0 indicates a school that totally reflects the percentage of a group in the overall district.

5. It is our impression that most of the discipline problems have occurred at nonmagnet schools. One of the most widely publicized incidents took place outside of Taft High School in the West End. A student was shot and later died a week after President Bush visited the school.

6. Our understanding and interpretation of this incident draws heavily from Downs's "law of dominance" presented in a 1968 article. He argues that racially segregated schools are not due to an unwillingness among white parents to share schoolrooms with blacks. Whites want to make sure that their cultural and social values dominate not only their residential neighborhood but their children's school as well: "This desire in turn springs from the typical middle-class belief of all racial groups that everyday life should be primarily a value-reinforcing experience for both adults and children, rather than primarily a value-altering one" (1338). Downs notes that although there is no intrinsic reason why race is linked to values that can have a functional impact on adults or children, most whites perceive race as a relevant fact in assessing the type of homogeneity that they want to attain. Therefore in deciding whether a school or a neighborhood exhibits the kind of environment in which their own values are and will be dominant, they consider blacks to be members of another group. If educational experts and others interpret incidents of uncivil behavior like the one above as a reflection of racial/cultural difference, this can only contribute to the tendency among whites to view blacks as members of another group.

7. Nor are such problems limited to urban, as compared to suburban and rural schools; see Celis 1993.

8. Rossell (1990) has criticized the use of the Taeuber Index and called for a measure of black exposure to white students because the racial balance measure masks the possibility of falling white enrollments. She views the Index of Dissimilarity as a measure of racial balance, indicating the proportion of black students who would have to be reassigned to white schools to achieve a perfect racial balance. Rossell (1990: 35) argues that since "racial balance can be achieved with very little interracial exposure," one should also examine a measure of interracial exposure. She warns against relying on the Index of Dissimilarity and therefore regarding a situation where all but a few whites have left a school system, but these few whites are spread evenly throughout the system, as a positive one. In fact, since interracial exposure cannot be achieved without a good deal of racial balance, Rossell utilizes the racial balance measure in her work. The reader will not be surprised that Rossell's approach has also been criticized, specifically for not adequately counting the number of black students in totally segregated schools. That is, where the distribution of students is not normal, the "average" does not do a good job of describing the distribution (Kelly and Miller 1989).

9. A quantitative analysis of the district's success in retaining upper-income pupils was cited by two interviewees, but could not be located.

10. Although the archdiocese defines greater Cincinnati as including Hamilton, Butler, Warren, and Clermont counties, the bulk of the student population comes from Hamilton County. The latter is the appropriate geographic unit of analysis for this section, because many students from the city attend Catholic schools elsewhere within Hamilton County. The reverse is true as well.

11. Interview with Margo Aug, Social Action and World Peace Office, Archdiocese of Cincinnati, March 11, 1994.

12. Interview with Sister Kathryn A. Connelly, superintendent of schools, Archdiocese of Cincinnati, Department of Educational Services, March 11, 1994.

CHAPTER 12

1. Wilmington and Cincinnati illustrate the difficulty American cities have in maintaining lively downtowns. By now, most of Wilmington's retail and entertainment functions have relocated to the suburbs. While Cincinnati's downtown is in better shape than Wilmington's, it is far from healthy. The first obvious sign of trouble occurred in 1987 when the L.S. Ayres department store closed. Since then numerous specialty stores have closed

as the downtown has lost market share to thriving suburban malls. A recent report by a team from the Urban Land Institute (Bolton 1993a, 1993b) painted a more dismal picture than most local leaders had known. The team recommended that the city hire a consultant to negotiate a contract within 90 days to help relocate one of the two remaining major department stores (Lazarus) two blocks to be closer to the heart of the downtown retail district. It also recommended the creation of a new group, city funded and composed of officials from the city, chamber of commerce and other downtown committees, as well as downtown property and business owners, to monitor the downtown's marketing and management. A more recent (March 1994) plan, the "Downtown Marketplace" prepared by the Downtown Cincinnati Inc. (DCI) business group outlines an ambitious strategy that depends on achieving a "critical mass" to attract business. This follows the example of suburban malls luring other retail developments (Crowley 1994c). However, for this most recent plan to succeed, it will have to overcome the same obstacles that have stymied recent downtown revitalization efforts: suburban flight that has yanked shoppers from the central city, perceptions that the downtown is crime-ridden and inconvenient, and the challenge of attracting stores and shoppers downtown (Crowley and Reese 1994).

2. See Ashworth and Voogd (1990) for an excellent discussion of city marketing efforts from a European perspective.

3. One possible problem with the plan—that it would result in substantial revenue loss—is not a real concern, according to Morton Schussheim, Senior Economist, Congressional Research Service. Revenue losses would be minimal. Interview, October 26, 1993. Although it seems reasonable to assume that the implementation of Bier's recommendation would promote movement to central city locations, little if any research has been conducted on this issue. Nor have there been any studies on whether the provision for excluding from taxation gains of up to $125,000 for those 55 years and over has contributed to moves to central city locations.

4. HUD is taking a number of steps towards achieving these goals. High-level officials expect to create a new office to oversee a consolidated planning process (combining the CHAS with a number of other planning documents) and are considering an awards program to recognize and reward examples of excellent strategic local and regional planning, innovative urban design and community institution building (Stegman 1993).

5. Obviously, one needs to be cautious in generalizing from Paris to American cities like Cincinnati and Wilmington. To start off with, the French are more strongly attached to their downtowns than Americans. Our main reason for citing the Paris school is to dispel the stereotype that central city schools are inherently inferior to suburban ones.

6. Wilmington High School, on the edge of the city, now has a banking program. One classroom has been converted to serve as a bank for the school. As noted in chapter 10, the Red Clay School District is trying to convert this school to one with several magnet programs. A program for performing arts presently serves middle school students, and a program based on Ted Sizer's Coalition of Essential Schools serves high school students.

7. A few examples of such coordination appear in the literature. In the 1970s Chicago tried to tie school construction to urban renewal. Wong (1992) reports that "in Chicago, the opening of the Whitney Young Magnet High School in 1975 was clearly designed to complement the city's urban renewal efforts" (20). Campbell and Levine (1977) argue that "with attractive public schools . . . the future of the city [Chicago] could be different" (141). Chicago had areas of urban renewal with populations large enough to support local schools to serve the population, but what was needed was "a school that parents can be assured will not become an inner-city school with a majority of students with low socioeconomic status" (141). Whitney Young was designed to provide middle-class parents, white and black, with an outstanding secondary school. It was built near the downtown area close to several major urban renewal projects. Whitney Young, however, received far more applications from blacks than whites for the original 500 openings. But the board stuck to its policy of not giving any preference to neighborhood students to maintain the magnet school (and please the middle-class).— Jonathan Kozol (1991) describes with disdain another example of school-housing cooperation in Chicago: "A mostly middle-income condominium development was built close to a public housing project known as Hilliard Homes. The new development, called Dearborn Park, attracted a number of young professionals, many of whom were fairly affluent white people, who asked the school board to erect a new school for their children. This request was honored and the South Loop Elementary School was soon constructed. At this point a bitter struggle ensued. The question: Who would get to go to the new school?" (60). According to Kozol, the board had earlier refused to build a new school for the housing project children. Local leaders argued that the new school should serve their children. The compromise was that the condominium parents could enter their children from kindergarten, but the housing project children were not allowed in the school until third grade. As a result of this agreement, the project children attend school in a prefabricated metal building surrounded by junkyards.

References

Abbott v. Burke, 575A.2d359 (N.J. 1990).

Abu-Lughod, J., and M. Foley. 1960. "Consumer strategies." In *Housing choices and housing constraints*, Part 2. N. N. Foote, J. Abu-Lughod, M. Foley, and L. Winnick, eds. New York: McGraw-Hill.

Adler, J. 1986. "A return to the suburbs: Boomers are acting like parents." *Newsweek.* July 21. 52–54.

Allen, Jodie T. 1992. "South Bronx cheer: A miracle grows amid the rubble." *Washington Post.* July 19. C3.

Alonso, William. 1982. "The population factor and urban structure." In *Internal structure of the city*, L. S. Bourne, ed. New York: Oxford University Press.

Anderson, Elijah. 1989. "Sex codes and family life among the poor inner-city youth." *Annals of the American Academy of Political and Social Science* 501. (Jan.) 59–78.

Apgar, William C., and Henry O. Pollakowski. 1986. *Housing, mobility and choice.* Working paper W 86-6. Cambridge: Joint Center for Housing Studies of M.I.T. and Harvard University.

Applebome, Peter. 1992. "Busing is abandoned even in Charlotte." *New York Times.* April 15. B9.

Applied Economic Research, Inc. 1989. *Delaware housing needs analysis.* Dover: Delaware State Housing Authority.

Archdiocese of Cincinnati, Office for Catholic Schools. n.d. Superintendent's Annual Report. 1990/1991. Cincinnati: Archdiocese.

———. n.d. Superintendent's Annual Report 1993/94. Cincinnati: Archdiocese.

Armor, David J. 1982. Testimony. School desegregation. Hearings before the subcommittee on civil and constitutional rights. House of Representatives. Ninety-Seventh Congress, Serial no. 26. Washington, D.C.: U.S. Government Printing Office. 192–242.

———. 1980. "White flight and the future of school desegregation." In *School desegregation*, Walter G. Stephan and Joe E. Feagin, eds. New York: Plenum Press.

Ashworth, G. J., and H. Voogd. *Selling the city.* London: Belhaven Press.

Baer, William C. 1988. "California's housing element: A backdoor approach to metropolitan governance and regional planning." *Town Planning Review* 59, (3). 263–76.

Baltimore Community Development Financing Corporation. n.d. Fact sheet. Baltimore: BCDFC.

Bass, Carole. 1992. "Schools of thought." *Connecticut Law Tribune* 18 (47). 1, 7–13.

Bates, Percy. "Desegregation: Can we get there from here?" *Phi Delta Kappan* 72 (1). 8–17.

Bell, Katrina. 1992. "Suburbanites find comforts of home in Cleveland." *Cleveland Plain Dealer.* Sept. 7.

Bell, W. 1958. "Social choice, life styles, and suburban residence." In *The Suburban community*, W. Dobriner, ed. New York: G. Putnam.

———. 1968. "The suburb and a theory of social choice." In *The new urbanization*, D. C. McElrath, D. W. Minar, P. Orleans, and S. Greer, eds. New York: St. Martin's Press.

Bennett, David A. "Choice and desegregation." In *Choice and control in American education*, Volume 2. William H. Clune and John F. Witte, eds. London: Falmer Press.

Berenyi, Eileen. 1989. *Locally funded housing programs in the United States: A survey of 51 most populated cities.* New York: Community Development Research Center, New School for Social Research.

Berry, Brian J. L. 1982. "Inner city futures: An American dilemma revisited." In *Internal structure of the city*, L. S. Bourne, ed. New York: Oxford University Press.

———. 1985. "Islands of renewal in seas of decay." In *The new urban reality*, Paul E. Peterson, ed. Washington, D.C.: Brookings Institution.

Berry, Brian J. L., and Donald C. Dahmann. 1980. "Population redistribution and public policy." In *Population redistribution and public policy,* Brian J. L. Berry and Lester P. Silverman, eds. Washington, D.C.: National Academy of Sciences.

Bier, Thomas and Ivan Maric. 1993. "IRS code sec. 1034, rollover of gain on sales of principal residence: Contributor to urban decline." Paper presented at the 23rd annual meeting of the Urban Affairs Association, Apr. 23, Indianapolis, Indiana.

Black, J. T. 1975. "Private market housing renovation in central cities: A ULI survey." *Urban Land* (34). Nov. 3–9.

Blank, Rolf K. 1990. "Educational effects of magnet schools." In *Choice and control in American education,* Volume 2. William H. Clune and John F. Witte, eds. London: Falmer Press.

Board of Education of Oklahoma City v. Dowell. 498 U.S. 237 (1991).

Bolton, Douglas. 1990. "High noon on hill: Condos garner more support." *Cincinnati Post.* Sept. 10.

———. 1993a. "Downtown plan: Move Lazarus now." *Cincinnati Post.* June 18. 1A, 10A.

———. 1993b. "Downtown plan draws city support." *Cincinnati Post.* June 19. 1A, 11A.

Boyle, Robin. 1990. "Regeneration in Glasgow: Stability, collaboration, and inequity." In *Leadership and urban regeneration,* Dennis Judd and Michael Parkinson, eds. Newbury Park, Calif.: Sage.

Bradley, Ann. 1993. "The business of reforming Cincinnati's schools." *Education Week.* May 19. 12 (34). 1, 16.

———. 1994. "The discipline dilemma." *Education Week,* 13 (17). 20.

Brecher, Charles, and Raymond D. Horton. 1985. *Setting municipal priorities.* New York: New York University Press.

"Bright ideas: Innovations that make state and local government work better." 1993. *Cincinnati Enquirer.* Nov. 23. A6.

Brown, L. A., and J. Holmes. 1971. "Search behavior in an intra-urban migration context. A spatial perspective." *Environment and Planning* 3 (3). 307–26.

Brown v. Board of Education. 347 U.S. 483 (1954).

Brown v. Board of Education. 349 U.S. 294 (1955).

Burns, John F. 1992. "The proud city of 'great events' has a great fall." *New York Times.* Feb. 5. 4.

Byrum, Oliver E. 1992. *Old problems in new times: Urban strategies for the 1990s.* Chicago: APA Planners Press.

Campbell, Connie, and Daniel U. Levine. 1977. "Whitney Young Magnet High School of Chicago and urban renewal." In *The future of big city schools*, Daniel U. Levine and Robert J. Havighurst, eds. Berkeley: McCutchan.

Cataldo, Everett F., Michael W. Giles, and Douglas S. Gatlin. 1978. *School desegregation policy: Compliance, avoidance, and the metropolitan remedy.* Lexington: Lexington Books.

Celis, William, III. 1992. "Businesslike with business's help Cincinnati schools shake off crisis." *New York Times.* Aug. 20. B10.

———. 1993. "Suburban and rural schools learning that violence isn't confined to cities." *New York Times.* April 21. B11.

Chatman, Angela D. 1993a. "Developer studies Hough expansion." *Cleveland Plain Dealer.* Feb. 17.

———. 1993b. "Middle-class families build dreams in Hough." *Cleveland Plain Dealer.* Mar. 22. 1.

Christensen, Karen S., and Michael B. Teitz. 1980. "Housing assistance plan: Promise and reality." In *Housing policy for the 1980's*, Roger Montgomery and Dale Rogers Marshall, eds. Lexington: Lexington Books.

Cibulka, James. 1990. "Choice and restructuring of American education." In *Choice in education: Potential and problems*, William L. Boyd and Herbert J. Walberg, eds. Berkeley: McCutchan.

Cincinnati City Planning Commission. 1979. *The coordinated city plan.* Cincinnati: Commission.

Cincinnati Department of City Planning. 1986. *Environmental quality/community revitalization district no. 1, East End Riverfront.* Cincinnati: Planning Department.

Cincinnati Park Board. 1992. *Cincinnati parks and greenways plan.* Cincinnati: Park Board.

City of Cincinnati Department of City Planning and Department of Neighborhood Housing and Conservation. 1991. *Eastern riverfront urban design plan.* Cincinnati: Planning Department.

———. 1992. *East End riverfront community development plan and guidelines.* Cincinnati: City of Cincinnati.

City of Hartford Department of City Planning. 1986. *Hartford plan of development: 1985–2000.* Hartford: City of Hartford.

City of Montreal. 1989. *Habiter Montréal.* Montreal: City of Montreal.

City of Vancouver Planning Department. 1989. *Evaluation of False Creek South social objectives.* Vancouver: Planning Department.

"City's missing 'big picture' leaders say." 1993. *Cincinnati Post.* Aug. 4.

Clark, Michael D. 1990a. "Magnet schools: Alternative programs attract praise, blame." *Cincinnati Post.* July 24. 1C, 8C.

———. 1990b. "City schools confirm student violence up." *Cincinnati Post.* Aug. 4. 1A, 16A.

———. 1990c. "Fear factor grows in city classrooms." *Cincinnati Post.* Dec. 7. 1A, 8A.

Clark, Terry Nichols. 1985. "Fiscal strain: How different are snow belt and sun belt cities?" In *The new urban reality,* Paul E. Peterson, ed. Washington, D.C.: Brookings Institution.

Clark, Thomas A. 1979. *Blacks in suburbs: A national perspective.* New Brunswick: Center for Urban Policy Research.

Clavel, Pierre, and Nancy Kleniewski. 1990. "Space for progressive policy: Examples from the United States and the United Kingdom." In *Beyond the city limits: Urban policy and economic restructuring in comparative perspective,* John R. Logan and Todd Swanstrom, eds. Philadelphia: Temple University Press.

Cleary, Paul, and Ronald Angel. 1984. "The analysis of relationships involving dichotomous dependent variables." *Journal of Health and Social Behavior* 25. 33–48.

Clinchy, Evans. 1993. "Needed: A Clinton crusade for quality and equality." *Phi Delta Kappan* 74 (8). 605–12.

Clune, William H. 1990. "Educational governance and student achievement." In *Choice and control in American education,* Volume 2, William H. Clune and John F. Witte, eds. London: Falmer Press.

Coleman, James S., Ernest Q. Campbell, Carol J. Hobson, James McPartland, Alexander M. Mood, Frederick D. Weinfeld, and Robert G. York. 1966. *Equality of Educational Opportunity.* Washington, D.C.: U.S. Government Printing Office.

Colton, David, and Susan Uchitelle. 1992. "Urban school desegregation: From race to resources." In *The politics of urban education in the United States,* James G. Cibulka, Rodney J. Reed, and Kenneth K. Wong, eds. Washington, D.C.: Falmer Press.

Crain, Robert L. 1972. *Discrimination, Personality, and Achievement: A survey of northern blacks.* New York: Seminar Press.

Crain, Robert L. 1982. Testimony. School desegregation. Hearings before the subcommittee on civil and constitutional rights. House of Representatives, Ninety-Seventh Congress, Serial No. 26. Washington, D.C.: U.S. Government Printing Office. 382–389.

Crowley, Patrick. 1994a. "Qualls: Think globally; act locally." *Cincinnati Enquirer.* Jan. 6. B1.

———. 1994b. "Area cooperation urged by Qualls in 'state' address." *Cincinnati Enquirer.* Jan. 7. D4.

———. 1994c. "Downtown plan: Mirror the malls." *Cincinnati Enquirer.* March 10. A-1.

Crowley, Patrick, and Shelly Reese. 1994. "Old obstacles block 'new' downtown." *Cincinnati Enquirer.* March 11. A-1.

Curnutte, Mark. 1993. "Cincinnati no. 1: 'Places rated' calls it North America's most livable city." *Cincinnati Enquirer.* Oct. 26.

"D.C. schools plan new programs to attract more white students." 1993. *Education Week.* March 10. 12 (24).

Davis, Matthew G. 1992. "Low-interest loans draw high interest." *Saint Paul Pioneer Press.* Feb. 4.

Dennison, Sandy. 1992. "Red Clay doesn't cloak the problem—jackets OK in class." *Wilmington News Journal.* July 16. B3.

Deurloo, M. C., W. A. V. Clark, and F. M. Dieleman. 1990. "Choice of residential environment in the Randstad." *Urban Studies.* 27 (3). 335–51.

De Witt, Karen. 1992. "'Clustering' of white students stirs Richmond furor." *New York Times.* Dec. 9. B15.

DiLonardo, Mary Jo. 1993a. "Cleveland is crowing about its comeback." *Cincinnati Post.* June 12. 1A, 10A.

———. 1993b. "Revitalized Cleveland on a roll." *Cincinnati Post.* June 14. 1A, 4A.

Downs, Anthony. 1968. "Alternative futures for the American ghetto." *Daedalus* 97 (4). 1331–78.

———. 1980. "Using the lessons of experience to allocate resources in the community development program." In *Housing urban America,* Jon Pynoos, Robert Schafer and Chester Hartman, eds. New York: Aldine.

———. 1981. *Neighborhoods and urban development.* Washington, D.C.: Brookings Institution.

———. 1985. "The future of industrial cities. In *The new urban reality,* Paul E. Peterson, ed. Washington, D.C.: Brookings.

———. 1990. "A strategy for designing a fully comprehensive national housing policy for the federal government of the United States." In *Building Foundations,* Denise DiPasquale and Langley C. Keyes, eds. Philadelphia: University of Pennsylvania Press.

"East End controls likely to remain." 1991. *Cincinnati Post.* April 10.

Egan, Timothy. 1992. "Seattle mayor breaks with the past seeking growth in 'urban villages.'" *New York Times.* April 24. A9.

———. 1993. "Seattle has a plan: Urban renewal for fun." *New York Times.* April 4. 12.

Egerton, John. 1976. *School desegregation: A report card from the south.* Atlanta: Southern Regional Council.

Fainstein, Susan. 1990a. "Economics, politics, and policy development: The convergence of New York and London." In *Beyond the city limits: Urban policy and economic restructuring in comparative perspective,* John R. Logan and Todd Swanstrom, eds. Philadelphia: Temple University Press.

———. 1990b. "Neighborhood planning: Limits and potentials." In *Neighborhood policy and programs: Past and present,* Naomi Carmon, ed. Houndmills, Basingstoke, Hampshire, and London: MacMillan Academic and Professional.

Farley, Reynolds, Howard Schumann, Suzanne Bianchi, Diane Colasanto, and Shirley Hatchett. 1978. "Chocolate city: vanilla suburbs: Will the trend toward racially separate communities continue?" *Social Science Research* 7. 319–44.

Felix, Joseph L., and James N. Jacobs. 1977. "Issues in implementing alternative programs in Cincinnati." In *The future of big city schools,* Daniel U. Levine and Robert J. Havighurst, eds. Berkeley: McCutchan.

Finder, Alan. 1990a. "Non-profit groups rebuilding housing for the poor." *New York Times.* March 11.

———. 1990b. "Should the poor get the housing that Koch built?" *New York Times.* March 18.

Finn, Chester, Jr. 1990. "Why we need choice." In *Choice in education: Potential and problems,* William L. Boyd and Herbert J. Walberg, eds. Berkeley: McCutchan.

Fitzpatrick, Kevin M., and John R. Logan. 1985. "The aging of the suburbs: 1960 to 1980." *American Sociological Review* 50 (1). 106–17.

Frey, William H. 1979. "Central city white flight: Racial and non-racial causes." *American Sociological Review* 44 (June). 425–48.

———. 1985. "Mover-destination selectivity and the changing suburbanization of metropolitan whites and blacks." *Demography* 22 (2). 223–43.

———. 1993. "The new urban revival in the United States." *Urban Studies* 30 (4/5). 741–74.

Frey, William H., and Frances E. Kobrin. 1982. "Changing families and changing mobility: Their impact on the central city." *Demography* 19 (3). 261–77.

Frieden, Bernard, and Marshall Kaplan. 1990. "Rethinking neighborhood strategies." In *Neighborhood policies and programmes: Past and present,* Naomi Carmon, ed. Houndmills, Basingstoke, Hampshire, and London: MacMillan Academic and Professional.

Frieden, Bernard, and Lynne B. Sagalyn. 1990. *Downtown inc.: How America rebuilds cities.* Cambridge: MIT Press.

Friedman, Thomas L. 1993. "Clintons pick private school in capital for their daughter." *New York Times.* Jan. 6. A1.

Fuerst, J. S., and Roy Petty. "Quiet success: Where managed school integration works." *American Prospect* 2 (Summer). 65–73.

Gale, Dennis. 1984. *Neighborhood revitalization and the postindustrial city.* Lexington: D.C. Heath.

———. 1987. *Washington D.C.: Inner-city revitalization and minority suburbanization.* Philadelphia: Temple University Press.

Galster, George C. 1987. *Homeowners and neighborhood investment.* Durham and London: Duke University Press.

Gans, Herbert. 1962a. *The urban villagers.* New York: Free Press.

———. 1962b. "Urbanism and suburbanism as ways of life: A reevaluation of definitions." In *Human behavior and social processes,* A. M. Rose, ed. Boston: Houghton, Mifflin.

Gastright, Joseph F. 1992. Report of achievement test results, April 1992 administration of the California achievement test, form E. Cincinnati: Planning, Research, and Evaluation Branch, Cincinnati Public Schools. July.

Goodman, John L., Jr. *Urban residential mobility: Places, people, and policy.* Washington, D.C.: Urban Institute.

Green, Richard. 1994a. "Two-state port authority gathers steam." *Cincinnati Enquirer.* Jan. 7. 1.

——. 1994b. "Qualls: Downtown hasn't hit bottom yet." *Cincinnati Enquirer.* Jan 8. 1.

Greenhouse, Steven. 1992. "Why Paris works." *New York Times Magazine.* July 19. 29.

Griffin, Virginia K. 1977. "Desegregation in Cincinnati: The legal background." In *The future of big city schools,* Daniel U. Levine and Robert J. Havighurst, eds. Berkeley: McCutchan.

Grimes, Kenneth. 1991. "The San Diego housing trust fund: A successful affordable housing strategy." *Housing and Human Services Newsletter* (Winter 1991/1992.) 3–4.

Gross, Jane. 1991. "A milestone in the fight for gay rights: A quiet suburban life." *New York Times.* June 30.

Gursky, Daniel. 1992. "Cincinnati cuts more than half of central office." *Education Week.* May 20, 11 (35). 1, 13.

Gurwitt, Ron. 1992. "Getting off the bus." *Governing.* 5 (8), (May). 30–36.

Hanz, J. E. 1971. Socio-economic characteristics as criteria for market segmentation: A multivariate approach. PhD. dissertation, University of Cincinnati.

Henig, Jeffrey R. 1992. "Defining city limits." *Urban Affairs Quarterly* 27 (3). 375–95.

Herbert, David. 1973. *Urban geography: A social perspective.* New York: Praeger.

Hill, Paul T., Arthur E. Wise, and Leslie Shapiro. 1989. *Educational progress: Cities mobilize to improve their schools.* Santa Monica: Rand Corporation.

Hinds, Michael deCourcy. 1993. "Belatedly, Philadelphia faces busing." *New York Times.* March 1. A12.

Hoben, James, and Todd Richardson. 1992. *The local CHAS: A preliminary assessment of first year submissions.* Washington, D.C.: U.S. Department of Housing and Urban Development.

Holthaus, D. 1991. "City's population drops to 1910 levels." *Cincinnati Post.* April 27. 4A.

Horn, Dan. 1993. "Indian Hill, Mariemount face large increases." *Cincinnati Post.* July 1.

Housing Blueprint Technical Working Group. 1989. *A blueprint for housing production in Cincinnati.* Cincinnati: Department of Neighborhood Housing and Conservation.

Housing Opportunities Made Equal. 1991. *Over-the-Rhine: A permanent ghetto.* Cincinnati: HOME.

Hula, Richard. 1990. "The two Baltimores." In *Leadership and urban regeneration,* Dennis Judd and Michael Parkinson, eds. Newbury Park, Calif.: Sage.

Hulchanski, J. David, Margaret Eberle, Michael Lytton, and Kris Olds. 1990. *The municipal role in the supply and maintenance of low cost housing: A review of Canadian initiatives.* Vancouver: University of British Columbia Centre for Human Settlement.

Johnson, Joseph E. 1982. Testimony. School desegregation. Hearings before the subcommittee on civil and constitutional rights. House of Representatives, Ninety-Seventh Congress, Serial no. 26. Washington, D.C.: U.S. Government Printing Office. 425–32.

Johnson, Kirk. 1993. "Schools need race balance, Weicker says." *New York Times.* Jan. 7. B1.

Jones, Judith Denton. 1988. "The six school complex." *Equity and choice.* (Winter). 31–38.

Jones, Thomas. 1990. "The politics of educational choice." In *Choice in education: Potential and problems,* William Lowe Boyd and Herbert J. Walberg, eds. Berkeley, Calif.: McCutchan.

Jossi, Frank. 1992. "Holding on to the middle-class." *Planning* 58 (8) (April). 34.

Judd, Dennis and Michael Parkinson, eds. 1990. *Leadership and urban regeneration: Cities in North America and Europe.* Volume 37. Urban Affairs Annual Review. Newbury Park, Calif.: Sage.

Judson, George. 1992. "Integrating Hartford." *New York Times.* Dec. 21. B14.

———. 1993. "New Haven's task: Tying city to region to promote growth." *New York Times.* June 1. A1, A9.

Kain, John F. 1986. "The influence of race on racial segregation and housing policy." In *Housing desegregation and federal policy,* J. M. Goering, ed. Chapel Hill: University of North Carolina Press.

———. 1988. Racial residential segregation in Hamilton County, Ohio: Its extent and causes and role of government. Report prepared for Legal Aid Society of Cincinnati in relation to expert testimony on *Martin v. Taft.* Jan. 10.

Kasarda, John D. 1985. "Urban change and minority opportunities." In *The new urban reality*, Paul E. Peterson, ed. Washington, D. C.: Brookings Institution.

———. 1989. "Urban industrial transition and the underclass." *Annals of the American Academy of Political and Social Science* 501 (Jan.). 26–47.

Katzman, Martin. 1980. "Contributions of crime to urban decline." *Urban Studies* 17 (3). 277–86.

Keating, W. Dennis, and Norman Krumholz. 1991. "Downtown plans of the 1980s." *Journal of the American Planning Association* 57 (2) (Spring). 136–52.

Kelly, Patrick, and Will Miller. 1989. "Assessing desegregation efforts: No 'best measure.'" *Public Administration Review* 49 (5). 431–37.

Kemme, Steve. 1992. "East End group goes to grass roots." *Cincinnati Enquirer.* Feb. 11 (extra). 1, 6.

Kendig, Hal L. 1984. "Housing careers, life cycle and residential mobility: Implications for the housing market." *Urban Studies* 21. 271–83.

Kennedy, Carolyn. 1991. "Housing plans and elements for the 1990s." *PAS Memo.* July. 1–3.

Kent, Cheryl. 1993. "Seeding a huge Chicago railyard project." *New York Times.* March 7. 30.

Kent, Jennifer, 1990. "Looking at life from a luxury condo." *Cincinnati Post.* July 31. 2.

Kephart, George. 1991. "Economic restructuring, population redistribution, and migration in the United States." In *Urban life in transition*, M. Gottdiener and Chris G. Pickvance, eds. Newbury Park, Calif.: Sage.

Kerr, Peter. 1992. "Building homes and hope in Watts." *New York Times.* June 12.

Klaff, Vivian Z. 1982. "Metropolitan school desegregation: Impact on racial integration of neighborhoods in the United States." *Population Research and Policy Review.* 1. 259–82.

———. 1984. *The consequences of school desegregation programs for residential segregation: The case of Wilmington, Delaware.* Final report submitted to the National Science Foundation. Newark, Delaware: Department of Sociology, University of Delaware.

Knack, Ruth Eckdish. 1993. "Schools 'R' us." *Planning* 59 (11). 22–28.

Knox, Paul. 1982. *Urban social geography: An introduction.* New York: Longman.

Koven, Andrea C., and Steven G. Koven. 1993. "Tax reform: Housing incentives in Des Moines, Iowa." *Journal of Urban Affairs* 15 (6). 491–504.

Kowinski, William S. 1980. "Suburbia: End of the golden age." *New York Times Magazine.* March 16.

Kozol, Jonathan. 1991. *Savage inequalities.* New York: Crown.

Krumholz, Norman, 1982. "A retrospective view of equity planning: Cleveland, 1969–1979." *Journal of the American Planning Association* 48 (2) (Spring). 163–83.

Krumholz, Norman, and Pierre Clavel. 1994. *Regenerating cities: Equity planners tell their stories.* Philadelphia: Temple University Press.

Krumholz, Norman, and John Forester. 1990. *Making equity planning work: Leadership in the public sector.* Philadelphia: Temple University Press.

Krumholz, Norman, and Richard Shatten. 1992. Cleveland: "Are you better off now than you were twenty years ago?" Mini-plenary session, 22nd annual meeting, Urban Affairs Association, April 30. Cleveland.

La Pierre, D. Bruce. 1988. "The St. Louis plan: Substantial achievements and unfulfilled promises." *Equity and Choice.* Feb. 4. 34–44.

Lacayo, Richard. 1992. "This land is my land." *Time.* May 18. 30–33.

Land Design Research Inc. 1989. *Eastern Riverfront Redevelopment Strategy.* Columbia, Md.: LDR.

Laska, Shirley, and Daphne Spain, eds. 1980. *Back to the city.* New York: Pergamon.

Lee, Felicia. 1993. "Disrespect rules." *New York Times.* April 4. 16. (Education section).

Lemann, Nicholas. 1994. "The myth of community development." *New York Times Magazine.* Jan. 9. 26.

Lemmon, Wayne A. 1992. Eastern Riverfront financial analyses. Silver Spring, Md.: Wayne A. Lemmon consultant.

Léveillée, Jacques, and Robert K. Whelen. 1990. "Montreal: The struggle to become a world city." In *Leadership and urban regeneration,* Dennis Judd and Michael Parkinson, eds. Newbury Park, Calif.: Sage.

Levin, Melvin. 1987. *Planning in government.* Chicago: APA Planners Press.

Levine, Daniel, and Eugene E. Eubanks. 1986. "The promise and limits of regional desegregation plans for central city school districts." *Metropolitan Education* 1 (Spring). 36–51.

Levine, Marc. 1990. *The reconquest of Montreal.* Philadelphia: Temple University Press.

Levy, Paul. 1993. "Philadelphia CCD works at linking public programs and private-sector jobs." CUPREPORT. 4 (4) (Fall). 6.

Lewis, Jade L., and Betty Elsey. 1989. Taeuber index values for the 1989–90 school year. Cincinnati: Planning, Research, and Evaluation Branch, Cincinnati Public Schools. November.

Listokin, David. 1976. *Fair share housing allocation.* New Brunswick, N.J.: Center for Urban Policy Research.

Logan, John R., and Todd Swanstrom. 1990. *Beyond the city limits: Urban policy and economic restructuring in comparative perspective.* Philadelphia: Temple University Press.

Long, Larry H., and Donald C. Dahmann. 1980. *The city-suburb income gap: Is it being narrowed by a back-to-the-city movement?* Special demographic analyses. CDS-80–1. Washington, D.C.: Bureau of the Census, U.S. Department of Commerce.

Lowery, David and William E. Lyons. 1989. "The impact of jurisdictional boundaries: An individual level test of the Tiebout Model." *The Journal of Politics* 5 (1). 73–97.

Lowry, I. 1980. "Bringing mobility research to bear on public policy." In *Residential mobility and public policy.* Volume 19. Urban Affairs Annual Review. Beverly Hills, Calif.: Sage.

Lubasch, Arnold H. 1989. "Reports contrast housing in New York City." *New York Times.* July 30.

Lubinger, Bill. 1992. "Incentives lure home buyers to city." *Cleveland Plain Dealer.* May 17.

Lyall, K. 1980. "A bicycle built-for-two." In *Public-private partnership in American cities,* R. S. Fosler and R. A. Berger, eds. Lexington, Mass.: D. C. Heath.

Lyall, Sarah. 1992. "Loneliness on downtown streets: Closing of Syracuse's last department store leaves a void." *New York Times.* Aug. 21. B1, B4.

MacNeil/Lehrer News Hour. 1993. February 7.

Mahard, Rita E., and Robert L. Crain. 1983. "Research on minority achievement in desegregated schools." In *The consequences of school desegregation,* Christine H. Rossell and Willis D. Hawley, eds. Philadelphia: Temple University Press.

Maloney, Michael E. 1974. *The social areas of Cincinnati: Toward an analysis of social needs.* Cincinnati: Cincinnati Human Relations Commission.

Mandelker, D. R., G. H. Feder, and M. R. Collins. 1979. *Reviving cities with tax abatement.* New Brunswick, N.J.: Center for Urban Policy Research.

Marcuse, Peter. 1990. "New York City's community boards: Neighborhood policy and its results." In *Neighborhood policy and programs: Past and present,* Naomi Carmon, ed. Houndmills, Basingstoke, Hampshire: MacMillan Academic and Professional.

Marriott, Michel. 1991. "Louisville debates plan to end forced busing in grade school." *New York Times.* Dec. 11.

Marrison, Benjamin. 1993. "Detroit friends pick up the tab: White expected to net $50,000 in campaign fund-raiser." *Cleveland Plain Dealer.* March 6.

Marshall, Harvey, and Kathleen O'Flaherty. 1987. "Suburbanization in the seventies: The push-pull hypothesis revisited." *Journal of Urban Affairs* 9 (3). 249–62.

Mayer, Neil S. 1984. *Neighborhood organizations and community development: Making revitalization work.* Washington, D.C.: Urban Institute Press.

McAuliffe, Bill. 1991. "St. Paul plan aims to keep middle-income homeowners in the city." *Star Tribune.* Sept. 14.

McCarthy, K. F. *The household life cycle and housing choices.* RAND paper P-5565. Santa Monica, Calif.: Rand.

McClure, Jane. 1991. "Low-interest loans offered to keep middle-income families in St. Paul." *Highland Villager.* Nov. 20.

McConahay, John B., and Willis D. Hawley. 1977. *Is it the busing or the blacks? Self-interest versus symbolic racism as predictors of opposition to busing in Louisville.* Durham, N.C.: Center for Policy Analysis, Institute for Policy Analysis and Public Affairs, Duke University.

Mead, Lawrence M. 1989. "The logic of workfare: The underclass and work policy." *Annals of the American Academy of Political and Social Science* 501 (Jan.). 156–69.

Menahem, Gila, Shimon E. Spiro, Ellen Goldring, and Rina Shapira. 1993. "Parental choice and residential segregation." *Urban Education* 28 (1) (April). 30–48.

Merriweather, James. 1993. "Oberly: No firm time for deseg order." *Wilmington News Journal.* April 2. B8.

Metropolitan Area Religious Coalition of Cincinnati (MARCC). 1993. Enrollment and racial compositions of Hamilton County school districts. Mimeographed. Cincinnati: MARCC.

Metz, Mary H. 1990. "Potentialities and problems of choice in desegregation plans." In *Choice and control in American education.* Volume 2, William H. Clune and John F. Witte, eds. London: Falmer Press.

Meyer, Leon. 1991. Eastern riverfront-chronology of planning process. Memorandum from Leon Meyer, Director, Department of City Planning, to Gerald E. Newfarmer, City Manager, October 23.

Michael Maloney and Associates and Applied Information Resources. 1991. *East End community report: A community survey and report with observations and recommendations regarding the eastern riverfront redevelopment strategy.* Cincinnati: Michael Maloney and Associates.

Michelson, William. 1977. *Environmental choice, human behavior, and residential satisfaction.* New York: Oxford University Press.

Mieszkowski, Peter, and Edwin S. Mills. 1993. "The causes of metropolitan suburbanization." *Journal of Economic Perspectives* 7 (3). 135–47.

Miller, Nick. 1991. "Residents demand a say." *Cincinnati Post.* May 20.

Miller, Nick, and Molly Kavanaugh. 1991a. "Housing hassles split city poor." *Cincinnati Post.* March 16. 1A, 7A.

———. 1991b. "Where the Ohio flows, neighbors feel tide of time." *Cincinnati Post.* March 30. 1A, 7A.

Milliken v. Bradley. 418 U.S. 717 (1974).

Molotch, Harvey. 1990. "Urban deals in comparative perspective." In *Beyond the city limits: Urban policy and economic restructuring in comparative perspective,* John R. Logan and Todd Swanstrom, eds. Philadelphia: Temple University Press.

Monti, Daniel J. 1986. "*Brown's* velvet cushion: metropolitan desegregation and politics of illusion." *Metropolitan Education* 1 (Spring).

———. 1990. *Race, redevelopment and the new company town.* Albany: State University of New York Press.

———. 1991. "The carrot or the stick for school desegregation policy: Magnet schools or forced busing, review." *School Forces* 69 (3). 943–46.

Moore, Donald R., and Suzanne Davenport. 1990. "School choice: The new improved sorting machine." In *Choice in education: Potential and problems*, William Lowe Boyd and Herbert J. Wallberg, eds. Berkeley: McCutchan.

Moore, Eric G. 1972. *Residential mobility in the city*. Association of American Geographers resource paper no. 13. Washington, D.C.: Commission on College Geography, A.A.G.

Moynihan, Daniel P. 1965. *The negro family: The case for national action*. Washington, D.C.: U.S. Department of Labor, Office of Policy Planning and Research.

Murray, Charles A. 1984. *Losing ground: American social policy 1950–1980*. New York: Basic Books.

Nathan, Joe. 1990. "Progress, problems, and prospects of state educational choice plans." In *Choice in education: Potential and problems*, William L. Boyd and Herbert J. Wallberg, eds. Berkeley: McCutchan.

Nathan, Richard P. 1989. "Institutional change and the challenge of the underclass." *Annals of the American Academy of Political and Social Science* 501 (Jan.). 170–81.

National Conference of State Legislatures. 1988. *Shaping a national housing policy: Recommendations for state and federal action*. Denver and Washington, D.C.: National Conference.

Nemy, Enid. 1991. "More singles jilt the cities for the suburbs." *New York Times*. May 9.

Nenno, Mary K. 1989. *Housing and community development: Maturing functions of state and local governments*. Washington, D.C.: NAHRO.

Nenno, Mary K., and Paul C. Brophy, 1982. *Housing and local government*. Washington, D.C.: International City Management Association.

Nenno, Mary K., and George C. Colyer. 1988. *New money and new methods: A catalog of state and local initiatives in housing and community development*. Washington, D.C.: National Association of Housing and Redevelopment Officials.

Newman, Sandra J., and Greg J. Duncan. 1979. "Residential problems, dissatisfaction and mobility." *Journal of the American Planning Association* 45 (2) (April). 154–66.

New York City Department of City Planning. 1969. *Plan for New York City 1: Critical issues*. Cambridge: MIT Press.

New York City Housing Partnership. 1992. *Building homes, not just housing.* New York: City Housing Partnership.

Norusis, M. J. 1985. *SPSS-X advanced statistics guide.* Chicago: SPSS-Inc.

Olson, Lynn. 1991. "Cincinnati business group urges 'mini-district' to drive reforms." *Education Week* 11 (3) (September 18). 20.

O'Neill, John. 1990. "Housing prices balloon leaving wage earners adrift." *Wilmington News Journal.* Jan. 28. N4.

Orfield, Gary. 1975a. "How to make desegregation work: The adoption of schools to their newly-integrated student bodies." In *The courts, social science, and school desegregation, law and contemporary problems.* Part II, Betsy Levin and Willis D. Hawley, eds. 39 (2) (Spring).

——. 1975b. "White flight research: Its importance, perplexities, and possible policy implications." In *Symposium on school desegregation and white flight,* Gary Orfield, ed. Washington, D.C.: Center for National Policy Review.

——. 1978. *Must we bus: Segregated schools and national policy.* Washington, D.C.: Brookings Institution.

——. 1983. *Public school desegregation in the United States, 1968–1980.* Washington, D.C.: Joint Center for Political Studies.

——. 1985. "Ghettoization and its alternatives." In *The new urban reality,* Paul E. Peterson, ed. Washington, D.C.: Brookings Institution.

——. 1990. "Do we know anything worth knowing about educational effects of magnet schools?" In *Choice and control in American education.* Volume 2, William H. Clune and John F. Witte, eds. London: Falmer Press.

Orfield, Gary, and Franklin Monfort. 1988. *Racial change and desegregation in large school districts. Trends through the 1986–87 school year.* Alexandria: National School Boards Association.

——. 1992. *Status of school desegregation: The next generation.* Arlington: National School Boards Association.

Orfield, Gary, Franklin Monfort, and Melissa Aaron. 1989. *Status of school desegregation 1968–1986.* Alexandria: National School Boards Association.

Palen, J. John, and Bruce London. 1984. *Gentrification, displacement, and neighborhood revitalization.* Albany: State University of New York Press.

Peirce, Neal R. 1993. *Citistates: How urban America can prosper in a competitive world.* Washington, D.C.: Seven Locks Press.

Percy, Stephen L., and Brett W. Hawkins. 1992. "Further tests of individual-level propositions from the Tiebout model." *Journal of Politics* 54 (4) (Nov.). 1149–57.

Peterson, Paul E. 1981. *City limits.* Chicago: University of Chicago Press.

———, ed. 1985. *The new urban reality.* Washington, D.C.: Brookings Institution.

Pettigrew, Thomas, and Robert Green. 1976. "School desegregation in large cities: A critique of the Coleman 'white flight' thesis." *Harvard Educational Review* 46 (1) (Feb.). 1–53.

Piche-Cyr, Claire. 1990. The municipality's role in the production of affordable units for young families, Second housing awards symposium, Housing young families affordably, Sept., Vancouver, Canada.

Pollakowski, Henry O., and John G. Edwards. 1987. *Life cycle, class, city vintage and probability of suburbanization.* Working paper W 87–4. Cambridge: Harvard-M.I.T. Joint Center for Urban Studies.

Quercia, Roberto, and William M. Rohe. 1993. "Models of housing adjustment and their implications for planning and policy." *Journal of Planning Literature* 8 (1) (Aug.). 20–31.

Raffel, Jeffrey A. 1976. "Desegregation dilemmas." *Integrateducation* 6 (14). 38-41.

———. 1992. Public opinion in Delaware: Public schools and educational issues. Newark, Del.: College of Urban Affairs and Public Policy, University of Delaware. August.

———. 1980a. *The politics of school desegregation: The metropolitan remedy in Delaware.* Philadelphia: Temple University Press.

———. 1980b. "The voters grade the metropolitan desegregation plan in Delaware." *Integrateducation* 18 (1–4). 64–71.

———. 1982. Testimony. School desegregation. Hearings before the subcommittee on civil and constitutional rights. House of Representatives, Ninety-Seventh Congress, Serial no. 26. Washington, D.C.: U.S. Government Printing Office. 453–530.

———. 1985. "The impact of metropolitan school desegregation on public opinion: A longitudinal analysis." *Urban Affairs Quarterly* 21 (2) (Dec.). 245–65.

Raffel, Jeffrey A., William L. Boyd, Vernon M. Briggs, Jr., Eugene E. Eubanks, and Roberto Fernandez. 1992. "Policy dilemmas in urban education: Addressing the needs of poor, at-risk children." *Journal of Urban Affairs* 14 (3/4). 263–290.

Raffel, Jeffrey A., Nancy Colmer, and Donald Berry. 1983. Public opinion toward the public schools of New Castle County. Newark, Del.: College of Urban Affairs and Public Policy, University of Delaware. May.

Raffel, Jeffrey A., and Robert Warren. 1987. *Racial patterns in special education in New Castle County 1977–78/1984–85.* Newark, Del.: College of Urban Affairs and Public Policy, University of Delaware.

Ramsey, Krista. 1993. "White balance achieved, was education improved?" *Cincinnati Enquirer.* Oct. 28. 1,16.

———. 1994. "Suspensions, expulsions defy reformers." *Cincinnati Enquirer.* March 12. A1.

Rasey, Keith P., W. Dennis Keating, and Philip D. Star. 1991. "Management of neighborhood development: Community development corporations." In *Managing local government,* Richard Bingham, ed. Sage: Thousand Oaks, Calif.

Rasmussen, David W., and Raymond J. Struyk. 1981. *A housing strategy for the city of Detroit.* Washington, D.C.: Urban Institute.

"Readers Choice: Your ninth annual guide to area dining." *Wilmington News-Journal.* Section K. March 22.

Real Estate Research Corporation. 1972. *Comprehensive housing strategy.* Phase 1 final report. Prepared for the Working Review Committee on Housing, city of Cincinnati. Chicago: RERC.

———. 1973. Description and partial analysis of Cincinnati's 44 statistical areas, prepared for Cincinnati Working Review Committee on Housing, for the meeting of May 18, 1973. Chicago: RERC.

Reischauer, Robert D. 1989. "Immigration and the underclass." *Annals of the American Academy of Political and Social Science* 501 (Jan.). 120–31.

Riverfront Advisory Council and the Cincinnati Department of City Planning. 1988. *Eastern riverfront concept plan.* Cincinnati: Planning Department.

Rogers, Joseph P., Jr., and Howard Zucker. 1989. *ABCs of housing bonds.* 4th edition. New York: Hawkins, Delafield and Wood.

Rosdil, Donald. 1992. "Cultural change and regime restructuring: A dissenting view." Paper presented at 22nd annual meeting of the Urban Affairs Association, April 30, Cleveland, Ohio.

Rosenbaum, James E. 1991. "Black pioneers—do their moves to the suburbs increase opportunity for mothers and children?" *Housing Policy Debate* 2 (4). 1179–1213.

Rossell, Christine H. 1983. "Desegregation plans, racial isolation, white flight, and community response." In *The consequences of school desegregation,* Christine H. Rossel and Willis D. Hawley, eds. Philadelphia: Temple University Press.

———. 1987. "The Buffalo controlled choice plan." *Urban Education.* 22 (3). 328–54.

———. 1990. *The carrot or the stick for school desegregation policy: Magnet schools or forced busing.* Philadelphia: Temple University Press.

———. 1992. The classification of school segregation remedies. Unpublished paper.

Rossell, Christine H., and Ruth C. Clarke. 1987. The carrot or the stick in school desegregation policy? Boston: Report to the National Institute of Education. Boston University. March.

Rossi, Peter H., and Anne B. Shlay. 1982. "Residential mobility and public policy issues: 'Why families move,' revisited." *Journal of Social Issues* 38 (3). 21–34.

Rusk, David. 1993. *Cities without suburbs.* Baltimore: Johns Hopkins University Press.

Ruth, Eric. 1992. "Probe sought in school expulsion of blacks." *Wilmington News Journal.* July 16. B3.

Salins, Peter D. 1993. "Cities, suburbs, and the urban crisis." *The Public Interest* 113 (Fall). 91–104.

Salisbury, Robert H. 1967. "Schools and politics in the big city." *Harvard Educational Review* 37 (3). 408–24.

San Antonio Independent School District v. Rodriguez. 411 U.S. 1 (1973).

Savitch, H. V., and John Clayton Thomas, eds. 1991. *Big city politics in transition.* Volume 38, Urban Affairs Annual Review. Newbury Park, Calif.: Sage.

Schmidt, Julie A. 1979. "School desegregation in Wilmington, Delaware: A case study in non-decision-making." M.A. thesis, Department of Political Science, University of Delaware.

Schmidt, Peter. 1992a. "Palm Beach shifts integration focus to housing." *Education Week.* Feb. 11 (23). 1, 9–10.

———. 1992b. "N.J. school board can merge districts, court rules." *Education Week.* Aug. 5. 10.

———. 1992c. "Las Vegas officials must call to revise busing plan." *Education Week.* Oct. 14. 12 (6). 4.

————. 1993. "Governor seeks scrutiny of Milwaukee busing plan." *Education Week.* May 12. 14.

Schoenberg, Sandra P., and Patricia Rosenbaum. 1980. *Neighborhoods that work: Sources for viability in the inner city.* New Brunswick: Rutgers University Press.

Schwab, W. A. 1987. "The predictive value of three ecological models." *Urban Affairs Quarterly* 23. 295–308.

Shanker, Albert. 1992. "Cincinnati's smart trade." *New York Times.* Aug. 2. 7.

————. 1994. "Discipline by the numbers." *New York Times.* Jan 16, E7.

Shevky, E., and W. Bell. 1955. *Social area analysis: Theory, illustrative application, and computational procedures.* Stanford, Calif.: Stanford University Press.

Sills, James H. 1982. "Equalizing teacher salaries: Racial and policy implications in a new metropolitan public school district." *Urban Education* 17 (Oct.). 351–74.

————. 1993. "Preserving the city's schools." *Wilmington News Journal.* Aug. 8. H1, H4.

Simmons, James W. 1968. "Changing residences in the city: A review of intra-urban mobility." *Geographical Review* 58. 622–51.

Sims, Calvin. 1994. "Leader to quit post-riot panel in Los Angeles." *New York Times.* Jan. 12. 8.

Sleeper, Jim. 1993. "The end of the rainbow." *The New Republic.* Nov. 1. 20. 22–25.

Small, Kenneth A. 1985. "Transportation and urban change." In *The new urban reality,* Paul E. Peterson, ed. Washington, D.C.: Brookings Institution.

Smith, Marjorie. 1990. "Struggling in St. Louis." *American School Board Journal* 177 (2). 24–25.

Smothers, Ronald. 1993. "City seeks to grow by disappearing." *New York Times.* Oct. 18. A8.

Spain, Daphne. 1980. "Reasons for intra-metropolitan mobility: Are schools a key issue?" *Review of Public Data Use* 8 (1). 59–67.

————. 1987. "Why higher income households move to central cities." Paper presented to the Association of Collegiate Schools of Planning meeting, Nov. 8, Los Angeles.

Speare, Alden, Jr., Sidney Goldstein, and William H. Frey. 1974. *Residential mobility, migration and metropolitan change.* Cambridge: Ballinger.

Stanback, Thomas M., Jr. 1991. *The new suburbanization: Challenge to the central city.* Boulder: Westview Press.

Stegman, Michael A. 1993. "The role of planning in the Clinton administration's community empowerment agenda." Speech to the Association of Collegiate Schools of Planning meeting. Oct. 29, Philadelphia.

Stegman, Michael A., and J. David Holden. 1987. *Nonfederal housing programs: How states and localities are responding to cutbacks in low-income housing programs.* Washington, D.C.: Urban Institute.

Sternlieb, George, and David Listokin. 1985. "Housing." In *Setting municipal priorities 1986,* Charles Brecher and Raymond D. Horton eds. New York: New York University Press.

St. John, Craig, and Frieda Clark. 1984. "Race and social class differences in the characteristics desired in neighborhoods." *Social Science Quarterly* 65 (3). 803–13.

Sturmon, Sarah. 1989. "Cincinnatians staying put, census shows." *Cincinnati Post.* Nov. 17.

———. 1992. "Don't spoil East End river view, hillsiders ask." *Cincinnati Post.* March 11.

Sullivan, Mercer L. 1989. "Absent fathers in the inner city." *Annals of the American Academy of Political and Social Science* 501 (Jan.) 48–58.

Sviridoff, Mitchell. 1988. "The seeds of urban revival." *The Public Interest* 114 (Winter). 82–103.

Swann v. Charlotte-Mecklenburg Board of Education. 402 U.S. 1 (1971).

Swanstrom, Todd. 1988. "Urban populism, uneven development, and the space for reform." In *Business elites and urban redevelopment: Case studies and critical perspectives,* Scott Cummings, ed. Albany: State University of New York Press.

Szanton, P. L. 1986. *Baltimore 2000: A choice of futures.* Baltimore: Morris Goldseeker Foundation.

Tatel, David S., Kevin J. Lanigan, and Maree Sneed. 1986. "The fourth decade of *Brown:* Metropolitan desegregation and quality education." *Metropolitan Education* 1 (Spring). 15–35.

Teaford, Jon C. 1990. "Rough road to renaissance." *LaFollette policy report.* Madison: Robert LaFollette Institute of Public Affairs. 1 (Spring). 8–12.

Testa, Mark, Marie Nan, Marilyn Astone Krogh, and Kathryn M. Neckermann. 1989. "Employment and marriage among inner-city fathers."

Annals of the American Academy of Political and Social Science 501 (Jan.). 79–91.

Tiebout, Charles M. 1956. "A pure theory of local expenditures." *Journal of Political Economy* 64 (5). 416–24.

Timmermans, H., A. Borgers, J. van Dijk, and H. Oppewal. 1992. "Residential choice behaviour of dual earner households: A decomposed joint choice model." *Environment and Planning A.* 24. 517–33.

Tuchfarber, Alfred, Jr., David P. Varady, and Dev Saggar. 1980. "Return to the city: Who, why, how many and from where." Paper presented to the national meeting of the Regional Science Association, Nov. 14–16, Milwaukee.

Urban Land Institute. 1990. *ULI market profiles: 1990.* Washington, D.C.: Urban Land Institute.

U.S. Bureau of the Census. 1983. Census of housing: Detailed housing characteristics. Washington, D.C.: U.S. Government Printing Office.

———. 1988. *County and City Data Book.* Washington D.C.: U.S. Government Printing Office.

———. 1991a. *Census and you.* 26 (6) (June).

———. 1991b. *Metropolitan areas and cities.* 1990 Census profile (Sept.), no. 3. Washington, D.C.: U.S. Bureau of Census.

———. 1992a. *Census of housing. General housing characteristics.* Washington, D.C.: U.S. Government Printing Office.

———. 1992b. *Census of population. General population characteristics.* Washington, D.C.: U.S. Government Printing Office.

———. 1993a. *Census of population and housing. Population and housing counts.* Washington, D.C.: U.S. Government Printing Office.

———. 1993b. *Census of population and housing.* Summary tape 3. Washington, D.C.: U.S. Government Printing Office.

U.S. House. 1982. *Hearings before the subcommittee on civil and constitutional rights.* 97th Congress. Serial no. 26.

U.S. National Advisory Commission on Civil Disorders. 1969. *Report of the National Advisory Commission on Civil Disorders.* Washington, D.C.: U.S. Government Printing Office.

Van Arsdol, Maurice D., Jr., Georges Sabagh, and Edgar W. Butler. 1968. "Retrospective and subsequent metropolitan mobility." *Demography* 5 (1). 249–67.

Varady, David P. 1983. "Determinants of residential mobility decisions: The role of government services in relation to other factors." *Journal of the American Planning Association* 49 (2) (Spring). 184–99.

———. 1984. "Residential mobility in the Urban Homesteading Demonstration neighborhoods." *Journal of the American Planning Association* 50 (3) (Summer). 346–51.

———. 1989. The impact of black suburbanization on racial integration: A Cincinnati study. Final report submitted to the Cincinnati Housing Resources Board. Cincinnati: School of Planning, University of Cincinnati.

———. 1990a. "Influences on the city-suburban choice: A study of Cincinnati home buyers." *Journal of the American Planning Association* 56 (1) (Winter): 22–40.

———. 1990b. "Tax abatements and below market-rate mortgages to attract middle-income families to the central city: A Cincinnati study." *Journal of Urban Affairs* 12 (1). 59–74.

Varady, David P., and Charlotte T. Birdsall. 1991. "Local housing plans." *Journal of Planning Literature* 6 (2) (Nov.). 115–35.

Voluntary Interdistrict Coordinating Council. 1993. Report to the community. St. Louis: VICC.

———. 1993c. "Schools cut costs, 404 jobs." *Cincinnati Enquirer.* April 23. A1.

Wacquant, Loic J. D., and William Julius Wilson. 1989. "The cost of racial and class exclusion in the inner city." *Annals of the American Academy of Political and Social Science* 501 (Jan.). 8–25.

Waddel, Paul. 1991. "Exogenous workplace choice in residential location models: Is the assumption valid?" *Geographical Analysis* 25 (1) (Jan.). 65–82.

Wald, Matthew. 1986. "The three home stages in the lives of Americans." *New York Times.* Sept. 7.

Waldrip, Donald R. 1977. "Alternative programs in Cincinnati or 'what did you learn on the river today?'" In *The future of big city schools,* Daniel U. Levine and Robert J. Havighurst, eds. Berkeley: McCutchan.

Waste, Robert J. 1993. "City limits, pluralism, and political economy." *Journal of Urban Affairs* 15 (5). 445–55.

Weiher, Gregory R. 1991. *The fractured metropolis: Political fragmentation and metropolitan segregation.* Albany: State University of New York Press.

Weintraub, Adam. 1993a. "Fewer students sent home." *Cincinnati Enquirer.* Dec. 24. B1, B3.

———. 1993b. "Racial balance drops in Cincinnati schools." *Cincinnati Enquirer.* Nov. 16. B1.

Wessel, David, and Larry Reich. 1992. "Baltimore's HarborView redevelopment project." *Planner's Casebook.* 3 (Summer).

Wilson, William Julius. 1987. *The truly disadvantaged: The inner city, the underclass and public policy.* Chicago: University of Chicago Press.

———. 1989a. Special edition of the volume, "*The ghetto underclass: Social science perspectives.*" *Annals of the American Academy of Political and Social Science.* 501 (Jan.).

———. 1989b. "The underclass: Issues, perspectives, and public policy." *Annals of the American Academy of Political and Social Science.* 501 (Jan.). 182–92.

Witte, John F. 1990. "Introduction." In *Choice and control in American education,* Volume 1. William Clune and John F. Witte, eds. London: Falmer Press.

Witte, John F., and Daniel J. Walsh. 1990. "A systematic test of the effective schools model." *Educational and Policy Analysis* 12 (2). 188–212.

Wolinsky, Frederick D., and Robert Johnson. 1991. "The use of health services by older adults." *Journal of Gerontology-Social Sciences* 46 (6). S345–57.

Wolters, Raymond. 1984. *The Burden of Brown: Thirty years of school desegregation.* Knoxville: University of Tennessee Press.

Wong, Kenneth K. 1990. *City choices: Education and housing.* Albany: State University of New York Press.

———. 1992. "The politics of urban education in the United States: Introduction and overview." In *The politics of education in the United States,* James G. Cibulka, Rodney J. Reed, and Kenneth K. Wong, eds. Washington, D.C.: Falmer Press.

Yudof, Mark G., David L. Kirp, Tyll van Geel, and Betsy Levin. 1987. *Educational policy and the law: Cases and material.* Berkeley: McCutchan.

Zimmer, Basil G.,, and Amos H. Hawley. 1968. *Metropolitan area schools: Resistance to district reorganization.* Beverly Hills, CA.: Sage.

N